Introduction to Systematic Theology

Introduction to Systematic Theology

Louis Berkhof

BAKER BOOK HOUSE
Grand Rapids, Michigan

Reprinted 1979 by
Baker Book House Company
from the 1932 edition published by
Wm. B. Eerdmans Publishing Company
ISBN: 0-8010-0768-2

Fourth printing, January 1988

PHOTOLITHOPRINTED BY CUSHING - MALLOY, INC.
ANN ARBOR, MICHIGAN, UNITED STATES OF AMERICA

PREFACE TO THE REVISED EDITION

IT is not necessary to say very much now that the revised edition of my *Introduction to the study of Systematic Theology* appears on the market. I can only say that I am truly grateful for the reception which this work has enjoyed, and for its use in ever-increasing circles. While the general plan of the work remained the same, it has been re-written and revised from cover to cover. In some cases small changes were brought on, in order to clarify the thought, while in others the modifications were considerable. A great deal of historical material has been added, and more attention has been paid to recent movements in theology. This brings the Introduction more in harmony with the second edition of my *Systematic Theology*. My only prayer is that the work in this new form may be of even greater usefulness, and may contribute in some small measure to the study of Reformed theology in our Country.

L. BERKHOF

TABLE OF CONTENTS

The Idea and History of Dogmatic Theology

I. Names Applied to the Systematic Presentation of Theology 15
II. The Nature of Dogmas:
   A. *The Name 'Dogma'*:
      1. Derivation and Meaning of the Term 18
      2. The Biblical Use of the Word 18
      3. Various Uses of the Term in Theology 19
   B. *The Formal Characteristics of Dogmas*:
      1. Their Subject-Matter is Derived from Scripture 21
      2. They are the Fruit of Dogmatic Reflection 23
      3. They are Officially Defined by Some Competent Ecclesiastical Body 24
   C. *The Necessity of Dogmas*:
      1. Causes of Present Day Opposition to Dogmas 26
      2. Dogmas Essential to Christianity 28
   D. *The Elements Involved in Dogmas*:
      1. The Social Element 31
      2. The Traditional Element 32
      3. The Element of Authority 33
III. The Idea of Dogmatic Theology:
   A. *The Relation of Dogmas to Dogmatics*: 35
      1. Dogmas Arise out of the Necessity of the Believing Community 36
      2. Theology May and Has Frequently Served as an Auxiliary in the Formation of Dogmas 37
      3. Dogmatic Theology Finds the Nucleus of its Subject-Matter in the Dogmas of the Church 37
   B. *The Object of Dogmatic Theology*:
      1. The Conception of the Object of Dogmatic Theology in the Early Church 39
      2. The Development of a New Conception in Modern Subjective Theology 40
      3. Recognition of the Objective Character of Dogmatic Theology in Recent Times 41
   C. *Theology as a Science*
      1. The Scientific Character of Theology Denied 44
      2. The Possibility of Maintaining the Scientific Character of Theology 46
   D. *The Encyclopaedic Place of Dogmatics*:
      1. The Group of Studies to Which it Belongs 48
      2. The Relation of Dogmatics to Apologetics 49
      3. The Relation of Dogmatics to Ethics 50

TABLE OF CONTENTS

IV. The Task, Method, and Distribution of Dogmatics:
- A. *The Task of Dogmatics*:
  1. Modern Conceptions of the Task of Dogmatics 53
  2. The Reformed Conception of the Task of Dogmatics 58
- B. *The Method of Dogmatics*:
  1. Various Views as to the Source from Which the Content of Dogmatics is Derived 59
  2. The Manner in Which the Material is Secured and Treated 67
- C. *Distribution of the Material of Dogmatics*:
  1. The Trinitarian Method 72
  2. The Analytical Method 73
  3. The Covenantal Method 73
  4. The Christological Method 74
  5. The Method Based on the Kingdom-Idea 74
  6. The Synthetic Method 74

V. History of Dogmatics:
- A. *The Period of the Old Catholic Church*:
  1. Origen's *Peri Archon* 76
  2. Augustine's *Enchiridion ad Laurentium de Fide, Spe, et Caritate* 76
  3. John of Damascus *Ekdosis Akribes tes Orthodoxus Pisteos* 77
- B. *The Period of the Middle Ages*:
  1. Works of Anselm 78
  2. The Sentences of Peter the Lombard 78
  3. The *Summa* of Alexander of Hales 78
  4. The *Summa* of Thomas Aquinas 78
- C. *The Period of the Reformation*:
  1. Melanchton's *Loci Communes* 79
  2. Zwingli's *Commentarius de Vera et Falsa Religione* 79
  3. Calvin's *Institutio Christianae Religionis* 80
- D. *The Period of Protestant Scholasticism*:
  1. Dogmatical Study Among the Lutherans 80
  2. Dogmatical Study Among the Reformed 81
  3. Dogmatical Study Among the Roman Catholics 82
- E. *The Period of Rationalism and Supranaturalism*:
  1. Pietistic Dogmatics 83
  2. Rationalistic Dogmatics 83
  3. Supranaturalistic Dogmatics 84
- F. *The Period of Modern Theology*:
  1. Schleiermacher and His School 84
  2. The Speculative School 85
  3. The Neo-Lutheran School 86
  4. The Mediating School 87
  5. The School of Ritschl 88
  6. Reformed Theology 88

TABLE OF CONTENTS

The Principia of Dogmatics

I. Principia in General:

    A. *Principia in Non-Theological Sciences*:
- 1. Definition of 'Principium' 93
- 2. Principia of the Non-Theological Sciences 93

    B. *Principia in Religion or Theology*:
- 1. God is the *Principium Essendi* 95
- 2. The *Principium Cognoscendi Externum* is God's Special Revelation .. 96
- 3. The *Principium Cognoscendi Internum* is Faith 97

II. Religion:

    A. *The Essence of Religion*:
- 1. The Derivation of the Word 'Religion' 98
- 2. Scriptural Terms for Religion 99
- 3. Historical Conceptions of the Essence of Religion 100

    B. *The Seat of Religion*:
- 1. It has Its Seat in the Intellect 106
- 2. It has Its Seat in the Will 107
- 3. It has Its Seat in the Feelings 107
- 4. It has Its Seat in the Heart 108

    C. *The Origin of Religion*:
- 1. The Historical Method 109
- 2. The Psychological Method 111
- 3. The Theological Method 113

III. The *Principium Cognoscendi Externum* (Revelation):

    A. *Name and Concept of Revelation*:
- 1. Connection Between Religion and Revelation 116
- 2. The General Idea of Revelation 117
- 3. Historical Conceptions of Revelation 117
- 4. The Idea of Revelation in Modern Theology 119
- 5. The Proper Conception of the Nature of Revelation 124
- 6. Distinctions Applies to the Idea of Revelation 126

    B. *General Revelation*: 128
- 1. The Value and Significance of General Revelation 130
- 2. The Insufficiency of General Revelation 132

    C. *Special Revelation*:
- 1. The Scriptural Idea of Revelation 133
- 2. The Means of Special Revelation 134
- 3. The Contents of Special Revelation 136
- 4. The Purpose of Special Revelation 137

TABLE OF CONTENTS

    D. *Special Revelation and Scripture*:
        1. Historical Views of the Relation Between the Two 139
        2. The Reformed Conception of the Relation Between the Two 141

IV. The Inspiration of Scripture:
    A. *The Doctrine of Inspiration in History*:
        1. Before the Reformation 144
        2. After the Reformation 145
    B. *Scriptural Proof for the Inspiration of the Bible* 146
        1. Proofs for the Inspiration of the Secondary Authors of Scripture Considered Apart from Their Writing 147
        2. Proofs for the Inspiration of the Secondary Authors in Writing the Books of the Bible 148
    C. *Nature and Extent of Inspiration*: 150
        1. The Nature of Inspiration 151
        2. The Extent of Inspiration 153
    D. *Attempts to Discredit the Doctrine of Inspiration*:
        1. They who Defend it are Reasoning in a Circle 156
        2. Jesus Did not Teach the Doctrine of Inspiration 157
        3. The Phenomena of Scripture Contradict the Doctrine of Inspiration 158
        4. The Doctrine of Inspiration Applies only to the Autographa, and Therefore Has no Real Practical Value 158
    E. *Objections to the Doctrine of Inspiration* 159
        1. General Nature of the Objections 160
        2. General Remarks on the Objections Raised 160
    F. *The Perfections of Scripture* 162
        1. The Divine Authority of Scripture 163
        2. The Necessity of Scripture 165
        3. The Perspicuity of Scripture 167
        4. The Sufficiency of Scripture 167

V. The *Principium Cognoscendi Internum*:
    A. *The Human Understanding*:
        1. Historical Statement of This Position 170
        2. Evaluation of This Position 172
    B. *Speculative Reason*:
        1. Historical Statement of This Position 173
        2. Evaluation of This Position 174
    C. *Devout Feeling or Religious Intuition* 175
        1. Historical Statement of This Position 176
        2. Evaluation of This Position 177
    D. *The Moral Consciousness*:
        1. Historical Statement of This Position 178
        2. Evaluation of This Position 179
    E. *Faith the Proper* Principium Internum:
        1. The Name of the *Principium Cognoscendi Internum* 181
        2. Distinctive Nature of the Knowledge of Faith 181

    F. The Ground of Faith 182
        1. The Doctrine of the *Testimonium Spiritus Sancti* in the Church 183
        2. Mistaken Notions of the *Testimonium Spiritus Sancti* 184
        3. Correct View of the *Testimonium Spiritus Sancti* 185

Select Literature 187
Index of Authors 193
Index of Subjects 197

THE IDEA AND HISTORY OF
DOGMATIC THEOLOGY

I. Names Applied to the Systematic Presentation of Theology

There was little or no attempt in the first two centuries of the Christian era to present the whole body of doctrinal truth, gathered from the Word of God, in a systematic way. Yet the urge of the human mind to see the truth as much as possible as a whole could not long be suppressed. Man is endowed with reason, and the human reason cannot rest satisfied with a mere collection of separate truths, but wants to see them in their mutual relationship, in order that it may have a clearer understanding of them. It involuntarily begins to group disconnected truths, to classify them, and to integrate them, so that their interrelation becomes evident. Objections have frequently been raised against a systematic presentation of the doctrinal truths of Scripture; and also in the present day some are decidedly averse to it. There seems to be a lurking fear that the more we systematize the truth, the farther we wander from the presentation of it that is found in the Word of God. But there is no danger of this, if the system is not based on the fundamental principles of some erring philosophy, but on the abiding principles of Scripture itself. God certainly sees the truth as a whole, and it is the duty of the theologian to think the truths of God after Him. There should be a constant endeavor to see the truth as God sees it, even though it is perfectly evident that the ideal is beyond the grasp of man in his present condition.[1]

The Church has never hesitated on this point. From the beginning of the third century on several works appeared which aimed at giving a complete presentation of the doctrinal truths of Scripture. Their aim was similar, but they differed in character and did not always bear the same title. Origen was the first one of the Church Fathers who gave a systematic presentation of doctrinal theology under the title *Peri Archon*. Only fragments of the original have been preserved; but the whole work has come down to the present in the Latin translation of Rufinus, dating from the fourth century, under the title *De Principiis*. By 'First Principles' Origen meant the "fundamental doctrines and leading articles of the faith." Lactantius was the second to write a work of that nature. He entitled his work *Divinarum Institutionum Libri VII*. It is really an Apology for the Christian religion characterized by great elegance of style. Augustine followed in the fifth century with his *Enchiridion* (meaning, 'Handbook'), and designated its contents by adding "*sive de fide, spe et caritate.*" It is really an exposition of the Creed, in which the author exalts the sovereign grace of God and the saving work of Christ as connected with His death on

---

1. *Cf.* Bavinck, *Het Voor en Tegen van een Dogmatisch Systeem in Kennis en Leven,* p. 57 ff.

the cross. This work became almost as authoritative in the Church as the Creed itself. Toward the end of the patristic period John of Damascus wrote a systematic treatise under the title *Ekdosis Akribes Tes Orthodoxou Pisteos* (an Accurate Exposition of the Orthodox Faith). This is more like a modern work on Dogmatics than any of the preceding. It was divided into four books, dealing with (1) God and the Trinity; (2) Creation and the Nature of Man; (3) Christ and His Incarnation, Death, and Descent into Hades; and (4) the Resurrection and Reign of Christ, including the rest of theology.

During the Middle Ages the nature of the doctrinal works that appeared were of a somewhat different nature. They were not grounded on Scripture to the same extent, but were based largely on what the earlier Fathers had written. It was then that the name *Sententiae* came into use. The name itself indicates that the works consisted largely of compilations from the Fathers. The most important of these was that of Peter the Lombard, *De Libres Sententiarum*. This is not merely a compilation, but also contains a great deal of original material. It remained *the Handbook* for the study of theology *par excellence* for three centuries. Along-side of the name *Sententiae* the name *Summa* gradually came into use, and in course of time supplanted the earlier title. The most important of the *Summae* is that of Thomas Aquinas, the great authority of the Roman Catholic Church. The author did not live to finish the work. Additions to it from some of his other works supply at least in a measure what is lacking.

At the time of the Reformation, and after that, still other titles of doctrinal works came into use. Melanchton was the first great dogmatician of the Lutheran Church. He entitled his work *Loci Communes rerum theologicarum* (Common-places of Theological Matters). It grew out of a course of lectures on the Epistle to the Romans. Several other Lutheran theologians used very similar titles. In course of time, however, it also fell into disuse. Zwingli wrote a *Commentarius de vera et falsa religione*, which has been called "the first systematic exposition of the Reformed faith." And Calvin entitled his principal work *Institutio Religionis Christianae*, a title which was adopted by several others. Even in the nineteenth century it appeared in a modified form in Richard Watson's *Theological Institutes*, and without any change in Gerhart's *Institutes of the Christian Religion*.

After the Reformation, however, the name *Theologia* became increasingly prevalent among Lutheran and Reformed theologians. And when the number of theological studies increased, it became quite apparent that this name required some delimitation, and the adjectives *didactica, systematica, theoretica, positiva,* and *dogmatica* served the purpose. L. Reinhart (1659) seems to have been the first one to use the last term. He entitled his work *Synopsis theologiae dogmaticae*. Since the contents of the Christian faith had long been designated as *dogmata*, the modifier was gradually used independently, and the principal term (theologia) was dropped, though it is always understood. Under the influence of Schleiermacher, who called his principal work *Christlicher Glaube nach den Grundsaetzen der evengelischen Kirche*, the title *Doctrine of Faith* (Dutch: Geloofsleer) came into use.

In more recent works we find a variety of titles, such as *The Christian Faith* (Haering, Curtis); *Christian Theology* (Knapp, Pope, Valentine); *Dogmatics, Dogmatik, Gereformeerde Dogmatiek, Christliche Dogmatik* (Kaftan, Bavinck, Honig, Barth); Dogmatic Theology (Shedd, Hall); and *Systematic Theology* (Raymond, Hodge, Miley, Strong). Reformed scholars in Germany and in the Netherlands show a decided preference for the title *Dogmatics*, with or without a modifier. In our own country, however, the term *Systematic Theology* seems to have a more popular appeal. From an ideal point of view the former certainly deserves preference, (1) because it is the more specific of the two, and designates the real object of study with greater precision; and (2) because the modifier 'systematic' in 'Systematic Theology' is apt to create the impression that the study under consideration is the only theological study which treats its subject-matter in a logical order, or that among the theological *discipline* there is no other that is systematic in structure; and this is not true. For practical reasons, however, it seems more desirable, especially in our country and in our day, to use the title *Systematic Theology*. This does not require the sacrifice of any principle. Dr. Warfield even considers this title better than the other, and therefore comes to its defense.[1]

---

1. *Presbyterian and Reformed Review*, April 1896, p. 243.

II. The Nature of Dogmas

A. The Name 'Dogma'

SYSTEMATIC Theology or Dogmatics deals with the dogmata, the accepted doctrines of the Church. This makes it necessary to consider their general character first of all. In this connection the name 'dogma' deserves brief consideration.

1. DERIVATION AND MEANING OF THE TERM. The word 'dogma' is derived from the Greek verb *dokein*. In classical Greek the expression *dokein moi* meant not only, *it seems to me*, or, *I am of the opinion*, but also, *I have come to the conclusion, I am certain, it is my conviction*. And it is especially this idea of certainty that finds expression in the word 'dogma'. While a dogma might in the abstract be a mere private opinion, in common parlance it was generally regarded as an axiomatic or self-evident truth, an official ordinance, or a well founded and formulated article of belief. There are not only religious dogmas, but scientific, philosophical, and political dogmas as well. The fundamental and supposedly unchangeable principles of science, the established teachings of philosophy, the decrees of governments, and the generally accepted doctrines of religion,—they are all dogmata. Modern liberal theologians might well bear this in mind, for a great deal of their criticism of the concept of dogma proceeds from the mistaken assumption that it is something entirely peculiar to religion. All dogmata have this in common, that they are clothed with a certain authority. Naturally, the basis of this authority differs. Scientific dogmas have the authority of axiomatic or self-evident truth. Philosophical dogmas derive their authority from the generally admitted arguments by which they are established. Political dogmas are clothed with the authority of the government by which they are decreed. And religious dogmas are based on divine revelation (either real or supposed), and are therefore authoritative.

2. THE BIBLICAL USE OF THE WORD. The word 'dogma' is found both in the Greek translation of the Old Testament (the Septuagint), and in the New Testament. It is used several times to denote governmental decrees, Esth. 3:9; Dan. 2:13; 6:8; Luke 2:1; Acts 17:7. In two passages it serves as a designation of the Mosaic ordinances, Eph. 2:15; Col. 2:14. And in Acts 16:4 it is applied to the decisions of the assembly of the apostles and elders recorded in the preceding chapter. The use of the term in this passage is particularly important, because it speaks of an ecclesiastical decision, and therefore virtually furnishes a basis for the theological use of the term. It is true that the assembly at Jerusalem did not formulate any doctrine, but its decision certainly had

doctrinal bearings. Moreover, this decision was clothed with divine authority, and was absolutely binding on the churches for which it was intended. It was not a mere advice which these churches could follow up or ignore, as they saw fit, but a burden placed upon them to which they had to submit. The passage under consideration therefore contains at least an intimation of the fact that a religious dogma is a doctrine officially defined by the Church and declared to rest upon divine authority.

3. VARIOUS USES OF THE TERM IN THEOLOGY. In theology the word 'dogma' has not always been used in the same sense. The theological literature of the past sometimes employs the word in a rather loose sense, as practically equivalent with 'doctrine'. But when it speaks of dogmas with precision, it refers to those statements or formulations of doctrines which are regarded as established truths by the body of Christians which formulated them, and which are therefore clothed with authority. The early Church Fathers speak of the truths of the Christian faith, as they were recognized in the Church, as *dogmata*, and also apply this term to the teachings of the heretics. During the Middle Ages a somewhat more specific conception of dogmas was developed by the Roman Catholic Church. In that Church a dogma has come to be regarded as "a revealed truth which has in some way been defined by an infallible teaching authority, and as such is proposed to the acceptance of the faithful."[1] Such a truth need not necessarily be revealed in Scripture, but may also be revealed in oral tradition. The important thing is that the Church declares it to be revealed, and imposes it as such upon the Church. Thus it is really made to rest on the authority of the Church.

The Reformers, and Protestant theology in general, broke with this hierarchical view, and regarded dogmas as divine truths, clearly revealed in the Word of God, formulated by some competent Church body, and regarded as authoritative, because they are derived from the Word of God. Though they ascribed to them a great measure of permanence and stability, they did not, and do not now, regard them as infallible.

A notable change came about through Schleiermacher, who veered from the objective to the subjective in his conception of the source of dogmas. Since he considered Christian experience as their source, he saw in them the intellectual expressions, authorized by the Church, of the inner meaning of the religious experiences of the Christian community. Ritschlian theology pretends to be more objective in its conception of dogmas, but is, as a matter of fact, just as subjective. It regards dogmas as the scientific affirmations of the faith of the Church, that is, not of the contents of this faith, but of that which is involved in it. In this representation faith, the *fides qua creditur*, becomes the source of dogmas, and this is just as subjective as religious experience. While it is perfectly true that this faith does not arise apart from the divine revelation, this is equally true of the religious experience of which Schleiermacher speaks.

---

1. Otten, *Manual of the History of Dogmas I*, p. 2.

The Schleiermacherian and Ritschlian conceptions of dogmas still prevail in many circles. But in more recent theology a new tendency is manifesting itself to recognize their objective character. P. T. Forsyth, of whom McConnachie speaks as "a Barthian before Barth," speaks of dogma as "final revelation in germinal statement," and as "God's act put as truth."[1] The fundamental redemptive acts of God, revealed in the Bible (and therefore expressed in words), constitute the dogma, which is the foundation of the Church. In distinction from it, doctrine is the interpretation of the revealed dogma, and therefore not the foundation, but the product of the Church. Even the interpretations of the acts of God found in Scripture must be regarded as doctrines rather than as dogmas.

There is indeed some agreement between the position of Forsyth and that of Barth, though there are also points of difference. Barth distinguishes between 'dogma' in the singular and 'dogmas' in the plural. He defines 'dogma' as "Church proclamation, so far as it really agrees with the Bible as the Word of God."[2] In another place he speaks of it as "the agreement of Church proclamation with the revelation attested in Holy Scripture."[3] And this revelation is not to be regarded as a doctrinal proposition, but rather as divine action, as a behest or decree, calling for action on man's part. 'Dogmas' in the plural, however, are "the doctrinal propositions acknowledged and confessed by the Church, which are deposited in the Church Symbols, with their relative authority." They are the word of man which comes out of the Word of God, worthy of veneration and respect indeed, yet only the word of man. They do not constitute the *object*, (like 'dogma'), but only the *expression* of faith.[4]

Finally, Micklem is also very much in line with these two men, when he says: "The fundamental and distinctive dogmas of the Christian faith are not in terms of abstract truth, but in terms of the mighty acts of God. That which forms an essential part of the gospel story is dogma; that which is interpretation of the story is theology."[5] The final statement also applies to the interpretation that is found in the Bible itself. It need hardly be said that the views of these men are moving along lines which are quite foreign to Reformed theology.

B. The Formal Characteristics of Dogmas.

Some have spoken of dogmas simply as the substance of the Christian faith, but this view is too indefinite and finds no support whatsoever in Scripture. It does not do justice to their official character. They are truths derived from the Word of God, but the fact that they are so derived does not yet make them dogmas in the strict sense of the word. There are no dogmas *as such* in the Bible, though the doctrinal teachings which they embody are found there. But these become dogmas only when they are formulated and officially adopted

---

1. *Theology in Church and State*, p. 13.
2. *The Doctrine of the Word of God*, p. 308.
3. *op. cit.*, p. 304; cf. also *God in Action*, p. 53.
4. *op. cit.*, pp. 304-315.
5. *What is the Faith*, p. 70.

THE NATURE OF DOGMAS

by the Church. It may be said that religious dogmas have three characteristics, namely: their subject-matter is derived from Scripture; they are the fruit of the reflection of the Church on the truth, as it is revealed in the Bible; and they are officially adopted by some competent ecclesiastical body.

1. THEIR SUBJECT-MATTER IS DERIVED FROM SCRIPTURE. The Bible is God's Word, the book which is His continuous revelation of redemption for all successive generations. It acquaints us with the mighty redemptive acts of God, and also furnishes mankind with a reliable interpretation of these acts. It may therefore be said to be both a word—and a fact—revelation; and both these words and facts have doctrinal significance. Naturally, the meaning of the facts can only be expressed in words. Both the facts and the words have doctrinal significance, and therefore furnish the subject-matter of dogmas. The position of those who find the real revelation of God in Scripture only in the mighty redemptive acts of God (as Forsyth, Barth, Bultmann, Micklem) involves a denial of the fact that every part of the Bible is equally the Word of God. Moreover, it does not take sufficient account of the fact that we have no reliable information respecting the acts of God apart from the words in which He Himself describes these. And the idea that only the acts of God put as truth, or proclaimed by the Church, form the real foundation for dogma(s), clothed with divine authority, really makes an unwarranted distinction between the Scriptural words which describe the facts and the words which interpret them, by regarding the latter as less authoritative. According to our Reformed conception the Bible does not contain dogmas, but does contain the doctrinal truths which they embody. Doctrinal propositions, which are not derived from the Word of God, can never become ecclesiastical dogmas.

Roman Catholics speak of dogmas in the strict sense of the word as "truths contained in the Word of God, written or unwritten—i.e. in Scripture or tradition—and proposed by the Church for the belief of the faithful." The Vatican Council expresses itself as follows:[1] "Further all those things are to be believed with divine and Catholic faith which are contained in the Word of God, written or handed down, and which the Church, either by a solemn judgment, or by her ordinary and universal magisterium, proposes for belief as having been divinely revealed." Historical Protestantism, of course, does not thus coördinate Scripture and tradition. It maintains that the doctrinal truths embodied in dogmas are either contained explicitly in Scripture, or are deduced from it by "good and necessary consequence." Dogmas are not mere repetitions of Scripture statements, but careful, albeit human and therefore fallible, formulations of doctrines contained in the Word of God. Their subject-matter is derived from Holy Writ. If it were not so derived, they would not be dogmas.

It is not superfluous to stress this fact at the present time. Since the beginning of the nineteenth century another view of the derivation of dogmas gradually gained the ascendancy in some Protestant circles. Schleiermacher,

---

1. *Chapter III, On Faith.*

the father of modern theology, does not derive the material content of the dogmas of the Church from the facts or truths revealed in Scripture, but from the Christian consciousness or Christian experience. He declares the articles of faith to be "conceptions of pious feeling set forth in language." On that view they cease to be statements of the truth respecting God and His will, and become mere expressions of the meaning of the ever changing experience of man. Mackintosh correctly says: "If words mean anything, doctrine is for him a statement about our feeling, not about God."[1] And from this it also follows that for Schleiermacher it is not the question, whether the dogmas of religion are objectively true, but only whether they rightly express the various states of feeling. Edghill says that he conceives of dogma as the expression of "ever varying life," and points out that this involves the denial of any permanent authority in the statement of religious "belief."[2]

The Ritschlian view does not differ from this materially, though it pretends to be more objective by taking its starting point in the revelation of God given in Jesus Christ. It seems rather encouraging to find Kaftan saying: "Voraussetzung ist dabei, dass die Dogmen aus goettlicher Offenbarung stammen und, auf evangelischem Gebiet, dass sie dem Glauben und Bekenntniss der Gemeinde entsprechen."[3] But it soon becomes apparent that, while he certainly wants to take account of the objective revelation of God in Jesus Christ, he interposes the faith of the Church between this revelation and the dogmatician. And when he speaks of faith, he is not thinking of faith in the objective sense, as it is expressed in the symbols of the Church, the *fides quae creditur*, but of faith in the subjective sense, the *fides qua creditur*. Moreover, he does not even conceive of this faith as an intellectual apprehension of the truth revealed in the Word of God, but as *fiducia*, trust, that is, as a practically conditioned spiritual relationship to its object, which is presented in the Word of God. This faith includes knowledge, but this knowledge is practical, experiential rather than intellectual, knowledge resulting from a life in communion with God. Man cannot know God, except as He is mirrored in faith. (Kantian) And this practical knowledge, involved in faith, is expressed in dogmas. Thus dogmas are not the object, but the expression of faith. Faith becomes the source of dogmas. This means that Ritschlian theology rejects the older Protestant conception of dogmas as formulations of the truth that is found in the Word of God, and seeks to derive their content from the Christian faith as this is determined in a rather speculative way by value judgments. "Dogma," says Lobstein, another Ritschlian scholar, "is the scientific exposition of the Protestant faith."[4] On page 75 of the same work he states explicitly that "the source of dogmatics is faith."

A somewhat similar subjective view is also found among the Ethicals in the Netherlands. J. Van der Sluis in his work on *De Ethische Richting*, p 23, quotes a word of Prof. D. Chantepie de la Saussaye, which is very much in

---
1. *Types of Modern Theology*, p. 66.
2. *Faith and Fact*, p. 35.
3. *Dogmatik*, p. 2.
4. *An Introduction to Protestant Dogmatics*, p. 61.

harmony with the Ritschlian position: "De leer onstaat na en door het leven. Zij is de vrucht van het nadenkend verstand over de waarheid, wanneer die waarheid tot leven geworden is in de ziel."[1]   And Dr. Is. Van Dijk says: "Indien wij een bepaling van dogme moesten geven, wij zouden het aldus doen: Het dogme is de vrucht der poging, een bepaalde relatie van het leven der gemeente in de taal des verstands om te zetten."[2]

2. Dogmas are the Fruit of Dogmatic Reflection.

The Church does not find her dogmas in finished form on the pages of Holy Writ, but obtains them by reflecting on the truths revealed in the Word of God. The Christian consciousness not only appropriates the truth, but also feels an irrepressible urge to reproduce it and to see it in its grand unity. While the intellect gives guidance and direction to this reflection, it is not purely an intellectual activity, but one that is moral and emotional as well. The understanding, the will, the affections, in short, the whole man, is brought into play. All the faculties of his soul and all the movements of his inner life contribute to the final result. Broader still, it is not merely the individual Christian, but rather the Church of God as a whole, under the guidance of the Holy Spirit, that is the subject of this reflective activity. The spiritual man is the only one that is fit for this work, and even he can obtain a proper and adequate understanding of the truth in all its relations, and in all its fulness and grandeur, only in communion and in coöperation with all the saints. When the Church, led by the Holy Spirit, reflects on the truth, this takes a definite shape in her consciousness and gradually crystalizes into clearly defined doctrinal views and utterances. The formation of dogmas is not always a short process, nor is it a simple one. Its course is frequently determined more or less by long-drawn controversies. These are not always edifying, since they often generate a scorching heat and frequently lead to unholy antagonisms. At the same time they are of the greatest importance, and serve to focus the attention sharply on the question in debate, to clarify the issue at stake, to bring the different aspects of a problem into the open, and to point the way to a proper solution. The Church is largely indebted to the great doctrinal controversies of the past for its progress in the understanding of the truth. Seeberg calls attention to the various elements that entered into the construction of dogmas when he says: "Dogma is an exceedingly complicated historical structure. It has in it various constituent parts, constructed as they have been in the face of multifarious forms of opposition, and under the inspiration of many practical (ethical and devotional) impulses and external (political and canonical) occasions, received the impress of different theological tendencies."[2] Not all periods of history have been equally con-

---

1. Translation: "Doctrine arises after and through life. It is the fruit of the mind reflecting on the truth, when that truth has become life in the soul."
2. Translation: "If we had to give a definition of dogma, we would do it as follows: Dogma is the fruit of the attempt to express a certain relation of the life of the church in the language of the intellect."
1. *Begrip en Methode der Dogmatiek*, p. 14.
2. *History of Doctrines*, I, p. 19. Cf. also Harnack, *History of Dogma* I., p. 12.

ducive to the reflection required for the formation of dogmas. It calls for deep spirituality, for religious fervor, for willing subjection to the truth as it is revealed in the Word of God, for a consuming passion to gain an ever-increasing insight into the truth in all its bearings, for diligent exegetical study, and for constructive ability. Cold Rationalism and sentimental Pietism are equally inimical to it. And certainly such an age as ours, in which philosophical speculations and psychological analyses have largely taken the place of real theological study, is not favorable to the construction of theological dogmas. There is very little recognition of the supreme importance of reflecting on the truth as it is revealed in the Word of God. In fact, there is a widespread and decided opposition to the idea that man must lead his thoughts captive to the obedience of Christ, and must in his search for the truth respecting God and man, sin and redemption, life and death, base his thought on the word of authority, the inspired Word of God, rather than on the discoveries of fallible human reason.

3. DOGMAS ARE OFFICIALLY DEFINED BY SOME COMPETENT ECCLESIASTICAL BODY. The final step in the formation of dogmas is their specific formulation and formal acceptance by some official Church body. It is generally agreed that such an official action of the Church is necessary. Roman Catholics and Protestants are of the same opinion on this point. And even modern theologians, in spite of their subjectivism, voice their concurrence, because they believe that "dogma must have attached to it an idea of collectivity and an idea of authority." Schleiermacher recognized only those religious truths as dogmas, which were accepted as such by the Church. Lobstein says: "It is very evident, in effect, that dogma, in its precise and historical sense, is nothing other than a creed officially defined and formulated by a competent authority, that is to say, in this case, by the Church going hand in hand with the State."[1] And even George Burman Foster declares: "Dogmas are deliverances concerning faith, sustained by ecclesiastical authority."[2]

The question may arise, What Church body has the power to determine what should be believed? Harnack virtually takes the position that only an ecumenical council, representing the Church as a whole, can do this. For that reason he also denies the existence of a Protestant dogma. He points out that Protestantism broke up the unity of the Church, and itself does not present a united front. Naturally, the Churches of the Reformation do not share this view. Reformed Churches particularly have always stressed the fact that every local church is a complete representation of the Church of Jesus Christ, and therefore also has the *potestas dogmatica* or *docendi*, the power to determine what shall be recognized as a dogma in her own circle.

But if such a local church is affiliated with a number of similar churches in a larger organization, it will naturally have to leave this matter to major assemblies. It goes without saying that the dogmas officially defined by the ecumenical councils best satisfy the communal consciousness of the Church; but

---
1. *An Introduction to Protestant Dogmatics*, p. 21.
2. *Christianity in Its Modern Expression*, p. 4.

it is arbitrary to speak of the dogmas formulated by these councils as the only real dogmas.

The dogmas officially attested by the church have authority in the circle in which they are recognized. There is a difference of opinion, however, as to the nature of this authority. The Roman Catholic Church ascribes to its dogmas absolute authority, not only because they are revealed truths, but even more particularly because they are infallibly apprehended and proposed by the Church for the belief of the faithful. The following statement in *A Catholic Dictionary*, Article *Dogma* is significant: "Hence with regard to a new definition—such, e.g., as that of Transubstantiation, Christians have a two-fold duty. They are obliged to believe, first, that the doctrine so defined is true, and next that it is a part of the Christian revelation." Here the declaration of the Church has priority. Scripture and tradition, says Wilmers, are "only the remote or mediate rules of faith, while the immediate rule is the teaching Church."[1] Faith consists in the implicit acceptance of the truth from the hands of the *ecclesia docens* (the priesthood). And the authority of dogmas is really based on the formal declaration of the Church. That authority is absolute, because the Church is infallible.

The Churches of the Reformation broke with this view. While they maintain that a doctrine does not become a dogma, and does not acquire ecclesiastical authority, until it is officially defined and accepted by the Church, they ascribe authority to it only because, and in so far as, it is founded on the Word of God. Their view of the matter can perhaps be best stated as follows. Materially (that is, as to contents) dogmas derive their authority exclusively from the infallible Word of God, but formally (that is, as to form) they derive it from the Church. Barth has a somewhat different view on this point. According to him dogma, in the singular, is Church proclamation in so far as it agrees with the revelation attested in Scripture. That revelation is not primarily a disclosure of truth, though this is involved, but a *kerugma*, a herald's call, a divine imperative, which calls for a response on the part of man. That kerugma, that behest, must be made contemporary in Church proclamation. Hence this should not introduce God as an object about which man must speak, but as a subject which addresses man, and to which man must respond. And in so far as it does this, and is therefore really in agreement with the revelation attested in the Bible, it is dogma. Church proclamation is an approximation to the original revelation, and not a perfect reproduction of it; but in so far as it does agree with it and is therefore really God speaking to sinners in the present, it is clothed with divine authority. The dogma so conceived should be distinguished from the dogmas (plural), in which it is not God who speaks, but the Church, and which for that reason have only relative authority. They are doctrinal propositions acknowledged and formulated by the Church, the word of man which comes out of the Word of God. In them the Church of the past speaks to present generations, and passes on or reproduces the truth of God's

---

1. *Handbook of the Christian Religion*, p. 134.

revelation in so far as it has learned to understand it under the guidance of the Holy Spirit.

Naturally, the followers of Schleiermacher, and even those of Ritschl, do not share the Reformed conception of the authority ascribed to the dogmas of the Church, though they pretend to be in agreement with the position of the Reformers. They regard the view, presented in the preceding as that of Reformed theology, as being in reality the mistaken idea of Protestant Scholasticism which came nigh wrecking the work of the Reformation. For them dogmas are not derived from Scripture, but from the Christian consciousness, that is, from religious experience or from the Christian faith. They are clothed with authority only because they are sanctioned by the communal consciousness of the Church (Schleiermacher), or by that of Church and State combined (Lobstein). Moreover, the authority which they have is not normative and regulative, so as to require submission and demand obedience, but is merely, as Lobstein calls it, "a manifestation of the intrinsic force of the truth, a demonstration of the spirit and of power."[1] Hence it is also regarded as a serious blunder to ascribe a legal character to the Creeds, which embody the dogmas of the Church, and to regard them as a possible basis for disciplinary action.

C. The Necessity of Dogmas.

The present age is an undogmatic age. There is a manifest aversion, not only to dogmas, but even to doctrines, and to a systematic presentation of doctrinal truth. During the last half a century very few dogmatical works made their appearance, while the market was flooded with works on the History of Religions, the Philosophy of Religion, and the Psychology of Religion. The assertion is often heard that Christianity is not a doctrine but a life, and that it makes very little difference what we believe, if we but share the life of Christ. There is an insistent cry, especially in our own country, for a Christianity without dogmas. Dogmatical preaching is not in favor and is therefore avoided in many circles. Many conservative Christians clamour for purely experiential preaching, while others of a more liberal type greatly prefer ethical or social preaching.

1. CAUSES OF PRESENT DAY OPPOSITION TO DOGMAS. The question naturally arises as to the possible explanation of this opposition to dogmas. In the Christian Church at large it can only be explained as the result of certain philosophical tendencies. Under the influence of Kant the dogmas of the Church gradually fell into disrepute. He denied the possibility of theoretical knowledge of those things that transcend the phenomenal world, and therefore also of such knowledge of divine things. His epistemology was of far reaching influence, and received a new impetus in the theology of Ritschl and his disciples. The result was that so-called theoretical knowledge of God and divine things soon fell into disrepute in many circles. Hegel complained about the

---

1. *op. cit.*, p. 33.

undogmatic spirit of his day and sought to rehabilitate Christian dogma by means of speculative philosophy. Like the Gnostics of the second century, he proceeded on the assumption that, if it were pointed out that Christianity is really a philosophy, it would naturally become popular in educated circles. And therefore he stressed the fact that true philosophy, consistently carried through, necessarily leads to the tenets of the Church; and that Christian doctrines are nothing less than speculative truths *in pictorial form*. In his opinion it was only necessary to strip off this form, in order to liberate and disclose the real spiritual kernel of philosophical truth. But the attempt to change the foolishness of God into the wisdom of the world proved abortive. In the hands of left-wing Hegelians, like Strauss and Biedermann, it soon became evident that, after the so-called husk was removed, there was very little Christianity left, and that the philosophical kernel was something quite different from the truth revealed in the Word of God. The Hegelian operation really resulted, as Kaftan says, in "the breaking-up of dogma."[1]

The reaction that arose took the form of Neo-Kantianism in the theology of Ritschl. Says Dr. Orr in his work on *The Ritschlian Theology*, p. 33f.: "As a primary service, Kant furnished Ritschl with a theory of knowledge precisely suited to the requirements of his system. That our knowledge is only of phenomena; that God is theoretically incognoscible; that our conviction of His existence rests on a practical, not on a theoretic judgment—these are thoughts which, we shall see, are raised in Ritschlian circles almost to the rank of first principles." Hence it is no wonder that the work of Ritschl, and of such followers of his as Lotze, Herrmann, Harnack, Sabatier, and others, was on the whole unfavorable to Christian dogma, though theoretically it did not rule it out altogether.

Finally, Dreyer in his *Undogmatisches Christentum* makes a plea for a Christianity without dogma. He argues (a) that the ancient dogmas were naturally cast in the conceptual forms of the day in which they arose, and that these forms become a hindrance in a time when religious views have undergone a fundamental change; and (b) that dogmas endanger the independence and freedom that is indispensable for the Christian faith. It will readily be seen that only the second argument bears against dogmas as such, but it is exactly this argument that marks the real tendency of the work under consideration. Kaftan and Lobstein quite agree with Dreyer, that dogmas have often been a hindrance to faith, but at the same time consider them necessary and plead for a new dogma. Troeltsch comes to the conclusion that "an Ecclesiastical Protestant system of dogma no longer exists," and that the Protestant Churches will have to seek "union and cohesion" in some other sphere than that of dogma.[2]

Alongside of this direction of philosophical thought, there have, of course, been many other influences, too many to enumerate, which have operated and continue to operate to make dogmas unpopular. Religious free-thinkers repeat-

---
1. *The Truth of the Christian Religion I*, p. 313.
2. *The Social Teaching of the Christian Churches*, p. 1009.

edly raise their voices against dogmas, as encroaching upon their religious liberty and call for freedom in the Church. They not infrequently pose as the real champions of the right of private judgment, one of the fundamental principles of the Reformation. On more than one occasion a one-sided dogmatism led to a pietistic reaction. And it is characteristic of Pietism that it is hostile to all intellectualism in religion and exalts emotionalism and experience as the only real manifestation of the religious life. It bids Christian people escape from the wrangling of doctrinal controversies by withdrawing into the citadel of the heart, the seat of the affections. In our own country Pietism has found a rather welcome ally in an Activism, which holds that it makes little difference what one believes, provided one is only busy in the work of the Lord. A great number of American Christians are much too busy in all kinds of church activities to concern themselves very much about the study of the truth. They are practical pragmatists and are interested only in a religion that promptly yields tangible results. Their knowledge of dogmas has been reduced to a minimum. In fact both Pietists and Activists often claim that Christian people should disengage themselves from the complexities of present day doctrinal systems and return to the simplicity of the Apostolic Age, and preferably to the words of Jesus, who did not concern Himself about dogmas. Many other anti-dogmatic tendencies might be mentioned, but these are sufficient to give us at least some understanding of present day opposition to dogmas.

2. DOGMAS ESSENTIAL TO CHRISTIANITY. The necessity of dogmas may be argued in various ways. Even the followers of Schleiermacher and Ritschl defend it in spite of their subjectivism, and notwithstanding their mysticism and moralism. Several reasons at once suggest themselves, why Christianity cannot dispense with dogmas.

a. *Scripture represents the truth as essential to Christianity.* The assertion often heard in our day, that Christianity is not a doctrine but a life, may have a rather pious sound, and for that very reason seems to appeal to some, but is after all a dangerous falsehood. It has been pointed out repeatedly, and has in recent years again been emphasized by Dr. Machen in his *Christianity and Liberalism*, that Christianity is a way of life founded on a message. The gospel is the self-revelation of God in Christ, which comes to us in the form of truth. That truth is revealed, not only in the Person and work of Christ, but also in the interpretation of these found in the Bible. And it is only by a proper understanding and a believing acceptance of the message of the gospel, that men are brought to the necessary self-surrender to Christ in faith, and are made partakers of the new life in the Spirit. The reception of that life is not dependent on some purely mystical infusion of grace, nor on the proper ethical conduct of man, but is conditioned by knowledge. "And this is life eternal," says Jesus, *"that they should know thee,* the only true God, and Him whom thou didst send, even Jesus Christ."[1] Paul says that God would have "all men to be saved, *and come to the knowledge of the truth.*"[2] He

---
1. *John* 17:3.
2. *I Tim.* 2:4.

represents it as one of the grand ideals of the ministry, that all believers may "attain unto the unity of the faith, *and of the knowledge of the Son of God*, unto a full-grown man, unto the measure of the stature of the fulness of Christ."[1] And Peter says that the divine power "hath granted unto us all things that pertain unto life and godliness, *through the knowledge of him that called us by his own glory and virtue.*"[2] Participation in the life of Christianity is everywhere in the New Testament made conditional on faith in Christ as He has revealed Himself, and this naturally includes knowledge of the redemptive facts recorded in Scripture. Christians must have a proper understanding of the significance of these facts; and if they are to unite in faith, must also arrive at some unitary conviction and expression of the truth. Jesus concludes His prayer for His immediate disciples with the words: "Sanctify them in the truth: thy word is truth," and then continues: "Neither for these only do I pray, but for them also *that believe on me through their word; that they may all be one.*"[3] The acceptance of the Word of God and spiritual unity go hand in hand. The same remarkable conjunction is found in the word of Paul: "Till we all attain unto the unity of the faith, and of the knowledge of the Son of God."[4] The Bible certainly does not create the impression that the Church can safely disregard the truth, as it is revealed in the Word of God. Jesus stressed the truth, Matt. 28:20; John 14:26; 16:1-15; 17:3, 17; and the apostles were very much in earnest about it, Rom. 2:8; II Cor. 4:2; Gal. 1:8; 3:1 ff.; Phil. 1:15-18; II Thess. 1:10; 2:10, 12, 13; I Tim. 6:5; II Tim. 2:15; 4:4; II Pet. 1:3, 4, 19-21; I John 2:20-22; 5:20. They who minimize the significance of the truth, and therefore ignore and neglect it, will finally come to the discovery that they have very little Christianity left.

b. *The unity of the Church demands doctrinal agreement.* The Bible teaches the unity of the Church of Jesus Christ, and at the same time speaks of it as "the pillar and ground of the truth."[5] In Ephesians 4 Paul stresses the unity of the Church of God, and clearly indicates as the ideal that its members all attain to the unity of the *knowledge* of the Son of God. This receives further emphasis in the 15th verse: "That we be no longer children, tossed to and fro and carried about with every wind of doctrine." He exhorts the Philippians that they shall "stand fast in one spirit, with one soul striving for the *faith* of the gospel."[6] In this passage the word "faith" has in all probability the same meaning as in Jude 3, where the writer exhorts his readers "to contend earnestly for the faith which was once for all delivered unto the saints." If it does not entirely have the same meaning, it certainly approaches it. The apostle admonishes the Corinthians, that they "all speak the same thing," and that there

---

1. *Eph.* 4:12.
2. *II Pet.* 1:3.
3. *John* 17:17, 20.
4. *Eph.* 4:13.
5. *I Tim.* 3:15, 4:13.
6. *Phil.* 1:27.

be no divisions among them.[1] They should be of one accord and of one mind. He considers this so important that he hurls his anathema at those who preach a gospel different from that which he had preached,[2] and even insists on the exclusion of heretical persons.[3] It is a stern judgment, which he pronounces in I Tim. 6:3-5; "If any man teacheth a different doctrine, and consenteth not to sound words, even the words of our Lord Jesus Christ, and to the doctrine which is according to godliness; he is puffed up, knowing nothing, but doting about questionings and disputes of words, whereof cometh envy, strife, railings, evil surmisings, wranglings of men corrupted in mind and bereft of the truth, supposing that godliness is a way of gain." Unity in the knowledge of the truth is evidently regarded as of the greatest importance to the well-being of the Church. If it includes men of all kinds of conviction, it will harbor in its bosom the seeds of discord, strife, and division. And that certainly will not minister to the edification of the saints and to the welfare of the Church, nor be conducive to its efficiency in the work of the Lord. And in striving for the unity of the Church it will hardly do to rest satisfied with the least common denominator in the confession of the truth, nor to say, Let us forget about doctrine, and get together by working together.

c. *The duty of the Church requires unity in doctrine.* Naturally, the Church as such can only be one in doctrine, if it has a common confession. This means that the Church must formulate and thus give expression to its understanding of the truth. Unity in doctrine therefore involves the confession of a common dogma. It will not do to admit that the Church may need doctrines, and at the same time to deny that she needs dogmas. The Church cannot perform her function in the world, unless she becomes conscious of, and gives clear expression to, the contents of her faith. The Church of Jesus Christ was appointed to be a depository, a guardian, and a witness of the truth, and can only be true to her calling, if she has a definite conception of the truth. Ministers are exhorted to hold fast the pattern of sound words,[4] and believers in general, to contend earnestly for the faith once delivered to the saints, but how can they accomplish their important task, if there is no agreement as to the "sound words" and as to what the Church believes. The Church must deal with errorists, correcting, rebuking, and possibly excluding them from the fold, but cannot do this intelligently and effectively, unless she has a clear apprehension of the truth and therefore a definite standard of judgment. History clearly teaches that, before a Church can really pass judgment on heresies, she must have some official standard or test. And it goes without saying that she can never bear a united and powerful testimony to the truth, unless she herself presents a united front.

d. *The position of the Church in the world calls for a united testimony.* Every Church owes it to other Churches and to the world round about her, to

---

1. *I Cor.* 1:10.
2. *Gal.* 1:8, 9.
3. *Tit.* 3:10.
4. *II. Tim.* 1:13.

make a public declaration of her teachings. If it is but natural that we desire to know something about the character and convictions of the people to whom we would entrust our material interests, it will certainly be considered highly desirable, and in fact quite essential, that we know exactly where a Church stands, in which we would seek spiritual guidance for ourselves and for our children. Moreover, one Church will have to know where another stands, in order to be able to determine in how far it can correspond, coöperate, and possibly affiliate with such a Church. The Church of Jesus Christ should never seek refuge in camouflage, should not try to hide her identity. And this is exactly what she does in the measure in which she fails to give a clear and unequivocal expression of her faith.

e. *Experience teaches that dogmas are indispensable.* Every Church has its dogmas. Even the Churches that are constantly decrying dogmas have them in effect. When they say that they want a Christianity without dogma, they are by that very statement declaring a dogma. They all have certain definite convictions in religious matters, and also ascribe to them a certain authority, though they do not always formulate them officially and acknowledge them candidly. History clearly proves that even the present day opposition, is not really an opposition to dogmas as such, but simply opposition to a certain kind of dogmas, or to certain specific dogmas, which do not find favor in the eyes of modern theologians. A Church without dogmas would be a silent Church, and this is a contradiction in terms. A silent witness would be no witness at all, and would never convince anyone.

D. The Elements Involved in Dogmas.

Christian dogmas involve various elements, which are of great importance for the life of the Church. Of these the following three deserve special mention.

1. THE SOCIAL ELEMENT. Religious dogmas are not the product of individual Christians, but of the Church as a whole. Though the appropriation of the truth revealed in the Bible is first of all personal, it gradually assumes a communal and corporate aspect. It is only in communion with all the saints that believers can understand and confidently reproduce the truth. The personal reflection of the individual Christian thus gains the advantage of collective control, and the confidence which he may have in his own findings is naturally greatly strengthened by the fact that thousands of others reach the same conclusion. The communal or social character, which the dogmas thus acquire, may not be regarded as something accidental and of only relative importance, but should be thought of as something that is absolutely essential. Personal opinions, however true and valuable they may be, do not constitute Christian dogmas. Some extremists object to the social element of dogmas. They admit the necessity of reflecting on the truth, but are of the opinion that personal self-respect should prompt each one to decide for himself what is true. Each one should construct his own system of the truth, and should not concern himself

about the ideas of others. It cannot be said, however, that they represent the prevailing tendency of our day in theological thought. Both Schleiermacher and Ritschl, in spite of the fact that their subjectivism makes for individualism in religion, strongly emphasize the communal element of dogmas. Harnack says, that there is "introduced into the idea of dogma a social element . . .; the confessors of one and the same dogma form a community."[1] Sabatier, in speaking of the origin of dogmas, expresses himself as follows: "Dogma only arises when the religious society, distinguishing itself from the civil, becomes a moral society, recruiting itself by voluntary adherents. This society, like every other, gives to itself what it needs in order to live, to defend itself, and to propagate itself."[2] And, finally, McGiffert says:[3] "Schleiermacher's recognition of the social element has been reinforced in modern times by the study of the history and psychology of religion which has made it abundantly evident that our beliefs are largely social products, and that the notion that our individual reasons work in isolation to create our own independent faiths is a pure fiction."

2. THE TRADITIONAL ELEMENT. Dogmas also contain a traditional element. Christianity rests on historical facts which come to our knowledge through a revelation given and completed more than nineteen centuries ago. And the correct understanding and interpretation of these facts can only result from the continual prayers and meditation, from the study and struggles, of the Church of all ages. No one Christian can ever hope to succeed in assimilating and reproducing properly the whole content of the divine revelation. Neither is one generation ever able to accomplish the task. The formation of dogmas is the task of the Church of all ages, a task which requires great spiritual energy on the part of successive generations. And history teaches us that, in spite of differences of opinion and protracted struggles, and even in spite of temporary retrogressions, the Church's insight into the truth gradually gained in clarity and profundity. One truth after another became, the center of attention, and was brought to ever greater development. And the historical Creeds of the Churches now embody in concentrated form the best results of the reflection and study of past centuries. It is at once the duty and the privilege of the Church of our day to enter into that heritage of bygone years, and to continue to build on the foundation that was laid.

There is a manifest tendency, however, on the part of modern liberal theology to break with the past. Many of its representatives are often rather loud in their praises of the Creeds of the Church *as historical documents,* but refuse to acknowledge their doctrinal value for the present. And, sad to say, the so-called Fundamentalists of our day join hands with the liberals on this point with their well-known slogan, "No Creed but the Bible." They do not seem to realize that this really involves a break with the historical past of the Church, a refusal to profit by the lessons which the Churches of the Reforma-

---

1. *History of Dogma I,* p. 14.
2. *Outlines of a Philosophy of Religion,* p. 237.
3. *The Rise of Modern Religious Ideas,* p. 291.

tion passed on as a precious heritage to following generations in their great Creeds and Confessions, and a virtual denial of the guidance of the Holy Spirit in the past history of the Church. But modern liberal theology does not stop even there; it also breaks with the Bible itself as the authoritative source of all doctrinal truth. This is stated without any hesitation by Reville[1] in the following words: "Not only has it (Liberalism) thrown off the yoke of the Protestant confessions of faith, because a thorough examination of these proved that they by no means faithfully reflected the teaching of Christ. But further, owing to the immense results reached by the historical and philological sciences during the nineteenth century, it has recognized that in the Bible itself there are many doctrines which come neither from the prophets, nor from Jesus, and which consequently are not to be considered as the faithful expression of the teaching of Christ." Such a position, of course, involves a rejection of the Bible as the Word of God, and further an utter disregard and denial of the guidance of the Holy Spirit in the past doctrinal history of the Church, a lack of respect for the prayers, the labors, and the struggles of the greatest and most pious teachers of the Church. It represents an unwarranted individualism in the development and formulation of the truth, an exaggerated notion of the ability of a single individual, or of the Church of a single generation to rear *de novo* a better structure of religious truth than the time-honored system of the past.

3. THE ELEMENT OF AUTHORITY. When the Churches of the Reformation officially define their doctrines and thereby turn them into dogmas, they also implicitly declare them to rest on divine authority and to be expressions of the truth. And because they regard their dogmas as embodiments of the truth revealed in the Word of God, they consider them as entitled to general recognition, and insist on such recognition in their own circles. The Roman Catholic Church claims absolute infallibility for its dogmas, partly because they are revealed truths, but especially because they are proposed for the faith of the faithful by an infallible Church. Her dogmas are absolutely unchangeable. The Vatican Council declared:[2] "If any one shall assert it to be possible that sometimes, according to the progress of science, a sense is to be given to the doctrines propounded by the Church different from that which the Church has understood and understands: let him be anathema." This absolutism is not shared by the Protestant Churches. While they expect acceptance of their dogmas, because they regard them as correct formulations of Scripture truth, they admit the possibility that the Church may have been in error in defining the truth. And if dogmas are found to be contrary to the Word of God, they cease to be authoritative.

It is exactly this element of authority that meets with the greatest opposition in the present day. Both Roman Catholics and Protestants regard religion first of all as something given and determined by God, and therefore

---

1. *Liberal Christianity*, p. 40.
2. (*de Fide IV.* 3.):

find the seat of authority in Him. According to the former it is especially the Church, while according to the latter it is the Bible, that is basic to this authority. Both recognize an objective standard of the truth, which finds expression in the dogmas of the Church and which demands submission, faith, and obedience. Eighteenth century Rationalism and Deism broke with the "medieval principle of religious authority," and substituted for it the standard of human reason, thus placing the seat of authority in man and making it purely individual. For Schleiermacher the content of dogmas is determined by religious experience, and for Ritschl, ostensibly by Jesus Christ as the Founder of the Kingdom of God, but in reality by the subjective faith of the Church. In the case of both the real seat of authority is in the religious consciousness; and the authority, of course, is not that of an objective norm, but that of an internal principle. Lobstein says: "From the point of view of the Protestant it is necessary to condemn every conception which makes of dogma an authoritative and obligatory decision of the church in the sense of a statutory and legal ordinance."[1] According to the dictum of Sabatier, another Ritschlian, "The outward authority of the letter has given place to the inward and purely moral authority of the Spirit."[2] This French scholar argues that the human spirit has finally been emancipated from the principle of authority, and has become autonomous, which means that "the consent of the mind to itself is the prime condition and foundation of all certitude." This is tantamount to the rejection of all real authority. Barth rejects both the Roman Catholic and the modern liberal conception of dogmas. He ascribes absolute authority to dogma (singular), since it agrees with revelation, and relative authority to dogmas, that is, to the doctrinal propositions formulated by the Church, in so far as they spring from the root of revelation.[3]

QUESTIONS FOR FURTHER STUDY: Has the Church of Rome power to make new dogmas? Does it assume that the Pope has this power? If not, does it not follow that, according to this Church, *dogmas as such* are contained in the Word of God? How does Cardinal Newman's conception of the development of dogmas fit in with the Roman Catholic view of the unchangeableness of dogmas? What is the Protestant view as to the formulation of new dogmas? Do science and philosophy also furnish a part of the content of dogmas, or do they affect their form only? What is Harnack's conception of dogma? How does he conceive of its origin? What objections are there to his view? What factors in present-day life serve to strengthen the aversion to dogmas? Is there any Church in existence that has no dogmas?

REFERENCES: Bavinck, *Geref. Dogm.* I, pp. 1-10; Hepp, *De Waarde Van Het Dogma*; Is. Van Dijk, *Begrip en Methode der Dogmatiek*, pp. 1-28; Hodge, *The Idea of Dogmatic Theology*, in *The Princeton Theological Review*, Jan., 1908. pp. 52-60; Lobstein, *An Introduction to Protestant Dogmatics*, pp. 1-57; Kaftan, *The Truth of the Christian Religion*, Vol. I, and *Dogmatik*, pp. 1-9; Ihmels, *Centralfragen der Dogmatik*, pp. 1-30; Sabatier, *Outlines of a Philosophy of Religion*, pp. 229-343; Otten, *Manual of the History of Dogmas* I, pp. 1-4; Meyrick, *Is Dogma a Necessity?*; Barth, *The Doctrine of the Word of God*, pp. 11-15, 284, 304 ff.; *The Word of God and the Word of Man*, 229.

1. *An Introduction to Protestant Dogmatics*, p. 49.
2. *Religions of Authority*, p. 259.
3. *The Doctrine of the Word of God*, p. 356f.

III. The Idea of Dogmatic Theology

A. The Relation of Dogmas to Dogmatics.

THE discussion of dogmas naturally leads on to an inquiry as to the relation in which they stand to Dogmatics. The very name 'Dogmatics' suggests a very close relation. It is derived from the singular *'dogma'* rather than from the plural *'dogmata,'* and as such points to the fact that it deals not merely with certain separate dogmas, but with the dogma of the Church as a whole. The exact relation between dogma and Dogmatics has not always been conceived of in the same way. The most common view is that dogma forms the subject-matter of Dogmatics, so that the latter might be called the science of Christian dogma. Thus it may be said that Dogmatics deals with the doctrinal truth of Scripture in a systematic way, and more particularly with that truth as it is confessed by the Church. It studies the doctrine of the Church as a whole, and considers each article of faith in its relation to the whole. As such it is not only Scriptural, though it must be this first of all, but also bears an ecclesiastical imprint. Schleiermacher's conception of dogma differs from that of the Protestant Church in general, since he does not acknowledge its derivation from Scripture, but agrees with it in its representation of dogma as the subject-matter of Dogmatics. According to him dogmatic theology is the science of the doctrine professed by a Christian Church at a given moment of its historical development. The Ritschlian view of the relation between dogma and Dogmatics does not differ from that just indicated. Kaftan says: "Die Dogmatik hat es demnach mit einem *gegebenen* object zu thun, mit der christlichen Wahrheit, die die Kirche auf grund der goettlichen Offenbarung glaubt und bekennt."[1] Harnack claims, however, that the Church has not been altogether honest in its representation of the relation between dogmas and Dogmatics. According to him history teaches that dogmas are the product of theology. The Church, however, obscured their real origin, declared them to be revealed truths, and as such made them basic for theology.[2] According to Forsyth dogma is "final revelation in germinal statement. It is God's act put as truth," and is therefore a part of God's revelation. "Doctrine is truth about dogma, dogma expanded . . . It is secondary theology, or the Church's grasp —as in the creeds. Theology is doctrine in the making. It is tertiary and tentative theology or the Church's reach—as in I Pet. 1:18, 19, 20."[3] Dogma is for him the marrow of the gospel, the vital core of revelation, and is therefore found in Scripture. It is the root, out of which doctrine develops through

---

1. *Dogmatik*, p. 2.
2. *History of Dogma I*, p. 9.
3. *Theology in Church and State*. p. 12f.

the theological study of the Church. "Theology is tentative doctrine; doctrine is selected theology." This is rather strikingly similar to the view of Barth. Defining dogma (singular) as Church proclamation, so far as it is in real agreement with the Word of God, Barth regards Dogmatics as the science, *not of dogmas, but of dogma*, which inquires into the agreement of dogma with the revelation attested in Scripture. It therefore serves to test dogma.[1] He does not believe that dogmas (plural) form the subject-matter of Dogmatics, though their understanding and formulation may be greatly promoted by Dogmatics. Forsyth looks upon dogma as a part, and in fact the vital core, of God's revelation, and Barth comes very close to the same evaluation; so close in fact that he too, like Forsyth, regards dogma as the object of faith. They further agree in denying that dogmas or doctrines should be regarded as objects of faith, and insist on it that these are mere expressions of the faith of the Church. Both are also of the opinion that the prevalent conception of dogma is that of Protestant Scholasticism, and not that of the Reformers. In the discussion of the historical conception of the Protestant Churches respecting the relation between dogmas and dogmatics attention must be called to several propositions.

1. DOGMAS ARISE OUT OF THE NECESSITIES OF THE BELIEVING COMMUNITY. Seeberg says in opposition to Harnack: "Although the form of dogma is the work of theology, its content is derived from the common faith of the Christian Church."[2] This is a welcome correction of Harnack's view that dogmas are the product of theology, but can hardly be considered as a correct designation of the source from which dogmas are derived. It is more in harmony with the Ritschlian position. Rainy is more Reformed in his thinking, when he first points out that doctrines (dogmas) are derived from Scripture, and then says: "I do not think that it is the scientific interest which primarily calls out Christian doctrine; nor is it an obligation to comply with the formal conditions of science, which this activity properly obeys; nor do I think that the scientific impulse has been, historically, the creative force in this department. . . . Doctrine is maintained to arise not primarily in obedience to the scientific interest or impulse, but out of the necessities of the believing mind."[3]

Dogmas cannot be made to order. They cannot be produced by individual theologians, nor by scientific theology in general, and then imposed upon the community of believers from without. Chances are that dogmas so constructed and proposed would not really express the faith of the Church, would not strike a responsive chord in the communal life of believers, and consequently would not be recognized as authoritative. They are formed only in periods of intense spiritual life, of wide-spread and earnest reflection on the truth, and of deep religious experience. It is only when the Church thinks deeply on the truths of Scripture, when under the stress of religious controversies she has learned to see the truth sharply and clearly, and when definite

---

1. *The Doctrine of the Word of God*, pp. 11 ff., 15, 284, 304 ff.
2. *Cf. History of Doctrine I*, p. 19.
3. *Delivery and Development of Christian Doctrine*, pp. 109, 367.

convictions have gradually become the common property of the religious community, and thus a *communis opinio* is formed,—it is only then that she will be ready to confess, and will feel within herself an irresistible urge to give expression to her faith. Only the truth so confessed really constitutes a confession of faith, is rooted in the life and experience of the Church, and therefore also has a grip on the Church. Only the dogmas that spring from this living soil can be called in the words of Rainy "the human echo to the divine voice," or "the human response to the divine message."

2. THEOLOGY MAY AND HAS FREQUENTLY SERVED AS AN AUXILIARY IN THE FORMATION OF DOGMAS. While denying that dogmas are merely the product of theology, we need not close our eyes to the fact that, for their final formulation, the Church was often greatly indebted to theology. It need hardly be said that in the reflective activity of the Christian community some would be far more influential than others; and that, if all other things were equal, those who had special religious training would form the vanguard. As the spiritual leaders of the people, and as the interpreters, the historians, and the systematicians of the Church, they would naturally point the way in the careful formulation of dogmas. And it was but natural that, when the science of theology developed, this should also be pressed into service and become a powerful auxiliary in the process. This could not be otherwise, because it has, in its own field, the special task of reflecting on the truth as it is revealed in the Word of God, and of reproducing this truth in systematic form. Yet it should be borne in mind that the work of theology in this sphere is of a purely formal nature. It does not furnish the subject-matter of the dogmas, but merely helps the Church in forming and defining her dogmas. Naturally, in the measure in which theology took a hand in the formation of dogmas, these assumed a more systematic form than they would otherwise have had.

3. DOGMATIC THEOLOGY FINDS THE NUCLEUS OF ITS SUBJECT-MATTER IN THE DOGMAS OF THE CHURCH. Though theology may serve as an auxiliary in the formation of dogmas, this is not its main concern with the dogmas of the Church. These form the nucleus of the material with which it must build and which it must rear into a systematic structure, and will therefore naturally have a determining influence on the texture and the complexion of the system as a whole. They will occupy a very important place in it and lend it a distinctive character. The dogmatician takes his stand in the confessional teachings of the Church to which he belongs; these form his bias, if you will. It may be objected that this naturally endangers his intellectual liberty, but this is not necessarily the case. As long as he remains a member of that particular Church, it may be assumed that he does this from conviction. And if this is the case, he will naturally regard the dogmas of his Church more as friendly guides, acquainting him with the direction in which he should move, than as hateful fetters that impinge on his liberty. Moreover, it is well to remember that no one is ever entirely unbiased in his scientific work; and that the dogmatician who refuses to be biased by the dogmas of his Church should not pose

as its dogmatician. To do so would be ethically reprehensible. We repeat that these dogmas constitute the most important part of the materials which he must use in the construction of his system, and will so enter into the structure of it as to form its nucleus and core, and also its unifying element.

But the theologian cannot limit himself to the dogmas that are contained in the Confession of the Church, for this is by no means an exhaustive expression of its faith. He must utilize all the doctrinal truths that are revealed in the Word of God, and doing that, of course, also draw upon the fruits of other studies, such as Exegesis, Biblical Theology, History of Doctrines, and others. He may find it profitable to levy contributions from individuals and groups. But whatever elements he incorporates in his system, he must present, not merely as historical data, but as component parts of the structure which he is rearing, and which he regards not merely as an expression of his own belief but as absolutely valid truth. Moreover, he cannot consider these doctrines as bare abstract intellectual formula, and as so many isolated truths, but will have to study and present them as living plants, which have come to development in the course of the centuries and strike their roots deep down into Scriptural soil, and must view them in their grand unity.

Naturally, modern theology, under the influence of Schleiermacher and Ritschl, has a somewhat different conception of the relation between dogmas and dogmatics. Litchtenberger states the position of Schleiermacher in a single sentence,[1] when he says that, according to the father of modern theology, "Dogmatics describes not doctrines nor facts which have been revealed in a supernatural manner, but experiences of the human soul, or the feelings which the religious soul experiences in its relations with Jesus the Savior." Lobstein represents the Ritschlian position. Says he: "Like dogma, like dogmatics. There obtains between the notion of dogma and the role of dogmatics a necessary and direct relation . . . . It is clear that a return to the vital principle of the Reformation and the corresponding transformation of the idea of dogma in the evangelical Church involves a parallel modification of the task entrusted to the dogmatician. Dogmatics . . . . is the scientific exposition of the Protestant faith . . . . Dogmatics creates nothing; it merely formulates the problems whose elements are given to it by the religious experience of the Christian in the presence of the living realities of the gospel. Dogmatics is an experimental and positive science, but it receives its material from faith; rather its material is faith itself with the divine content of faith."[2]

Is. Van Dijk, a representative of the Ethical Movement in the Netherlands, which reminds one somewhat of both Schleiermacher and Ritschl but seems to owe its greatest debt to Vinet, puts it as follows: "Het dogme is de vrucht der poging om een bepaald moment, een bepaalde relatie van het leven der gemeente in de taal des verstands om te zetten, terwijl de dogmatiek dan is de

---
1. *History of German Theology in the Nineteenth Century*, p. 142.
2. *An Introduction to Protestant Dogmatics*, pp. 58-62.

beschrijving, de omzetting in begrippen van dat leven in zijn geheel."[1] The objection that this obliterates the distinction between dogmatics and ethics, is met by the remark that, though both describe life, they do not contemplate life in the same sense: . . . "de dogmatiek beschrijft den *grond* en den *inhoud*, de ethiek de *openbaring* en het *ideaal* van het leven."[2]

B. The Object of Dogmatic Theology. (Its Definition)

The question of the object of theology, and therefore also of dogmatic theology, can be considered very appropriately in connection with its definition. Theology has not always been defined in the same way. A brief consideration of the most important definitions that have been suggested in course of time may be helpful in determining what has been and should be considered as the object of theology.

1. THE CONCEPTION OF THE OBJECT OF DOGMATIC THEOLOGY IN EARLY PROTESTANT THEOLOGY. Previous to the Reformation there were various ideas respecting the object of Dogmatic Theology. According to Augustine it deals with God, the world, man, and the sacraments. Peter the Lombard shared this view. Others (Alexander of Hales, Bonaventura) regarded the mystical body of Christ, that is, the Church, and still others (Hugo of St. Victor), the redemptive work of God, as the object of Dogmatic Theology. Thomas Aquinas expressed himself as follows: *"Theologia a Deo docetur, Deum docet, et ad Deum ducit"* ("Theology is taught by God, teaches God, and leads unto God"). This is more in harmony wth the etymology of the word in so far as it represents God as the object of theology. A considerable number of both Lutheran and Reformed theologians of the post-Reformation period defined theology as the knowledge or science of (concerning) God. Some objected to this on the ground that it is not possible for us to have a perfect knowledge of God on earth. But the men who used this definition were generally quite careful to point out that they did not have in mind the knowledge which God has of Himself (archetypal knowledge), but the knowledge which man has of God *in virtue of His Self-revelation* (ectypal knowledge.) They considered such knowledge of God possible, because He revealed Himself. The desire to stress the practical nature of this science prompted some seventeenth century theologians to define it with reference to its end or purpose rather than with a view to its object. They conceived of it as teaching man *the true religion unto salvation, the life for God in Christ,* or *the service of God that is well-pleasing to Him.* These and other, somewhat similar, descriptions are found in the works of Hollaz, Quenstedt, Gerhard, Amesius, Mastricht, and

---

1. Translation: "Dogma is the fruit of the attempt to reproduce a certain point, a certain relation of the life of the Church in the language of the intellect, while dogmatics is then the description, the transformation into concepts of that life as a whole."
2. Translation: "Dogmatics describes the *ground* and the *content*, Ethics the *manifestation* and *ideal* of life."

2. *Begrip en Methode der Dogmatiek*, pp. 14, 16. For a criticism of this position cf. Honing, *Dogmatiek en Ethiek*, pp. 40-46.

à Marck. In general it may be said, however, that Reformed theologians conceived of theology as the science of (concerning) God. However, this simple definition frequently received certain complementary additions. It often assumed some such form as the following: Theology is the science of God and of divine things; or .... of God and His relations to the universe; or .... of God as He is in Himself and as He is related to all His creatures.

2. THE DEVELOPMENT OF A NEW CONCEPTION IN MODERN SUBJECTIVE THEOLOGY. The phenomenalism of Kant had a rather revolutionary effect on the common conception of theology. It limited all theoretical knowledge, scientific or otherwise, to the phenomenal world. This means that according to it man can have no theoretical knowledge of that which transcends human experience, and therefore theology as the science of God is an impossibility. The practical reason is the only reliable guide in religion, and its propositions are not susceptible of rational proof, but must be accepted by faith. God is highly exalted above our observation and experience. We can accept Him and the relations in which He stands to His creatures only by faith, and what is so accepted cannot be constructed into a scientific system. God is an object of faith, and not of science.

The epistemological principles of Kant paved the way for that subjectivism in religion, of which Schleiermacher became the great spokesman. He defined Dogmatics as "the science of the Christian faith," that is, of the contents of the Christian faith. This content does not consist in truths or facts supernaturally revealed, but in religious experiences, primarily under the inspiration of the personality of Jesus, by which man becomes conscious of the supernatural and eternal. The intellectual expressions of the devout feeling, or of Christian experience, which are current in the preaching and teaching of a particular Church, constitute the raw material of theology. And an inquiry into the cause of this experience will naturally lead the mind to God. Ritschlians also define Dogmatics as "the scientific exposition of the Protestant faith." Yet they do not agree with Schleiermacher's conception of the object of Dogmatics, for with respect to his work Lobstein says: "The classical work of the great theologian is not, to tell the truth, a systematic exposition of the Protestant faith; it is composed of reflections upon the soul of the Christian, upon the different modifications of the religious consciousness of the subject."[1] Ritschlians generally claim greater objectivity, and it sounds somewhat more objective, when the author just quoted says: "Dogmatics . . . receives its material from faith; rather its material is faith itself with the divine content of faith, that is, the gospel." Yet in the end the Ritschlian view turns out to be just as subjective as that of Schleiermacher, as we shall show in one of the following chapters.

This subjective tendency in course of time gave rise to the definition, so popular in our day, according to which theology is defined as "the science of religion" or, more specifically, as "the science of the Christian religion." In this definition, as it is generally used in modern theology, the word 'religion'

---
1. *An Introduction to Protestant Dogmatics*, p. 63.

THE IDEA OF DOGMATIC THEOLOGY

is used in the subjective sense, to denote religion as a phenomenon of human life. Moreover, this religion is often conceived of in a very one-sided and unsatisfactory way, and is sometimes represented in a purely naturalistic fashion. Thus that aspect of human life, which is indicative of man's relation to a divine Being, became the object of theology. This view resulted in an increased emphasis on the study of the history of religion, of the philosophy of religion, and of the psychology of religion.

There are, of course, serious objections to this conception of theology: (a) it divorces theology from its objective foundation in the Word of God, and bases it entirely on subjective experiences which have no normative value; (b) it robs theology of its positive character and reduces it to a purely descriptive science, describing historical and psychological phenomena instead of aiming at absolute truth; and (c) it involuntarily leads to a representation of the Christian religion as merely one of the many religions of the world, differing from them indeed in degree, but not in essence.

Attention should be called to the fact, however, that the definition of theology as the science of religion is sometimes found in the works of the older Reformed theologians, and is still found in the theological writings of such men of a previous generation as Thornwell, A. A. Hodge, and Girardeau. But when these men so define theology, they use the term 'religion' in an objective sense, that is, as denoting the divine revelation, which is the standard for the true service of God, the rule of man's religious life, devotion, and worship. So understood, the definition is not exposed to the criticism that was offered. At the same time it is ambiguous, and therefore does not deserve commendation.

3. RECOGNITION OF THE OBJECTIVE CHARACTER OF DOGMATIC THEOLOGY IN RECENT TIMES. Though some conservative scholars adapted themselves more or less to the use of the new definition, and spoke of theology as the science of religion or of the Christian faith (McPherson), they did not at all mean to indicate thereby that they too regarded man's subjective religion or faith as the object of theology. Some of them evidently chose this definition as an indication of the fact that theology was not limited to the study of just one object, namely, God, but included the study of all the doctrines of religion or of the Christian faith. This means that in their definitions the terms 'religion' and 'faith' did not have a subjective, but an objective connotation.

The greater number of conservative scholars, however, continued to conceive of theology as the science of God, though frequently with the distinct understanding that they did not regard God *apart from His creation* as the object of theology, but God *as related to His creatures*. Thus Shedd says: "Theology is a science that is concerned with both the Infinite and the Finite, with both God and the Universe."[1] And A. H. Strong gives the following definition: "Theology is the science of God and of the relations between God and the universe."[2] Other well-known theologians, who regard God as the

---
1. *Dogmatic Theology I*, p. 16.
2. *Systematic Theology*, p. 1.

object of theology, and therefore speak of theology, as the science of God, are Hill, Dick, Heppe, Schmid, Dabney, Boyce, Hastie, Orr, and Warfield.

The preceding paragraph makes no mention of Dutch theologians. This does not mean, however, that their stand differs materially from that of the men just mentioned. They are named separately merely because some of them varied their definition somewhat, just as Charles Hodge did in our own country. This change was, at least in part, prompted by the desire to obviate the difficulty suggested by the consideration that we cannot make God the direct object of our scientific study. Hodge finds the object of theology in the "truths" and "facts" of Scripture, which the theologian must "collect, authenticate, arrange, and exhibit in their natural relation to each other."[1] In Kuyper's estimation this definition is "in the main not incorrect," but both he and Bavinck rightly object to the idea that the theologian must *authenticate* the truths and the facts of Scripture, because this virtually destroys the concept of the ectypal theology, and logically brings the theologian once more under the dominion of a naturalistic science.[2]

Kuyper proceeds on the assumption that God cannot be the direct object of scientific study. In such a study the subject rises superior to the object, and has the power to examine and to comprehend it. But the thinking man is not so related to God, I Cor. 2:11. According to Kuyper it is quite essential to distinguish between two kinds of theology, namely: (a) theology as the knowledge of God, of which God is the object, and (b) theology as a science, which finds its object in the divine Self-revelation. The former is the ectypal knowledge of God, contained in Scripture, and adapted to the cognitive faculties of man; while the latter is defined as "that science which has the revealed knowledge of God as the object of its investigation and raises it to *sunesis* (insight)."[3] By means of this distinction he seeks to establish an organic connection between theology and science in general. Now the question arises, whether this position is equivalent to a denial of the fact that God is the object of theology. On the one hand it certainly seems so, and as a matter of fact Kuyper clearly says that the revealed knowledge of God, and it only, is the object of theology as a science.[4] This point even became the subject of a theological debate in the Netherlands. At the same time he also says that this science would not yet be entitled to the name *theology*, if it did not deepen our insight in the ectypal knowledge of God.[5] The question arises, whether Kuyper's way of putting things is not merely another way of saying that God is the object of theology as a science only in so far as He has revealed Himself in His Word. Or, to put it in other words, that God is not the *direct*, though He is the *ultimate* object of theology; that He is not the *immediate* object, but the object as *mediated* through His divine Self-revelation.

---

1. *Systematic Theology I*, p. 1.
2. *Encyclopaedie der Heilige Godgeleerdheid II*, p. 268 f.; Bavinck, *Gereformeerde Dogmatiek* I. p. 81f.
3. *Encyclopaedie der Heilige Godgeleerdheid II*, p. 249.
4. *op. cit.*, p. 244.
5. *op. cit.*, *II*, p. 246.

After all, on his view, theology as a science deals with *the Knowledge of God*, seeks to appropriate and assimilate its various data, to represent them in their grand unity, and to cast them into a form that satisfies the human consciousness, and can be called theology only in so far as it deepens insight into the knowledge of God. Moreover, it deserves attention (a) that Kuyper asserts that the science of theology admits of no other motive than "to know God or to learn to know Him";[1] (b) that his denial that God can be the object of human science simply means that we cannot *of ourselves* attain to a scientific knowledge of God, but are bound to His Self-revelation;[2] (c) that he regards it as a very precarious phenomenon that in theology "no more the reality *God*, but the reality *religion* is the object of investigation.[3]

This view of the matter finds corroboration in the fact that Bavinck considers God as the object of theology, and yet defines Dogmatics as "the scientific system of the knowledge of God";[4] that Hepp, one of Kuyper's disciples and successors says that Dogmatics "is that part of science that has God for its object, as He can be known through His revelation, or to express it more briefly, that has Scripture for its object";[5] and that Honig, one of the earliest disciples of Kuyper, also maintains that both definitions, namely, that theology is the science of God, and that it is the science of the knowledge of God, are good, and that the dispute about this was largely a dispute about words.[6] Evidently Dr. Warfield too feels that these two do not conflict. He defines theology as "the science which treats of God and of the relations between God and the universe," but also says: "Now the object of theology, as Dr. Kuyper has often justly insisted, is the ectypal knowledge of God." For him this is not equivalent to saying that the Scriptures constitute the object of theology, for he explicitly says that "The Scriptures, after all, are not the object of theology, but only its source."[7]

In Germany a reaction arose in recent years against the subjectivism that was introduced into theology by Schleiermacher and resulted in placing man rather than God in the center. There are those who emphasize anew the fact that God is the proper object of theological study. This new tendency finds expression in the two-volume work of Schaeder. This author begins his second volume with these significant words: "Mit Gott hat es die Theologie zu tun; immer und ueberal mit Gott. Jede Frage der Theologie, auch wenn sie sich auf die Welt in Natur und Geschichte oder auf den Menschen und sein Leben richtet, ist nur unter der Bedingung eine wirklich theologische, dass sie sich im letzten Grunde um Gott dreht." The theology of crisis differs considerably from Schaeder's theocentric theology, and that among other things in break-

---

1. *op. cit., II*, p. 196.
2. *II*, p. 163f.;
3. *II*, p. 265.
4. *Gereformeerde Dogmatiek I*, p. 15.
5. *Christelijke Encyclopaedie II*, p. 348.
6. *Handboek van de Gereformeerde Dogmatiek*, p. 13.
7. *The Idea of Systematic Theology*, in *Studies in Theology*, p. 56, and the *Introductory Note to Beattie's Apologetics*, p. 23f.

ing more completely and radically with the method of Schleiermacher. While Schaeder makes the Word of God more prominent in his theology than Schleiermacher, he does not rise superior to the subjectivism of the latter. The theology of crisis on the other hand places the Word of God, that is, God's super-natural revelation, prominently in the foreground, and is therefore also called "the theology of the Word of God." Barth defines the task of Dogmatics as follows: "As a theological discipline, dogmatics is the scientific test to which the Church puts herself regarding the language about God which is peculiar to her."[1] In *Credo* he expresses himself as follows: "Dogmatics endeavors to take what is first said to it in the revelation of God's reality, and to think it over again in human thoughts and to say it over again in human speech. To that end dogmatics *unfolds* and *displays* those truths in which the truth of God concretely meets us."[2] It deals therefore with the doctrinal material which the Church has derived from God's revelation.

There is really no good reason why we should not continue to speak of theology as the science of (concerning) God. It is, of course, possible to consider the ectypal knowledge of God as the immediate object of theology, and under certain circumstances it may be desirable to represent it as such; but on the whole it would seem to be preferable to speak of Him, *as He has revealed Himself in His Word*, as the real object of theology. This does not imply that the thinking subject can place itself above God as the object, and can *of itself* elicit from Him knowledge of the divine Being; nor that the human subject can comprehend God and thus attain to a perfect knowledge of Him. In employing the old definition it is assumed: (a) that God has revealed Himself and thus conveyed true knowledge of Himself to man; (b) that man, created in the image of God, is capable of appropriating and apprehending this divine truth; and (c) that man has an urge within him to systematize this knowledge with a view to a better understanding of God and of His relations to His creatures. With Bavinck we may define Dogmatics as "the scientific system of the knowledge of God."

C. Theology as a Science.

1. THE SCIENTIFIC CHARACTER OF THEOLOGY DENIED.

a. *The ground for this denial.* Theology was once generally recognized as the queen of the sciences, but does not enjoy that distinction today. Duns Scotus already held that theology was not a science in the strict sense of the word, but simply a practical discipline. This view was rather exceptional, however, and did not meet with a great deal of favor. The Scholastics in general stressed the scientific character of theology and treated it as such; and in the theological works of the Reformation and post-Reformation periods it is also fully recognized. It is especially since the end of the eighteenth century that the right of theology to be called a science was called in question, and was even positively denied. This was due in part to Kant's criticism of the faculty of knowledge, according to which it is impossible to obtain any theoretical knowl-

---

1. *The Doctrine of the Word of God*, p. 1.
2. *op cit.*, p. 3.

edge of God and of the supersensible in general; and in part to the pretentious claim of the natural sciences to be the only sciences worthy of the name. This negative attitude was greatly strengthened by Positivism with its notion that each branch of knowledge passes, successively, through three different stages: the theological or fictitious stage, the metaphysical or abstract stage, and the scientific or positive stage. The man who has reached the final stage has left theology far behind. Herbert Spencer, the great agnostic, also invariably proceeded on the assumption that theology is outside of the domain of science.

The greatest objection to the scientific status of theology was especially twofold. In the first place theology is devoted to the study of an object that lies beyond the ken of human theoretical knowledge, since it cannot be observed nor subjected to experimental tests. And in the second place it finds its ground of certitude in an authoritative revelation rather than in human reason, the only authority recognized in science. In our day it is quite common to find scientists smiling significantly, when they hear people speak of the *science* of theology. Harry Elmer Barnes even declares the theologian utterly incompetent to deal with the subject-matter of his own chosen field of study. Says he: "The new view of matters makes it very evident that the clergyman can no longer pretend to be a competent expert in the way of discovering the nature, will and operations of the new cosmic God. If undertaken and solved at all, this is a problem for the coöperative endeavors of the natural scientist and the cosmic philosopher of the Dewey tradition. The theologian at best can be only a competent second —or third—hand interpreter of the facts and implications gathered about the cosmos and its laws by specialists in science and philosophy . . . . But now, when God must be sought, if at all, in terms of the findings of the test-tube, the compound microscope, the interferometer, the radium tube and Einstein's equations, the convential clergyman is rather hopelessly out of place in the premises."[1] There is more than a mere grain of truth in the following words of Macintosh: "Among the empirical sciences theology can find none so poor as to recognize her, much less do her reverence. Moreover, even the world at large, including hosts of persons who still think of themselves as religious, is coming to share in the contempt of the scientists for theology."[2]

b. *Reaction of theologians to this denial.* This widespread denial of scientists and philosophers, re-echoed by large numbers of lesser lights, who popularize the prevailing opinion, did not fail to affect the attitude of theologians and of religious people in general. The reaction on the part of those theologians who accepted the dictum of the scientists, has been especially twofold. Some simply relinquish the claim of theology to the high honor of being scientific. and appear perfectly willing to assign to it a lesser position. Says Macintosh: "Of late, under the stress of much hostile criticism, there has been a strategic retreat, and the definitions generally favored are modest statements to the effect that theology is the intellectual expression of religion."[3]

---
1. *The Twilight of Christianity,* p. 437.
2. *Theology as an Empirical Science,* p. 4.
3. *op. cit.,* p. 1.

Others, however, set themselves the task of reconstructing theology in such a manner as to vindicate its time-honored claim to a scientific position. They substituted religious experience, religious faith, or religion in general for God as the object of theology, which means that they turned from the objective to the subjective, from the divine to the human, from the supersensible to certain psychological phenomena, which fall under human observation. They have been seeking ever-increasingly to study and interpret the religious life by the application of the true scientific method, which Macintosh describes as "the method of observation and experiment, of generalization and theoretical explanation." This author adds that, "if theology is to become really scientific, it must be by becoming fundamentally empirical."[1] He does not believe that the methods of Schleiermacher, Ritschl, and Troeltsch have been successful, but does not on that account abandon all hope. Says he: "Systematic theology is not now and never has been an empirical science. And yet this does not mean that it cannot become a science, and that in the very near future."[2] It is rather remarkable that this modern theologian, like Schaeder in Germany, again stresses the fact that not religion but God is the object of theology, but then God as revealed in religious experience (taking experience in its broadest sense), and in the history of religions.

2. THE POSSIBILITY OF MAINTAINING THE SCIENTIFIC CHARACTER OF THEOLOGY.

a. *From one point of view it is impossible.* In our day many base the right of theology to be called a science on the fact that it is devoted to the study of Christianity or of religion, and therefore deals with historical data or data of experience, which can be studied according to the strictly scientific method of observation and experiment. Since we do not share this conception of theology, we cannot avail ourselves of the ground it affords for maintaining the scientific character of theology. For us the question is, whether it is possible to maintain the scientific status of a theology which aims at the study of God rather than of religion. And the answer one gives to this question will depend on one's conception of science. This means that it will be necessary first of all to come to a clear understanding as to what constitutes a science. Many present day scholars, especially in our country, regard the term 'science' as a proper designation of what are usually called "the natural sciences," and of them only, since they are the only studies that deal with matters that can be observed and that can be tested in the laboratory. The deciding question seems to be, whether a study deals with facts of observation. But the question may be raised, whether this is not a rather arbitrary limitation. Dr. Harris says that it can be justified only "by reverting to the complete Positivism of Comte, and avowing and maintaining that knowledge is limited to the observation made by the senses." But this is an utterly untenable position, for, says he, "if they do this, they must renounce the important part of their own sciences

---

1. *Theology as an Empirical Science*, p. 11.
2. *op. cit.*, p. 25.

THE IDEA OF DOGMATIC THEOLOGY

know by inferences depending for their validity on rational intuitions."[1] They who insist on taking this position will naturally exclude theology from the domain of science, for theology as the science of God does not deal with data given by observation or experience. It does not greatly improve matters to say, as Huxley does: "By science I understand all knowledge which rests upon evidence and reasoning *of a like character to that which claims our ascent to ordinary scientific propositions* (italics mine); and if any man is able to make good the assertion that his theology rests upon valid evidence and sound reasoning, then it appears to me that such a theology must take its place as a part of science." Macintosh refers to these words of Huxley on page 25 of his *Theology as an Empirical Science*, and is inclined to take up the challenge. But from our point of view this would seem to be quite hopeless. We may not lose sight of the fact that the methods of the natural sciences do not apply in the study of theology, nor even in the study of religion. Theology is entitled to its own method, a method determined by the nature of its subject-matter. Dr. Mullins correctly remarks: "It is a false issue when men deal with religion as if it were physics or chemistry or biology, or psychology, or sociology. There is no necessary conflict between any of these and religion. But when men crave religion and a solution of its problems, then religious criteria must be employed. When modern science offers any other it gives a stone instead of bread, a serpent instead of a fish."[2]

b. *From another point of view it is possible.* The situation is quite different, if 'science' is taken in the sense of the German 'Wissenschaft' or the Dutch 'wetenschap.' Eisler in his *Handwoerterbuch der Philosophie* defines Wissenschaft as "systematisiertes Wissen, der Inbegriff zusammengehoeriger. auf ein bestimmtes Gegenstandsgebiet sich bezienhender oder durch den gleichen Gesichtspunkt der Betrachtung verbundener, zu systematischer Einheit methodisch verknupfter, zusammenhaengender Erkenntnisse." According to this definition there is no good reason why we should not regard dogmatic theology as a science. Science is simply systematized knowledge. It is reared on the basis of the common knowledge of mankind. This knowledge may be obtained in various ways, depending on the nature of its object. It may be acquired by observation, by reflection, or by revelation, but must be true knowledge. Experimental tests may and should be applied in the case of the natural sciences, rational tests in the case of the *Geisteswissenschaften*, and Scriptural tests in the case of theology. The subject-matter of theology can only be given by revelation, and it is the duty of the theologian to systematize the knowledge so acquired, and to test it rigidly by the analogy of Scripture. If he takes a comprehensive view of the subject-matter, and unifies it, he is dealing with it in a systematic way, and the result of his work is scientific.

Theology has its own distinctive method, but there is after all a great deal which it has in common with the other sciences. If the matter with which

---
1. *Philosophical Basis of Theism*, p. 301.
2. *Christianity at the Cross Roads*, p. 62.

theology deals is given by revelation, so is, strictly speaking, also the matter which the other sciences build into a system. Reason cannot be regarded as the source of this matter, but only as the instrument by which it is grasped, analyzed, classified, and systematized. And if the sciences in general employ human reason in the construction of their system of knowledge, so does theology depend on sanctified human reason in its investigation and constructive work. It is true that the element of faith is fundamental in the work of the theologian, but there is not a single scientist who can exclude this from his work altogether. And if theology must leave a great many ultimate questions unsolved, this is true to a large degree also of every other science.

Theology, then, does not move in the sphere of the natural sciences, and therefore does not and cannot apply its methods. It would succeed only in destroying itself by the application of the experimental method. It has far more in common with the so-called *Geisteswissenschaften,* a term which Baillie renders "sciences of spirit." It should be borne in mind that theology is not merely a descriptive science, which yields only historical knowledge, but very decidedly a normative science which deals with absolute truth, given by revelation and binding on the conscience. Shedd speaks of it as an *absolute* science, which is true not only for the human intellect but for all rational intelligence. He also calls it a *positive* science, to indicate that faith yields real and true knowledge of its object, though it must leave many mysteries unexplained. If others occasionally deny that it is a positive science, they usually mean that it is not a positive science in the Comtian sense of the word.

D. The Encyclopaedic Place of Dogmatics.

Under this general caption we shall consider the question as to the group to which Dogmatics belongs, and more particularly the relation in which it stands to Apologetics and Ethics.

1. THE GROUP OF STUDIES TO WHICH IT BELONGS. There is very little difference of opinion as to the group of theological studies to which Dogmatics belongs. It is almost invariably classed with the Systematic or, as Kuyper calls it, the Dogmatological group, that is, the group which centers about the dogma of the Church. The most important of the other studies which he includes in this group are Symbolics, the History of Dogma, Ethics, Apologetics, and Polemics. Schleiermacher departed from the ordinary classification, however, and classified it under Historical Theology. This was due to the fact that he conceived of Dogmatics as the systematic exposition of the Christian faith *at a certain stage of its development,* and more specifically as the science of the doctrine confessed by a particular Christian Church *at a certain stage of its historical development.* According to him dogma is characterized by change rather than by stability. It is the product of the constantly changing religious experience of a Church, having real value and significance only in so far as it is in agreement with the immediate believing Christian consciousness. In accordance with this conception of dogma, dogmatic the-

ology is represented as "the science of the connected presentation of the doctrine prevailing in a Christian Church association at a given period." As an expression of ever varying religious life, Dogmatics in his estimation is not an expression of absolute truth, and is therefore entirely wanting in permanent authority.

This view of Schleiermacher, however, did not find great favor in the theological world, not even among liberal theologians. Rothe and Dorner are the most notable scholars who followed Schleiermacher in this respect. Raebiger correctly says: "According to the place assigned to it by Schleiermacher, dogmatics must be a history of doctrine current at the present time."[1] Even George Burman Foster raises objections to it in the following words: "But historical theology is concerned with facts, not with truth; with what was, not with what ought to be. And indeed this limitation of the dogmatic task to historical theology has not been adhered to, even by these evangelical theologians themselves, least of all by Schleiermacher, who is the great champion of the conception."[2]

2. THE RELATION OF DOGMATICS TO APOLOGETICS. There never has been and is not now general agreement as to the exact nature of Apologetics, and as a result opinions differ very much with respect to the place which it should occupy in the encyclopaedia of theology. Some have given it a place in the exegetical group of theological studies, and others have incorporated it with Practical Theology. It has been more customary, however, to regard it as a part of Systematic Theology, either as an introductory study or as something in the nature of an adjunct to Dogmatics.

In this matter also, as in many others, Schleiermacher struck out on an entirely new path, when he declared it to be an introductory discipline, basic to the whole system of theology, which as such should precede even the exegetical group of theological studies. He represents Apologetics as the science that is devoted to the vindication of Christianity as a whole by means of rational argumentation. It was rather inconsistent on the part of Schleiermacher to take this position, since he considered it imperative to exclude philosophy from theology, and yet in this way laid an elaborate philosophical basis for theology. Apologetics became a sort of *Fundamentallehr*, and has since his day sometimes been called *Fundamental Theology*.

This view of Schleiermacher was adopted by Ebrard, a Reformed theologian. Beattie also favors it in his work on *Apologetics*. Says he: "It may be best, therefore, to give Apologetics a place of its own, and to regard it as *an introductory discipline to the whole system of theology* .... This, no doubt, is the best view."[3] Dr. Warfield shares this view of Apologetics. He conceives of it as "the department of theology which establishes the constitutive and

---
1. *Encyclopaedia I*, p. 94.
2. *Christianity in its Modern Expression*, p. 3.
3. *Apologetics*, p. 66.

regulative principles of theology as a science; and in establishing these it establishes all the details which are derived from them by the succeeding departments, in their sound explication and systematization." He says further that it is the business of Apologetics "to establish the truth of Christianity as the absolute religion directly only as a whole, and its details only indirectly."[1] With a direct appeal to reason for its evidences, Apologetics is supposed to deal with the great topics of God, religion, revelation, Christianity, and the Bible. The remaining departments of theology can only build on the foundation laid by Apologetics. According to Bruce it thus becomes a sort of mediator between philosophy and theology and a mediator, in which he does not have the greatest confidence. He himself conceives of Apologetics as "a preparer of the way of faith, an aid to faith against doubts whencesoever arising, especially such as are engendered by philosophy and science."[2] This speaking of it as "a preparer of the way of faith" would seem to bring his view of it more or less in line with the conception of Schleiermacher, however different it may be in other respects. The position of Henry B. Smith is expressed in these words: "It is best to regard it as historico-philosophical Dogmatics. It is the whole contents and substance of the Christian faith, arrayed for defense and for (defensive) assault."[3]

Kuyper, Bavinck, and Hepp have serious objections to the Schleiermacherian conception of Apologetics, and their strictures would seem to be fully warranted. They register especially the following objections: (a) While, as the name indicates, Apologetics is properly a defensive science, it is on this view changed into a constructive science, which aims at the construction of an independent system from philosophical data and by means of purely rational arguments. (b) According to this view Apologetics precedes the four departments of theology as a sort of *Prinzipienlehre*, and theology must build on a foundation laid by human reason. (c) Theology is thus robbed of its independent character, and derives its principles from a system that is the product of pure reason; all of which conflicts with the nature of theology.

These theologians assign to it a place in connection with the study of Dogmatics, and ascribe to it the task of vindicating the Christian system of the truth over against the attacks of false philosophy and science. They try to avoid overrating Apologetics on the one hand, and underrating it on the other hand. They do not want to neglect it, nor to consider it as a study of purely practical significance, but assign to it the modest and yet important task of defending the dogma of the Church against all attacks, and of doing this in a constructive and principial manner, and not merely in an occasional way as determined by current controversies.

3. THE RELATION OF DOGMATICS TO ETHICS. No branch of theological study is so closely related to Dogmatics as Christian or Theological Ethics. Before and during the Reformation many theologians incorporated Christian

---
1. Art. on *Apologetics* in *Studies in Theology*, p. 9.
2. *Apologetics*, p. 37.
3. *Apologetics*, p. 10.

Ethics in their Dogmatics, and several theologians of the seventeenth century treat it in a second part after Dogmatics. Yet even at that early time some began to discuss it as a separate discipline, in order to do more justice to it than could be done in a week on Dogmatics. According to Geesink,[1] Daneau was the first to publish a Reformed Ethics in 1577. This separation of Dogmatics and Ethics did not at once become general, though theologians began to make a sharper distinction in their works between the dogmatical and the ethical material, the *credenda* and the *facienda*. Gradually, however, the practice of separating the two increased. While this was in itself quite harmless, it did have disastrous results, since Ethics gradually drifted from its religious moorings. Under the influence of the philosophy of the eighteenth century, Christian Ethics was gradually robbed of its theological character. In the philosophy of Kant religion was based on Ethics rather than Ethics on religion. And in the writings of such men as Schleiermacher, Ritschl, Rothe, Herrmann, and Troeltsch morality is divorced from religion and acquires an autonomous character.

Such writers as Dorner, Wuttke, and Luthardt, again linked Ethics up with the Christian religion, but in a rather unsatisfactory way. As a matter of fact there is no principial difference between Dogmatics and Ethics. The *principia* of the one are also those of the other. It is no wonder therefore that some have again sought a closer connection between the two. In the previous century Raymond included a separate system of Ethics in his *Systematic Theology*. George Burman Foster in his *Christianity in its Modern Expression* did the same thing. And such Reformed theologians as Charles Hodge and Robert L. Dabney incorporated a discussion of the ten commandments in their works on Systematic Theology. Kuyper considers it desirable to treat Theological Ethics separately, because (a) ethical truths have come to development in a different way than dogmatical truths; and (b) the study of each of these has its own requirements and methods. Dogmatics discusses the *articula fidei*, and Ethics the *praecepta decalogi*. And Geesink says that it is generally admitted that the separation of Dogmatics and Ethics is incorrect, even though their separate treatment is commendable.[2] It is undoubtedly true that the two should always be regarded and studied as standing in the closest relation to each other. The truth revealed in the Word of God calls for a life that is in harmony with it. The two are essentially inseparable.

QUESTIONS FOR FURTHER STUDY: Is it correct to speak of dogmas as the fruit of theology? What does history teach as to the function of theology in the formation of dogmas? Is the subject-matter of theology limited to what is found in the Creeds? How does Barth conceive of dogma, dogmas, and the Creeds? How do Schleiermacher, Ritschl, Wobbermin, Troeltsch, Schaeder, and Barth differ in their conception of Dogmatics? What objection is there to making Dogmatics a purely descriptive science? Does it still remain theology, if it consistently makes religion or the Christian faith its object? On what grounds is it denied that theology is a science? How can its scientific character be maintained? Is it important that this should be done? Do Barth and Brunner regard Dogmatics as a science?

1. *De Ethiek in de Gereformeerde Theologie*, p. 22.
2. *Gereformeerde Ethiek, I*, p. 174.

REFERENCES: Bavinck, *Geref. Dogm.* I, pp. 1-41; Kuyper, *Enc. der Heil. Godgel,* I, pp. 241-283; Hepp, *De Waarde van het Dogma;* id., *Geref. Apologetiek;* Honig, *Dogmatiek en Ethiek;* Van Dijk, *Begrip en Methode der Dogm.,* pp. 7-51; Hodge *Syst. Theol.* I, pp. 1-22; Shedd, *Dogm. Theol.* I, pp. 3-58; Strong, *Syst. Theol.,* pp. 1-24; McPherson, *Christian Dogm.,* pp. 1-9; Schmid, *Doct. Theol. of the Ev. Luth. Church,* pp. 25-35; Girardeau, *Discussions of Theol. Questions,* pp. 1-44; Hastie, *Theol. as a Science,* pp. 1-58; Lobstein, *An Introd. to Prot. Dogm.,* pp. 1-96; H. B. Smith, *Introd. to Chr. Theol.,* pp. 49-59; Meyrick, *Is Dogma a Necessity?;* Kaftan, *Dogm.,* pp. 1-9; id., *The Truth of the Chr. Rel.* I; Haering, *The Chr. Faith* I, pp. 1-31; Hall, *Dogm. Theol., Introduction,* pp. 10-32; Warfield, *Introd. to Beattie's Apologetics,* pp. 19-32; id., *The Idea of Syst. Theol. and Apologetics,* both in *Studies in Theology;* C. W. Hodge, *The Idea of Dogm. Theol., Princeton Review,* Jan. 1908, pp. 52-82; Raebiger, *Theol. Enc.* II, pp. 330-338, 362-367; Beattie, *Apologetics,* pp. 43-48-67; Barth, *The Doct. of the Word of God,* pp. 1-10, 284-335; Geeseink, *Geref. Ethiek* I, pp. 149-184.

IV. The Task, Method, and Distribution of Dogmatics

A. The Task of Dogmatics.

1. MODERN CONCEPTIONS OF THE TASK OF DOGMATICS. One's conception of dogma(s) and of Dogmatics will naturally determine one's view of the task of Dogmatics. Since the notion of dogma(s) and Dogmatics that became prevalent in the nineteenth century differs radically from the view prevailing in the theology of the Reformation, there is also a fundamental departure from the earlier view of the task of Dogmatics. We shall call attention only to some of the most important of the modern conceptions.

a. *Schleiermacher's conception.* According to Schleiermacher, it is the task of Dogmatics to describe the feelings which the Church experiences in union with Jesus Christ, the Saviour. For him religion is neither knowledge nor moral action, but feeling, more specifically, a feeling of dependence on an ultimate reality, which arises only within the Christian community; and dogma is merely the intellectual expression or interpretation of the inner significance of this religious feeling. Experience rather than the Word of God is therefore the source of dogmas, though Schleiermacher still regards the New Testament as the norm by which this experience must be tested. The materials furnished by the communal experience of the Church form the subject-matter of Dogmatics. Its task is to give a systematic exposition of the Dogma of a Christian Church at a given moment of its historical development, which can boast of historical exactness, but is not necessarily an expression of absolute truth. In this way it becomes something purely subjective, divorced from the external authority of the Word of God, a merely historical or descriptive science without any normative significance.

The Erlangen school, including such men as J. C. K. Hofmann, Thomasius, and Frank, represents a reaction against the subjectivism of Schleiermacher in favor of orthodox Lutheranism. It does indeed share the subjective starting point of Schleiermacher, and is in so far also a theology of experience, but from experience it works back to an objective basis, which is found not in certain isolated passages of Scripture, but in the doctrinal truth of Scripture *as a whole.* Speaking of Hofmann, Edghill really indicates its method clearly in the following words: "Starting with the personal experience of the Christian he worked backwards to the experience of the Christian Church, as expressed in its creeds and confessions; and thus further to the documentary proofs in Scripture upon which all is based."[1]

A position somewhat similar to that of Schleiermacher, though reflecting even more clearly the influence of Vinet, is that of the Ethicals in the Nether-

---

1. *Faith and Fact. A Study of Ritschlianism,* p. 40.

lands. It takes its starting point in the life of believers in communion with Christ, that is, not merely in the life of the individual believer, but in that of believers collectively, of the community of believers, which is the Church. When the Church reflects on this life, which consists not merely in feelings, but also in thought and action, this gives rise to dogmas, which are merely the intellectual expression of that life. And the task of Dogmatics is to describe the life of the Church at a particular time in a systematic and scientific way. Van Dijk, one of their prominent representatives, defines Dogmatics as the description of the life of the Church. He prefers the term 'life' to the Schleiermacherian term 'feelings,' because it points to something more permanent, and is also more comprehensive and Scriptural. Moreover, he maintains that this description of the life of the Church should be under the constant control of Scripture as a record of what the writers experienced of the life of the Lord, and refuses to consider Dogmatics as a purely historical discipline, devoid of normative authority.[1]

b. *The Ritschlian conception.* In Ritschlian circles it is quite customary to speak of Dogmatics as "the scientific exposition of the Christian faith" (Lobstein), or as "the science of the Christian faith" (Haering). This faith, however, is not always conceived in the same way. Herrmann divorces it as much as possible from all knowledge, and regards it purely as *fiducia* (trust). The content of this faith consists merely in religious-ethical experiences, which are always individual and cannot be systematized, and which develop out of faith itself. On this view Dogmatics can hardly be anything else than a description of religious-ethical experiences. Yet there is in the Ritschlian school a manifest desire to break away from the subjectivism of Schleiermacher. This tendency finds expression perhaps most of all in Kaftan, the real dogmatician of the school. He defines Dogmatics as follows: "Die Dogmatik ist die Wissenschaft von der Christlichen Wahrheit, die auf Grund der goettlichen Offenbarung in der Kirche geglaubt und bekannt wird."[2] This definition seems to acknowledge the objective character of Dogmatics. But his description of the task of Dogmatics on page 104 makes a different impression. Says he: "Die eigentliche Hauptaufgabe der evangelischen Dogmatik besteht darin, die Erkenntniss darzulegen, die sich dem Glauben aus der Aneignung der von der Schrift bezeugten Gottesoffenbarung ergiebt." This means that Dogmatics must set forth faith, that is, the knowledge-content involved in faith, which results from the appropriation of the divine revelation given in Scripture. In the study of Scripture faith fastens on certain truths and appropriates these. It does not accept them, however, because they are infallibly given by revelation and therefore authoritative, but because they commend themselves by their practical value for the religious subject. The knowledge-content of faith is therefore after all a content selected by man. Consequently, even Kaftan does not succeed in maintaining the objective character of Dogmatics.

---

1. *Begrip en Methode der Dogmatiek*, pp. 12-24.
2. *Dogmatik*, p. 1.

THE TASK, METHOD, DISTRIBUTION OF DOGMATICS

The position of Lobstein agrees with that of Kaftan. He speaks of faith as being both the object and the source of Dogmatics, but also mentions the gospel as the source. The synthesis of these two is expressed in the following words: "Faith is the legitimate and pure source of Dogmatics only when it is in union with the divine factor which inspires it and which, without ceasing, conditions and establishes it. The source of Dogmatics is that faith which has assimilated to itself the eternal essence of the gospel, or the gospel in its apprehension by the mysterious power of faith."[1] The knowledge-content of faith is inspired by the gospel, but its extent is determined by the selective activity of faith. It is only in the light of these facts that we can really understand his definition of Dogmatics as "the scientific exposition of the Protestant faith." Both of these men want to maintain the objective and normative character of Dogmatics, but in view of the fact that with them faith is really the immediate source of Dogmatics, it can hardly be said that they have succeeded.

c. *The view of Troeltsch.* Troeltsch was motivated by a desire to secure for Dogmatics a greater measure of objectivity, and therefore suggested a religious-historical norm of more universal validity than that of the Ritschlians, in order to establish the truth of the Christian religion. In his estimation this should not be sought merely in the study of what the history of the *Christian religion* has to offer, but in the study of *religions in general.* In his scheme Dogmatics really derives its subject-matter from history, the history of religions. According to him it has a threefold task. The first of these is to establish the supremacy of the Christian religion over other religions. The dogmatician must begin with the study of the history of the various religions. In the course of this study a standard or norm emerges in virtue of a religious *a priori* in the human consciousness, which cannot be demonstrated but is nevertheless real and determinative, and enables us to decide in favor of Christianity. The judgment so reached is not a mere value judgment, but one that has ontological significance. Having established the supreme character of the Christian religion, the dogmatician must, in the second place, determine the real meaning of Christianity or discover its essence. Troeltsch says that it is characteristic of Christianity that it ever leads to new interpretations, so that the conception of its essence will naturally change from time to time. He expresses his own view of it in these words: "Christian religious faith is faith in the regeneration of man who is alienated from God, a regeneration effected through the knowledge of God in Christ. The consequence of this regeneration is union with God and social fellowship so as to constitute the kingdom of God."[2] Finally, the third task of Dogmatics is to expound the content of Christianity so conceived, and to formulate the doctrines of God, man, and redemption that are involved in this general conception of it. This view is more objective than that of the Ritschlians in its appeal to the history of religions in general, but does not entirely break with the empiricism of Schleiermacher and Ritschl. In

---
1. *An Introduction to Protestant Dogmatics,* p. 91f.
2. *Cf. Gruetzmacher, Textbuch zur systematischen Theologie,* p. 211f.

distinction from the view of these men it does not want to exclude metaphysics. However, it does not represent a return to the objective basis found in the Word of God.

d. *The position of Schaeder.* Schaeder criticizes both the Ritschlian position and that of Troeltsch. The former simply postulates a God, in order to secure certain moral interests; and the latter leaves Jesus too much amid the relativism of history, instead of seeing in Him the unique revelation of God in history. History records man's search for God, and not God's finding man through His revelation. Theology must cease to be man-centered, and should become God-centered. In Schaeder's opinion the glory and the majesty of God were compromised too much in the anthropocentric theology that prevailed since the days of Schleiermacher. This sounds very promising, but Schaeder does not succeed in rising above the subjectivism of the theology which he condemns. He does not recognize the Word of God as the only source and norm of theology. His starting point is, after all, also purely subjective. It is the revelation wrought by the Spirit of God in man, a revelation which becomes ours only through the faith wrought in us. To this revelation Scripture, nature, history, and Christ also make their contribution. From this revelation, mediated to us through faith, Dogmatics must draw its material, all of which centers about God. Dogmatics must deal first of all with that which is most fundamental in God, namely, His majesty or absolute sovereignty; then it must treat of the holiness of God in its close and unqualified relationship to the majesty of God; and, finally, it must unfold the idea of the love of God, especially as it is revealed in Jesus Christ, in organic connection with both the majesty and the holiness of God. "Auf diese Weise ergeben sich drei einfache Teile des dogmatischen Entwurfes: Gott der Herr, Gott der heilige, Gott der liebende oder der Vater . . . So ist die ganze Theologie wirklich Gotteslehre. Sie ist aber aus dem Glauben und fuer den Glauben."[1] The method of Schaeder does not differ *fundamentally* from that of Schleiermacher; but while Schleiermacher's theology can hardly be said to rise above the level of anthropology, that of Schaeder strongly emphasizes the fact that it must be God-centered. And in striving to make it this he does not rule out the theoretic element.

e. *The Barthian view.* The conception of Barth respecting the task of Dogmatics can best be indicated briefly by quoting some of his own words. Says he: "As a theological discipline, dogmatics is the scientific test to which the Christian Church puts herself regarding the language about God which is peculiar to her."[2] The task of Dogmatics is therefore to test the language of the Church respecting God, in order to make sure that it is in agreement with the divine revelation. In *God in Action*, p. 53 Barth expresses himself as follows: "Dogmatics must test dogma (not dogmas) to see that dogma corresponds to the true object . . . Dogmatics has the task of interpreting the corresponding co-relation of the dogmas. But beyond that its task is to carry on a comprehen-

---
1. *Theozentrische Theologie II*, p. 313.
2. *The Doctrine of the Word of God*, p. 1.

sive investigation of the entire Church's language, concepts, phrases, and ways of thinking in the present." He rejects the Roman Catholic conception of Dogmatics, and the tendency towards a similar view in the old Protestant tradition, to the effect that the task of Dogmatics is merely "the combination, repetition, and transcription of a number of already present 'truths of revelation,' once for all expressed and authentically defined as to wording and meaning."[1] In *Credo* he expresses himself in a slightly different way: "Dogmatics endeavors to take what is first said to it in the revelation of God's reality, and to think it over again in human thoughts and to say it over again in human speech. To that end dogmatics *unfolds* and *displays* those truths in which the truth of God concretely meets us. It articulates again the articles of faith; it attempts to see them and to make them plain in their interconnection and context; where necessary it enquires after new articles of faith, i.e. articles that have not up to now been known and acknowledged."[2]

The fundamental idea from which to start, in order to understand the representation of Barth, is that of "Church proclamation." Just what does Barth mean by that? He tells us that not all language of the Church about God is Church proclamation. Words addressed to God in prayer, singing, and confession, do not form a part of it; neither do the social activities of the Church. Even the instruction of the youth cannot be so called, since it "has to teach, not to convert, not to 'bring to a decision,' and to that extent not to proclaim." Theology cannot claim to be such proclamation, though it is also language about God to men. "Proclamation is its presupposition, its raw material and its practical goal, not its content or its task. Naturally, proclamation also means to speak about God, but in it "is concealed, as the meaning of this action, the intention to speak the word of God Himself." It is speaking with the expectation that in it God Himself will be the speaker. "Proclamation is human language in and through which God Himself speaks, like a king through the mouth of his herald .... Where human language about God is proclamation, it raises this claim, it lives in this atmosphere of expectation."[3] Now dogma is Church proclamation in so far as it really agrees with the original revelation attested in Scripture, in which God is, of course, the speaker. It is revealed truth, and therefore quite different from dogmas, which are mere doctrinal propositions formulated by the Church, and therefore words of men. And now "Dogmatics must test dogma (not dogmas) to see that dogma corresponds to the true object."[4] "It is the inquiry about the Word of God in Church proclamation, must be the critical inquiry as to the agreement of Church proclamation. not with any norm of human truth or human value ... but with the revelation attested in Holy Scripture."[5] The goal of Dogmatics is dogma, that is, it aims at the agreement of Church proclamation with the original revelation. Barth

---

1. *The Doctrine of the Word of God*, p. 15.
2. p. 3.
3. *The Doctrine of the Word of God*, pp. 51-57.
4. *God in Action*, p. 53.
5. *The Doctrine of the Word of God*, p. 304.

reminds us, however of the fact that "the dogma after which Dogmatics inquires is not the truth of revelation, but it is on the way to the truth of revelation."[1]

2. THE REFORMED CONCEPTION OF THE TASK OF DOGMATICS. In distinction from the views discussed in the preceding, Reformed theologians maintain that it is the task of Dogmatics "to set forth in scientific form absolutely valid truth, and to embrace the entirety of Christian doctrine." (Hodge) Bavinck expresses it in these words: De dogmatiek heeft juist tot taak, om dien inhoud der openbaring, welke op de kennisse Gods betrekking heeft, denkend te reproduceeren."[2] It seeks to give a systematic presentation of all the doctrinal truths of the Christian religion. It may not rest satisfied with a description of what was at one time the content of the faith of the Church, but must aim at absolute or ideal truth. It is not a purely historical or descriptive science, but one that has normative significance. In the task to be performed by Dogmatics we can distinguish three different phases.

a. *A constructive task.* The dogmatician deals primarily with the dogmas embodied in the confession of his Church, and seeks to combine them into a systematic whole. He must do this in such a manner that the organic relations of the various elements of the divine truth stand out clearly. This is not quite as easy a task as Lobstein seems to think. It requires more than a mere logical arrangement of the truths that are clearly formulated in the confession of the Church. Many truths that are merely stated in general terms must be formulated; the connecting links between the separate dogmas must be discovered and supplied and formulated in such a way that the organic connection of the various dogmas becomes clear; and new lines of development must be suggested, which are in harmony with the theological structure of the past. For all its content it must draw directly on Scripture, and not on religious experience or faith (Schleiermacher, Ritschl, Kaftan, Schaeder), nor on history (Troeltsch), nor on Church proclamation (Barth), thus making God's revelation in Scripture merely a norm by which to test its content.

b. *A demonstrative and defensive task.* It is not sufficient to systematize the dogmas of the Church, since this would make Dogmatics merely descriptive. The dogmatician must demonstrate the truth of the system which he presents as his own. He must show that every part of it strikes its roots deep down into the subsoil of Scripture. Bible proof which takes account of the progressive character of the divine revelation should be given for the separate dogmas, for the connecting links, and for the new elements suggested. Dogmatics is in search of absolute truth. It may not be able to reach this in every particular, but should nevertheless seek to approach it as much as possible. Moreover, account must be taken of the historical departures from the truth, in order that this may stand out with greater clearness. All attacks on the dogmas embodied

---
1. *Ibid.*, p. 307.
2. "Dogmatics has exactly the task to reproduce intellectually that content of revelation that bears on the knowledge of God." *Gereformeerde Dogmatiek I*, p. 25.

in the system, should be warded off, so that the real strength of the position assumed may clearly appear.

c. *A critical task.* The dogmatician may not, with Harnack, proceed on the assumption that the doctrinal development of the past was one gigantic error, and that he must therefore begin his work *de novo*. This would reveal a lack of respect for the guidance of the Holy Spirit in the past history of the Church, and give evidence of an undue amount of self-confidence. At the same time he must be severely critical of the system which he proposes, and allow for the possibility of a departure from the truth at some point or other. If he detects errors even in the dogmas of the Church, he must seek to remedy them in the proper way; and if he discovers lacunae, he should earnestly endeavor to supply what is lacking. He should bend every effort to the advancement of the science of Dogmatics.

B. The Method of Dogmatics.

The word 'method' does not always have the same connotation, and is not always used with the same latitude in works on dogmatic theology. In some of them the discussion of the method of Dogmatics includes, if it is not limited to, a consideration of the necessary qualifications for the study of Dogmatics, and the distribution of the contents of Dogmatics in the construction of the system. Strictly speaking, however, the method of Dogmatics concerns only the way in which the content of Dogmatics is obtained, that is, the source or sources from which it is derived, and the manner in which it is secured. It is to the consideration of these two points that the present discussion will be limited.

1. VARIOUS VIEWS AS TO THE SOURCE FROM WHICH THE CONTENT OF DOGMATICS IS DERIVED. The first question that comes into consideration is therefore that of the source and norm of Dogmatics. Historically, there are especially three views that come into consideration, namely: (a) that Scripture is the source of Dogmatics; (b) that the teaching of the Church constitutes the real source; and (c) that the Christian consciousness must be regarded as the source. These three will be considered in succession.

a. *Holy Scripture.* Holy Scripture was generally recognized from the earliest times, if not as the *fons* or *principium unicum*, at least as the *fons primarius* of theology, and therefore also of Dogmatics. God's general revelation in nature was frequently, and is also now sometimes, recognized as a secondary source. Warfield says that "the sole source of theology is revelation." Taking into consideration, however, that God revealed Himself in divers manners, he also recognizes as "true and valid" sources God's revelation in nature, providence and Christian experience. They all furnish some data for theology. "But," says he, "it remains nevertheless true that we should be confined to a meager and doubtful theology were these data not confirmed, reinforced, and supplemented by the surer and fuller revelations of Scripture; and that the Holy Scriptures are the source of theology in *not only a degree but also in a sense in which nothing else is.*"[1] He would certainly call Holy Scripture the *fons primarius* of theology.

Other Reformed theologians, such as Turretin, Kuyper, Bavinck, Thornwell, and Girardeau, do not hesitate to speak of it as the *principium unicum* ('unicum' in the sense of 'only,' and not merely in that of 'unique'), or as the sole source and norm of theology. They, of course do not mean to deny that the theologian can also obtain some knowledge of God from His general revelation; but they maintain that, since the entrance of sin into the world, man can gather true knowledge of God from His general revelation only if he studies it in the light of Scripture, in which the elements of God's original self-revelation, which were obscured and perverted by the blight of sin, are republished, corrected, and interpreted. Consequently, the theologian must always turn to Scripture for reliable knowledge of God and of His relations to His creatures. Moreover, he can obtain no knowledge whatsoever of God's redemptive work in Jesus Christ, except from special revelation, and this is knowledge of supreme significance. It is only on the basis of Scripture therefore that one can construct a system of dogmatic theology.

In his use of Scripture the dogmatician will naturally take into account the results of his previous studies concerning Revelation and Inspiration, General and Special Introduction, Sacred History, and especially of the *Historia Revelationis or Biblical Theology*. In the opinion of some this means that he should regard the Bible as a collection of old Israelitish and early Christian literature of very unequal verity and value, should accept as historically true only those parts that are attested by historical criticism, and should ascribe normative significance only to the elements that approve themselves to the Christian consciousness. Such principles naturally lead to all kinds of arbitrary limitations of the special revelation of God as a source of theology.

Modern empirical theologians, averse to the idea of an authoritative revelation of God, and eager to secure the scientific character of their theology by applying scientific methods in its study, discredit the Bible as a source of theology entirely, though in some cases still ascribing to it some sort of normative significance. They seek the source of their theology in the Christian consciousness. The theology of Schleiermacher is purely subjective and experimental. The Ritschlians, it is true, still ascribe revelational significance to Scripture, but restrict it to the New Testament, and more particularly to those elements on which the faith of the Church fastens, and which are apprehended and verified by faith.

Reformed theologians, however, refuse to be led into that labyrinth of subjectivism, and accept the whole of Scripture as the divinely inspired revelation of God and as the source of theology. Nevertheless, they realize that all parts do not have equal doctrinal significance, that the earlier revelations are not as full and explicit as the later ones, and that doctrines should not be based on isolated passages of Scripture, but on the sum-total of the doctrinal teachings of the Bible. They feel that it is absolutely wrong to follow what a certain

---

1. *The Idea of Systematic Theology*, in *Studies in Theology*, p. 63.

writer calls "the cafeteria style" of using the Bible, selecting only what satisfies one's taste and ignoring all the rest. The dogmatician should always study Scripture according to the *analogia Scriptura*.

At the same time they do not follow the so-called Biblical method of Beck, who was strongly under the influence of Oetinger, though he avoided the mysticism of the latter. Beck opposed the subjectivism of Schleiermacher and his followers. He stressed the fact that the theologian must gather all his material from Scripture and from Scripture only, ignoring not only all philosophical theories, but also all Church doctrines. He regarded the divine revelation in Scripture as an organic whole, consisting of several interrelated parts, moving forward in a unitary development, and finally reaching its consummation under the guidance of the Holy Spirit. The theologian simply has the task to reproduce the truth as it is objectively given in Scripture, and in doing this should follow no other method than that which Scripture itself suggests. His exposition should follow the line of development indicated in Scripture, in which all parts of the truth are organically related.

This method does not sufficiently take into account the fact that Scripture does not contain a logical system of doctrine, which we can simply copy; that the order which it follows as the record of God's revelation is historical rather than logical; that dogmatic theology should be an exposition of the thoughts of God, appropriated and assimilated by the human consciousness, and expressed in a language and scientific form adapted to the dogmatician's own time; and that the dogmatician never comes to the study of Scripture without any prepossessions, but always represents a certain ecclesiastical standpoint and has certain positive personal convictions, which will naturally be reflected in his work.

One of the most recent names applied to the theology of Barth is "Theology of the Word of God." Barth denies general revelation, is violently opposed to the subjectivism of modern theology, and stresses the necessity of special revelation for the knowledge of (concerning) God. It would be a mistake, however, to infer from this that he agrees with the Protestantism of the Reformation in its conception of the Bible as the source of theology. In the first place the Bible should not be identified with the special revelation of God, but can only be regarded as a witness to that revelation. And in the second place special revelation is always simply *God speaking;* it can never be objectified and made static in a book, so that this becomes, in the words of Dr. Machen, "the supreme text-book on the subject of faith." God's special revelation is not a book, from which the theologian can simply gather his material. Consequently it is not the Bible, nor a part of the Bible, but simply God's speaking to man, to which the Bible bears witness, and by which the Church's speaking about God must be tested. And if the question be asked, Where does theology find its material, the answer can only be: in the Church's proclamation of the Word of God in so far as this is really the speaking of God. "In Dogmatics," says Barth, "it can never be a question of the mere combination, repetition, and summarizing of Biblical doctrine."[1] Says Mackintosh in stating Barth's view: "Dogmatics, therefore, starts from the message preached and taught by the Church, and finds the materials of its discussion there. When the Church speaks of God, it claims to be declaring His Word. And for Dogmatic the central question is this: how is the Church's language, in its intention and content, fit to serve and express the Word of God."[2] In view of all this it is no wonder that Barth says: "There is, to be sure, a history of the Reformed Churches, and there are documentary statements of their beliefs, together with classical expositions of their theory and practice, which command (and always will command) the attention, respect, and consideration of every one who calls himself a Reformed churchman; *but in the truest sense there is no such thing as Reformed doctrine*" (italics mine).[3]

b. *The teaching of the Church*. The teaching of the Church or its confession is also regarded by some as the source of theology. The Roman Catholic Church in a certain sense indeed regards Holy Scripture as a source of theology, but denies that it is the *complete* supernatural revelation of God and supplements it with what is called "apostolic tradition." These two in a way constitute the source of theology, and yet it is hardly correct to say that, in the estimation of this Church, these two together constitute *the* source and norm of theology, though Roman Catholic writers often speak as if they do. In reality they constitute the source and norm of theology only *as they are infallibly authenticated and interpreted by the Church*. Roman Catholics do say that Scripture and tradition are the sources of theology, but deny the right of private interpretation. They maintain that we receive both Scripture and tradition at the hands of the Church, which determines what books belong to the canon, and what tradition is authentic. Moreover, they hold that both must be read through the spectacles of the Church.

Consequently, though both Scripture and tradition may be regarded as sources of theology, only the teachings of the Church, which are irrevocable, constitute the real source and the rule of faith. In considering the question, whence the Church draws its teaching, or where revelation is deposited and preserved, Wilmers says: We answer: from two sources—Scripture and tradition. As these two sources contain the subject-matter of our faith, they are called *sources of faith;* and as they determine our faith, they are likewise called *rules of faith*. They are, however, only the remote or *mediate* rules of faith, while the *immediate* rule is the teaching Church.[4] And Gibbons asserts that "God never intended the Bible to be the Christian's rule of faith, independently of the living authority of the Church."[5] Dr. D. S. Schaff says: "The Tridentine position was reaffirmed by the Vatican Council when it stated that "all those things are to be believed with divine and Catholic faith which are contained in

---
1. *The Doctrine of the Word of God*, p. 16.
2. *Types of Modern Theology*, p. 274.
3. *The Word of God and the Word of Man*, p. 229.
4. *Handbook of the Christian Religion*, p. 134.
5. *Faith of our Fathers*, p. 77.

the Word of God, written or handed down and which the Church, either by solemn judgment or by virtue of her ordinary and universal teaching function offers for belief as having been divinely revealed."[1] The situation is this, that nothing can be accepted as true or received as an article of faith, which has not been defined and proposed by the Church. "She still retains the apostolic commission," says Thornwell, "and is the only accredited organ of God's Spirit for the instruction of mankind in all that pertains to life and godliness."[2] Strictly speaking, it is the voice of the Church that is heard in both Scripture and tradition. She only is the supreme oracle of God, and therefore it is no wonder that she does not regard the reading of the Bible as an absolute necessity, and even discourages this among the laity.

This Roman Catholic view is a misconception of the relation that obtains between the Church and the truth with which theology deals. It was the truth that gave birth to the Church, and not the Church that produced the truth. Consequently, she cannot be regarded as the *principium theologiae*. All her claims and all her teachings must be tested by Scripture, and are valid only in so far as they have Scriptural warrant. The Church of Rome cannot maintain her claim to a perpetual apostolic inspiration, and therefore even her so-called tradition must be submitted to the test of Scripture. The tests which the Roman Catholic Church herself applies are not sufficient.

But if the Church of Rome has an exaggerated view of the significance of the Church and its teachings, others are clearly inclined to minimize their importance. There is a widespread aversion at the present time to ascribe any binding character, any authority whatsoever, to the Church's creedal formulations of the truth. While the historical value of the creeds is frankly admitted, their normative significance is questioned, if not explicitly denied. Curtis regards it as a very dubious practice to demand of the officers of the Church that they subscribe to its creed.[3] Allen calls upon the members of the Anglican Church to stand fast in the liberty with which Christ has made them free, and to shake off the yoke of bondage placed upon them in the creed.[4] And William Adams Brown, while in his recent work, *A Creed for Free Men*, still pleading for a Creed, does not want to be misunderstood, and therefore says: "By a unifying Creed, let me hasten to explain, I do not mean a set of beliefs prescribed by authority, whether it be of Church or State, which one must take as it is given to one as a test of orthodoxy. I mean a definite grouping of the convictions which give meaning to life and direction to activity, which may serve as a guide for personal conduct and a means of understanding with one's neighbors."[5] Even Barth and Brunner, while regarding the Creeds as venerable and worthy of respect, refuse to ascribe to them authority and to regard them as rigid tests of orthodoxy. They stress the fact that the Creeds are

---
1. *Our Fathers' Faith and Ours*, p. 148.
2. *Collected Works I*, p. 43.
3. *History of Creeds and Confessions of Faith*, pp. 447-466.
4. *Freedom in the Church*, p. 194 ff.
5. p. 9.

expressions but not *objects* of faith.[1,2] Quite generally the position is taken that the theologian, while appreciating the historical value of the Creeds and Confessions of the Protestant Churches and gratefully using them as historical guides, should not feel himself bound by their teachings, but should be entirely untrammeled in his scientific investigations.

It is only proper, however, to avoid both of the extremes just described. Creeds and confessions, it goes without saying, may never be placed on a level with Holy Scripture as sources of theology. The Bible is the only source, and the Creeds should be interpreted in the light of Scripture, and not Scripture in the light of the Creeds. At the same time the Creeds contain the testimony of the Church respecting the truth revealed in the Bible; and the fact that she was guided in the development of the truth by the Holy Spirit is, to express it in the words of Thornwell, "a venerable presumption in favor of the divine authority of all that she proposes." The Church in drawing up a Creed proposes it as her carefully considered and prayerfully accepted conception and expression of the absolute truth revealed in the Word of God; and they who join that Church thereby signify their adherence to the truth of God's Word as it is confessed in its Creed. Common honesty demands of them that, as long as they remain members of that Church, they shall abide by her expression of the truth and teach nothing that is contrary to her standards.

This demand, of course, holds very emphatically for the officers and teachers of the Church. The theologian is always the theologian of a particular Church. He receives the truth in her communion, shares her convictions, and promises to teach and propagate these as long as they do not prove to be contrary to the Word of God. While he does not consider the Creed to be infallible, he accepts its teachings as the expression of absolute truth until the contrary appears. It may be said that these teachings constitute a bias, and this is perfectly true; but no one ever takes up a study without any prepossessions. Every theologian in entering upon his task has certain convictions which he cannot set aside at will, because he cannot eliminate himself.

c. *The Christian consciousness..* Under the influence of Schleiermacher and Ritschl it has become quite customary in many circles to regard the Christian consciousness as the source of theology, the only source from which it derives its material. For Schleiermacher the dogmas of the Church are the scientific expression of the pious feelings which the believer, on close and conscientious self-examination, perceives in his heart. The Christian consciousness of the individual, but especially of the religious community, is the goldmine from which the dogmas of the Church must be drawn. At the same time he believes that the truths derived from this source, in order to become an integral part of the organism of evangelical doctrine, should find support in the confessions of the Church and in the New Testament. While he does not recognize the Bible as the source of theology, he does ascribe a certain normative significance to the New Testament, since it contains the revelation of God in

---
1. Barth, *The Word of God and the Word of Man*, p. 229.
2. Brunner, *The Word and the World*, p. 70.

Jesus Christ, and describes the experiences of those who lived in immediate contact with Him. Because of their intimate association with Christ their experiences have normative significance for us.

Ritschlians criticize the subjectivism of Schleiermacher and his followers, which results in changing Dogmatics from a normative to a purely descriptive science, and make an attempt to safeguard the objective character of theology. They claim to derive their dogmas from a historical revelation, the revelation of God in Jesus Christ, as it is recorded in the Gospels, that is, the revelation embodied in the life and the teachings of Jesus, and especially in His work as the founder of the Kingdom of God. They often speak of that revelation as the source of theology. This does not mean, however, that they regard this as the *direct* source of theological doctrines. They even deny explicitly that it should be so considered, and this is but natural. Since they limit the Scriptural source to the historical revelation of God in Jesus Christ, the question naturally arises as to the ground for this limitation; and this is found only in the faith of the Church. Faith fastens on those elements of the historical revelation that are of real value for the Christian life, since they engender true piety. And the elements so appropriated constitute the material for the doctrinal system. Hence the faith of the Church is really the direct source of its theology, and so the contents of the theological system is after all subjectively determined. Faith comes in between the historical revelation in Christ and the theologian. The religious consciousness is still the source of theology. But even so the full subjectivity of the Ritschlian position does not yet appear. Dogmatics should not be regarded as "the science of the objects of faith," but as "the science of the Christian faith."[1] The task of the dogmatician, says Lobstein, "consists in analyzing the faith of the Church, in developing its content, in connecting together its affirmations."[2] He is concerned with *faith's understanding* of revelation, and considers the data of faith in the light of a particular theory of religious knowledge, and the test which he applies is primarily of a pragmatic kind. What works in religion is true in theology. Garvie says that according to Ritschl, "A doctrine is true, not because it is in the Bible, but because it verifies itself experimentally and practically."[3]

The idea that the Christian consciousness is the source of theology is rather common in present day theological literature. Even the Erlangen school takes it starting point in experience, and Troeltsch, in spite of his appeal to the history of religions in general, did not succeed in rising above the subjectivism of Schleiermacher and Ritschl. Wobbermin in principle goes back to Schleiermacher, and even Schaeder with his theocentric emphasis does not escape his subjectivism. The same experimental view is found in Lemme's *Christliche Glaubenslehre*, and in Schultz's *Grundriss der evangelischen Dogmatik*. It also characterizes the theology of the Ethicals in the Netherlands. And in our own country the Christian consciousness is regarded as the source of theology by

---

1. Kaftan, *The Truth of the Christian Religion II*, p. 409.
2. *An Introduction to Protestant Dogmatics*, p. 91.
3. *Encyclopaedia of Religion and Ethics*, X. p. 816.

such men as Wm. Adams Brown (*Christian Theology in Outline*), Beckwith (*Realities of Christian Theology*), D. C. Macintosh (*Theology as an Empirical Science*), and G. B. Foster (*Christianity in its Modern Expression*). Many of those who adopt this position are still inclined to recognize Scripture in some sense as an objective authority, though not as an infallibly inspired revelation of God.

Now there are some obvious objections to the notion that the Christian consciousness is *the* source, or even one of the sources of theology. (1) History and experience teach us that it is the acceptance and assimilation of the truth, which is revealed in the Word of God, that determines the nature of our Christian experience, and not *vice versa*. (2) In the interpretation of his experience man is always in danger of confusing what is from man with what is from God, and of allowing the imperfect thought of the individual or of the community to condition and limit his theology. (3) Many truths which are of the greatest importance in theology cannot be experienced. In the strict sense of the word man cannot experience God, though he may experience His operations. How can he experience such objective historical facts as the creation of the world, the fall of man, the incarnation of the Logos, the atoning death of Christ, His resurrection from the dead, His physical return, and so on? Consistency in this matter will result in one of two things: either it will impose upon experience a burden which it cannot bear, or it will seriously impoverish theology. (4) The interpretation of the data of the Christian consciousness with its currents and cross-currents, and with all its fluctuations, is a process, which is so delicate and in which man is so liable to error, that in all probability very few satisfactory inferences can be drawn from it. Absolute truth cannot be reached in that way, and yet this is the very thing at which dogmatic theology aims. (5) While it may be true that saving faith, at least in a general way, implicates a system of doctrine, it does not follow that such a system can be deduced from the Christian consciousness, even when this is more or less controlled by Scripture. Frank attempted to derive a whole system from the principle of regeneration, but it can hardly be said that he was successful. (6) It is a striking fact that they who so confidently speak of the Christian consciousness as the source of theology, frequently insist on it that its deliverances be brought to the touchstone of Scripture, and can be regarded as valid data for the construction of a system of theology only when they are in agreement with the written Word of God.

The fact that Christian experience or the Christian consciousness is not the source of theology does not mean that it is not a factor, and even an important factor, in the construction of the dogmatic system. Some Reformed theologians, such as H. B. Smith, Van Oosterzee, McPherson, and Warfield, even speak of it as a real, though subsidiary, source of theology. The latter says, however, "that probably few satisfactory inferences could be drawn from it, had we not the norm of Christian experience and its dogmatic implications

THE TASK, METHOD, DISTRIBUTION OF DOGMATICS

recorded for us in the perspicuous pages of the written Word."[1] If we bear in mind, however, that religious knowledge differs from all other knowledge in that it does not rest on one's own insight into the truth, nor on the authority of any man, but only on the authority of God, then we feel that the religious consciousness can hardly be an independent source of theology. The attempt to make man autonomous in this respect exposes one on the one hand to the danger of Deism, which makes man independent of God, and on the other hand, to the danger of Pantheism, which identifies him with God. Scripture never refers to the Christian consciousness as a source and norm of the truth. Moreover, the religious consciousness is determined to a great extent by the environment in which man lives, reveals significant variations, and therefore cannot be regarded as a dependable source.

At the same time the religious consciousness will always be an important factor in the construction of a system of dogmatic theology. Only the *Christian theologian* has a proper insight into the truth as it is revealed in the Word of God, and is therefore qualified to give a systematic representation of it. While his faith cannot be regarded as a fountain from which the living waters spring, it is nevertheless the channel that carries them to him from the perennial wellspring of Scripture. And his personal appropriation of the truths of revelation will naturally be reflected in his construction of the truth. The dogmatician, engaging in his work, will not be able to set aside his individual convictions, nor the convictions which he has in common with the Church to which he belongs. The product of his theological labors will necessarily bear a personal imprint. Moreover, Christian experience may serve to verify many of the truths of the Christian religion and to make them stand out as living realities in the Christian life. While it adds nothing to the truth of what is recorded in the Word of God, it may greatly strengthen the subjective apprehension of it, and therefore has great apologetical value.

2. THE MANNER IN WHICH THE MATERIAL IS SECURED AND TREATED. Several methods of obtaining and dealing with theological truth have been suggested and applied, of which the following may be regarded as the most important.

a. *The Speculative Method.* The term 'speculative' is not always used in the same sense in philosophy and theology. Speculative thought in one sense of the word is simply the antithesis of that Empiricism which maintains that all knowledge is based on experience. Consistent Empiricism reduces all knowledge to the comprehension of the things that fall directly under the observation of the senses, and is therefore called Sensualism. It yields knowledge of particular facts, but knows of no universal laws and principles, which unite them into an organic whole, and is therefore really equivalent to the negation of all scientific knowledge. It is the function of reason to go beyond the particular and contingent fact, and to seek the underlying general and necessary

---

1. *The Idea of Systematic Theology*, in *Studies in Theology*, p. 62.

principle, which unites the particular facts and ideas into a unity and gives them the coherence of a system. This function of reason is sometimes designated as 'speculation'. Now speculation in this sense is absolutely essential in raising any kind of knowledge to the level of a science, and therefore cannot be dispensed with in theology. Dogmatic theology aims at a systematic exposition of the knowledge of God in the relations in which He stands to His creatures, and will never be able to accomplish its task without the organizing function of reason.

This is not the ordinary meaning, however, which, in the sphere of theology, attaches to 'speculation' and 'the speculative method'. It denotes rather the method of philosophers and theologians who refuse to take their starting point in given facts and seek to construct a system in an *a priori* fashion, that, is, without taking account of the data given by observation and experience. It proceeds from the absolute and universal to the relative and particular in a purely deductive way. Fleming says that it is characteristic of this method "not to set out from anything given as its subject, but from determinations which thought finds in itself as the necessary and primary ground of all being as of all thinking."[1] In the application of this method the test of truth lies in its coherence or the consistency of its various propositions. Whatever a man must necessarily think according to the laws of logic must be regarded as true. This is the method which Bacon had in mind when he said: "The rationalists are like the spiders; they spin all out of their own bowels." The speculative method operates purely with abstract thought, and proceeds on the assumption that the world of thought is also the world of reality. Kaftan states the peculiarity of the speculative method, when he says: "It is based on the presupposition that there is a creative function inherent in human thought; that in the human mind there slumbers the power of extending our knowledge beyond all experience, and that it only requires to be awakened by the intercourse with things; that to the so-called Laws of Thought there accrues a supernatural significance."[2] Caldecott expresses himself on this point as follows: "The kernel of the full doctrine is that Necessary thought is constructive of intelligent experience, and that the 'idea' or 'object' which it presents is entitled to our full belief as Real. That we have some intelligent experience, and that it is veridical, is taken for granted; it is the fact to be explained: whatever idea, or thought, or belief can be shown to be necessarily involved or implied therein as its *prius* is a true thought; as veridical as the datum itself, to say the least."[3] According to this method human reason is not merely the instrument of thought, but is the very source of thought, and all necessary and coherent thought is also the Real. And not only philosophy but also theology (which Hegel regards as philosophy speaking in symbols) is spun out of the human mind. The philosophy of Hegel furnishes the classical example of this method, and this example is followed in the works of absolute Idealists.

1. *Vocabulary of the Philosophical Sciences*, p. 486.
2. *The Truth of the Christian Religion II*, p. 231.
3. *The Philosophy of Religion*, p. 30.

There are several obvious objections to the application of the speculative method, as it has been defined. (1) It proceeds on the assumption that the consciousness of man, which is here represented as absolute thought, is the source of theology; but, as we have seen in the preceding, it is quite impossible that the human consciousness should serve in that capacity. (2) In this method we are moving entirely in the realm of thought, and do not touch the objective in the sense of something independent of and, so to speak outside of our own mental life, while in theology we are concerned with objective realities. It may be said that what man necessarily thinks is objectively real, but this is an unwarranted idea. (3) It ignores the historical facts of Christianity, which exist independently of human reason and cannot be deduced from it. Moreover, it is limited to very general ideas, since, as Schleiermacher pointed out, pure thought is always limited to that which is general and can never yield particulars. (4) It obliterates the essential distinction between philosophy and theology and makes theology something purely intellectual. According to Hegel philosophy interprets ultimate reality in terms of pure thought, while theology represents the *same* reality in pictorial form, that is, in terms of the imagination. Philosophy is higher theology, and theology is lower philosophy. (5) It robs faith of its real Biblical character by reducing it to pure cognition. It is the knowledge of the ordinary Christian, which can only be raised to the level of true knowledge by means of speculative reason. Faith thus becomes something like the *pistis* of the Gnostics, as distinguished from the *gnosis* on which they prided themselves.

b. *The empirical method.* The terms 'empirical method' and 'experimental method' are often used interchangeably. Empiricism is quite the opposite of *a priorism*. In the acquisition of knowledge it proceeds inductively rather than deductively. It "allows nothing to be true nor certain but what is given by experience, and rejects all *a priori knowledge*." Theologians of the empirical school generally take experimental religion to be the object of theology. In the study of this object they desire to employ the method of modern science, that is, the method of observation and induction. Religion is made the object of careful observation, and all its manifestations are subjected to close scrutiny, in the historical study of the religions of the human race and in that of the psychology of religion. After these manifestations are carefully described and classified, their explanation is sought in general principles; and when these principles are carefully formulated, they are, in turn, tested by further observation. From the materials so gathered a system is constructed, which constitutes a philosophy of religion rather than a system of theological truth.

The preceding description is of a very general nature, and gives no indication of the different variations of the experimental method, which are rather numerous. Macintosh classifies under the empirical method what he calls the *mystical*, the *eclectic*, and the *scientific* types.[1] Wobbermin speaks of the *religio-*

---

1. *Theology as an Empirical Science*, p. 7 ff.

psychological method, which he also calls the *Scheiermacherian-Jamesian* method, and Lemme calls the method which he employs "die empirisch-descriptive Methode." The existing variations result from the various attempts that were made to overcome some of the weaknesses of the empirical method, and to meet such objections as the following: that it is altogether subjective; that it is purely individual and therefore has no general validity; and that it reduces theology to a rather highly specialized division of anthropology. Some modern theologians realize that they must deal with their subject-matter theologically, and that this requires a very special effort on their part. Macintosh wants it clearly understood that God is the object of his "Theology as an Empirical Science." And Schaeder very definitely wants his theology to be God-centered.

Schleiermacher may be regarded as the father of the empirical method in theology. Ritschl and the Ritschlians were opposed to his subjectivism and suggested a more objective method, but even their method is in the last analysis experimental. The Erlangen theologians continued this method, and even Troeltsch did not entirely break with it. Wobbermin's religio-psychological method is in fact a return to the position of Schleiermacher; and even Schaeder finds God primarily in the experiences of the soul. Thus it has been characteristic of modern theology to seek God in man, and to regard him as in some sense of the word continuous with man. Barth, it is true, stresses the infinite distance between God and man, and emphasizes the fact that man can only know God by means of a special divine revelation. But if the question is asked, Just where is God's revelation? Barth cannot tell, for it has no objective independent existence. It does not exist in a definite form, so as to enable one to say, Here it is. The Bible cannot be regarded as the infallibly inspired Word of God. It merely bears witness to the original divine revelation to the prophets and particularly in Christ. He can only say that God's revelation is there, where God speaks directly to the human soul, speaks a word which is recognized as the Word of God only by a special operation of the Holy Spirit in each particular case. The speaking of God is a revelation of God only for the one to whom God brings it home in faith. The reception of this revelation is a unique experience for those who receive it. Has Church proclamation, strictly speaking, any other source to draw on? And if not, how far does Barth then really get away from the experimental method? It may be said that, according to him, Church proclamation must be tested by the original revelation attested by Scripture, but that does not change matters. Most of the experimental theologians regard the Bible as, in some sense of the word, a norm for the study of theology. It is not surprising to find Rolston saying: "On Barthian premises, there is no way to prevent men from falling into a position which the Barthians themselves would abhor. The system would inevitably tend to a vast subjectivity in which each man decided for himself just what portion of Scripture had authority for him."[1]

---

1. *A Conservative looks to Barth and Brunner*, p. 101.

However much the empirical method may be in vogue in modern theology, it is nevertheless open to several serious objections. (1) The application of this method *eo ipso* rules out God as the object of theology, for it is not possible to investigate God experimentally. He cannot be brought to the tests of observation and experience. If some of those who apply this method feel that in the study of theology they should proceed beyond the knowledge of the phenomena of religion to the knowledge of God, and really make a serious attempt to move in that direction, they do it at the expense of their empirical method. (2) Because the empirical method deals with the phenomena of experimental religion rather than with God as its object, it does not really succeed in constructing a system of theology at all, but merely yields a study in religious psychology. James' *The Varieties of Religious Experience* is regarded as a classic production of this method. But however important this book may be, it is not theological. (3) The strict application of the empirical method does not enable one to get beyond the surface even in the study of religion. External tests can be applied to the phenomena of the religious life, but not to the inner life itself, not to the hidden depths of the soul from which the experiences of religion arise. The empirical method pure and simple ties one down to a bare phenomenalism without unity or conscience, which is not even entitled to the name of science. (4) Finally, the empirical method, even when it ceases to be purely empirical and allows the validity of reflection and inference, and admits of the application of general categories of thought, does not, as a rule, get beyond the description of subjective states of consciousness with their constant fluctuations. The result is a purely descriptive science, and not one that has normative significance. It abandons the field of objective religion, and seeks to achieve its triumphs in the realm of the subjective.

c. *The genetico-synthetic method.* This method is sometimes called *the theological method*, or *the method of authority*, because it proceeds on the assumption that the divine self-revelation in Scripture is the *principium cognoscendi externum* of theology. The presupposition is that God, and not religion, is the object of theology, and that the object can be known only because, and in so far as, it has revealed itself. Consequently the data with which theology deals are not given in the Christian consciousness, but in the objective special revelation of God. This self-revelation only can give us absolutely reliable knowledge of God. Whatever knowledge may be derived from other sources, such as nature and the Christian consciousness, must be tested by the Word of God.

According to this method the dogmatician, while taking his stand in the confession of his Church, yet in the construction of his system proceeds from the data given in Scripture. He enters into the rich harvest of the work that was done especially in exegesis and in the history of revelation or Biblical theology, and seeks to show how the dogmas of the Church are rooted, not in isolated passages of Scripture, but in Scripture as a whole, and are developed out of the divine revelation in an organic way. In so far as he gathers his materials from Scripture his method may be called inductive, but this should not be represented as a sort of experimental method, as is done in a measure by Hodge, and also by Edgar. For him Scripture not merely reveals certain facts which man may interpret as he sees fit and as he deems necessary in the age in which he lives, but also gives an infallible interpretation of the facts, an interpretation which he may not set aside at will, but must accept as authoritative.

In the application of the synthetic method the theologian will not merely receive isolated doctrines from Scripture, but rather the divine truth as a whole revealed in facts and words. The facts are the embodiments of the truths that are revealed, and the truths illumine the facts that stand out on the pages of Holy Writ. The teachings of Scripture are seen in their grand unity, since the Bible indicates in various ways how its separate doctrines are interrelated. Bearing all these data in mind, the dogmatician will seek to construct his system in a logical way, supplying whatever links may still be missing in the confession of the Church from the Bible as the fountain-head of religious truth, and calling attention to the various deviations from Scripture in the historical development of the truth. It will be his constant endeavor to set forth all the treasures of wisdom and knowledge that are hidden in Christ and revealed in Scripture.

C. Distribution of Dogmatics.

There has been quite a variety of opinion respecting the proper distribution of the material of Dogmatics. The principle of distribution has been derived from the subject-matter of theology, from the sources of its material content, from the manner in which this is treated, or from its historical development. Naturally, this principle may not be chosen arbitrarily, but should be germane to the subject, should cover the whole field and assure to each part a natural place, and should maintain the proper proportions of the separate parts. Logic would seem to require that in theology, as in all other sciences, the principle of division should be derived, not from its sources, its manner of treatment, or its historical development, but very decidedly from its subject-matter. The following are the most important methods of distributing the dogmatic material adopted in the Protestant Church since the days of the Reformation.

1. THE TRINITARIAN METHOD. To a certain extent Calvin and Zwingli paved the way for the trinitarian distribution of the dogmatic material. Their classification was not strictly trinitarian. but was derived from the Apostolic Confession. They followed up their discussion of God as Creator, God as Redeemer, and God as Sanctifier, with a separate book, dealing with the Church and the Sacraments. The Dutch theologian, Melchior Leydekker (born 1642), a follower of Voetius, was the first one to apply the strictly trinitarian method. It did not become popular, however. Hegel, who regarded the doctrine of the Trinity as the central doctrine of Christianity, brought it into prominence once more; and it is followed by Marheineke and Martensen. This

method naturally leads to an undue emphasis on the metaphysical in Dogmatics. Logically, it excludes the discussion of the doctrine of the Trinity. This can only be treated as a presupposition in a preliminary chapter. Moreover, this method, with its excessive emphasis on the separate persons of the Godhead tends to obscure the fact that the divine *opera ad extra* are all *opera essentialia*, that is, works of the divine Being as a whole, and to give them the appearance of *opera personalia*, works of the separate persons. Finally, the various elements of anthropology and soteriology do not find a natural place in such a scheme. For these reasons this method of distribution has found little favor, and does not deserve commendation.

2. THE ANALYTICAL METHOD. While the synthetic method begins with God, and then proceeds to discuss man, Christ, redemption, *et cetera*, until it finally reaches the end of all things, the analytical method, proposed by Calixtus (1614-1656), begins with what it considers the final cause or end of theology, namely, blessedness, then proceeds to the subject (God, angel, man, sin), and finally treats of the means by which it is secured (predestination, incarnation, Christ, justification, the Word, the Sacraments, and so on). It surely makes a strange impression that theology should begin with the end, and that the end should be blessedness rather than the glory of God. It is equally strange that in the second part God, angels, and men should be coördinated, as if blessedness were the end of theology for the one as well as for the other. Moreover, the third part does scant justice to Soteriology, since it is silent on such subjects as regeneration, calling, conversion, faith, sanctification, and good works. Notwithstanding this, the method of Calixtus was followed by several Lutheran theologians, though it meets with no favor at the present time.

3. THE COVENANTAL METHOD. Coccejus was the first to derive a *principium divisionis* from the covenant idea. He distinguished, and dealt successively with, the *foedus naturae et operum*, and the *foedus gratiae* with its three subdivisions: *ante legem, sub lege,* and *post legem*. Among the Reformed theologians of the Netherlands he was followed by Witsius and Vitringa, but in other circles his system found no favor. And even in Reformed theology it was short-lived. Among the Southern Presbyterians of our own country Dr. Thornwell followed a somewhat similar division. He derives his principle of distribution from the moral government of God, and treats of the moral government in its simple form, the moral government modified by the covenant of works, and the moral government modified by the covenant of grace. But in this division the principle of distribution is clearly not derived from the subject-matter as such, but from the history of its development. Taking its starting point in the covenant between God and man, it can naturally discuss the doctrine of God and of man only by way of introduction. Moreover, it virtually obliterates the distinction between the History of Revelation and Dogmatics, deprives Dogmatics of its absolute character, and leads to constant repetitions.

4. THE CHRISTOLOGICAL METHOD. Several theologians, both in Europe and in America, are of the opinion that all genuinely Christian theology should be *Christocentric*, and should therefore derive its principle of distribution from Christ or the saving operations of Christ. This position is taken by Hase, Thomasius, Schultz, T. B. Strong, A. Fuller, H. B. Smith, and V. Gerhart. Schultz treats of God and the world, and of man and sin, as presuppositions of the Christian salvation, and then proceeds to the discussion of the saving work of the Son of God (Person and work of Christ), and the saving acts of the Spirit of God (Church, means of grace, *ordo salutis*, perfecting of salvation). A somewhat similar course is followed by Smith, who treats successively of the antecedents of redemption, the redemption itself, and the consequents or (to use a later term) the kingdom of redemption. It is a sufficient condemnation of this method that the doctrines of God, of man, and of sin, must be placed outside of the system, and treated as prolegomena. Christ is indeed the center of God's revelation, but for that very reason cannot be the starting point. Moreover, this method is sometimes (as, for instance, in the work of Gerhart) combined with the false notion that Christ, and not Scripture, is the *principium cognoscendi externum* of theology.

5. THE METHOD BASED ON THE KINGDOM IDEA. Under the influence of Ritschl, who makes the Kingdom of God central in his theology, some theologians would derive the principle of distribution from this important concept. Ritschl himself does not apply this division; neither do Kaftan, Haering, and Herrmann, some of the most important theologians of the Ritschlian school. Van Oosterzee offers an example of it which is not very convincing. In reality he gives the customary synthetic division, and merely substitutes for the old titles of the various divisions designations derived from the idea of the Kingdom. He discusses successively God or the supreme King (theology), man or the subject (anthropology), Christ or the founder (Christology), redemption or the salvation (objective soteriology), the way of salvation or the constitution (subjective soteriology), the Church or the training school (ecclesiology), and the future coming of the Lord or the consummation, of the Kingdom (Eschatology). This division is purely formal, and is by no means organically deduced from the Kingdom idea. Moreover, a division based on the Kingdom idea robs Dogmatics of its theological character, and is logically impossible. The doctrine of God, of man in general, of sin, and of Christ in His many-sided significance cannot be derived from the idea of the Kingdom of God.

6. THE SYNTHETICAL METHOD. This is the only method that will yield the desired unity in Dogmatics. It takes its starting point in God, and considers everything that comes up for discussion in relation to God. It discusses the various doctrines in their logical order, that is, in the order in which they arise in thought, and which lends itself to the most intelligible treatment. In such an order of treatment each truth, except the first, must be so related to preceding truths that it will be seen in the clearest light. God is the fundamental truth in theology, and is therefore naturally first in order. Every follow-

ing truth, in order to be seen in its true perspective, must be viewed in the light of this primary truth. For that reason Anthropology must precede Christology, and Christology must precede Soteriology, and so on. Proceeding according to this logical method, we discuss:

I. The doctrine of God (Theology).
II. The doctrine of man (Anthropology).
III. The doctrine of Christ (Christology).
IV. The doctrine of applied salvation (Soteriology).
V. The doctrine of the Church (Ecclesiology).
VI. The doctrine of the last things (Eschatology).

QUESTIONS FOR FURTHER STUDY: What is the difference between biblical and dogmatical theology, and how are the two related? What objections have been raised to systematizing theological truth? What distinction do modern theologians make between the source and the norm of dogmatic truth? Is this distinction valid? Why should the Bible be regarded as the *principium unicum* of theology? How do Kuyper and Bavinck distinguish between a *principium* and a source or *fons*? What important truth is contained in the modern emphasis on the Christian consciousness? How do the views of Troeltsch, Schaeder, and Barth differ as to the task of Dogmatics? What is the Barthian view of the source of theology? Is it possible for a dogmatician to be unbiased in his theological studies? What is the mystical method? The religious-historical method of Troeltsch? The pragmatic method?

REFERENCES: Bavinck, *Geref. Dogm.* I, pp. 41-103; Kuyper, *Enc. der Heil. Godgel.* III, pp. 405-415; Hodge, *Syst. Theol.* I, pp. 1-150; Shedd, *Dogm. Theol.* I, pp. 3-15; Miley, *Syst. Theol.* I, pp. 7-54; McPherson, *Chr. Dogm.*, pp. 1-43; Thornwell, *Collected Writings* I, pp. 39-52; Macintosh, *Theol. as an Emp. Science*, pp. 1-46; Foster, G. B., *Christianity in its Modern Expression*, pp. 1-79; Van Oosterzee, *Chr. Dogm. I*, pp. 20-42, 84-109; Raebiger, *Theol. Enc.* II, pp. 335-339; Van Dijk, *Begrip en Methode der Dogm.*, pp. 7-89; Lobstein, *An Introd. to Prot. Dogm.*, pp. 58-275; Smith, H. B., *Introd. to Chr. Theol.*, pp. 60-83; Lemme, *Christl. Glaubenslehre*, pp. 14-31; Girardeau, *Discussion of Theol. Questions*, pp. 45-272; C. W. Hodge, *The Idea of Dogm. Theol., The Princeton Theol. Rev.*, Jan., 1908; Warfield, *The Idea of Syst. Theol., Studies in Theology*, pp. 49ff.; Schaeder, *Theozentrische Theologie*; Barth, *The Doctrine of the Word of God*, pp. 1-51.

V. History of Dogmatics

The history of Dogmatics does not go back to the time of the Apostles, but only to the beginning of the third century, when Origen wrote his *Peri Archon*. Several periods may be distinguished, namely, the period of the Old Catholic Church, the period of the Middle Ages, the period of the Reformation, the period of Protestant Scholasticism, the period of Rationalism and Supranaturalism, and the period of Modern Theology.

A. The Period of the Old Catholic Church.

In the beginning of this period some valuable preparatory work was done by the catechetical school of Alexandria, but it was not until the beginning of the third century that any important work appeared which purported to be a systematic presentation of theological truth. In fact, the period of the Old Catholic Church produced only three works of superior value in the field of systematic theology, and even these are rather deficient.

1. ORIGEN'S PERI ARCHON (DE PRINCIPIIS). Origen was the first to construct something like a system of theology. His work was written about the year 218 A. D. In it the author attempts to transform the doctrine of the Church into a speculative science, acceptable to the cultural and philosophical classes of his day. His great ambition was to develop the contents of faith into a science that did not rest on authority, but on its own inherent rational evidence. In this way he desired to raise *pistis* to the level of *gnosis*. While the work testifies to the intellectual clarity and profundity of the author, it also reveals a tendency to sacrifice theology to philosophy. It departs from the current teachings of the Church particularly (a) in the doctrine that human souls preëxisted, sinned in their previous existence, and are now for punishment imprisoned in material bodies; (b) in the notion that the human soul of Christ was already in its preëxistence united with the Logos; (c) in the denial of the physical resurrection; and (d) in the teaching of the restoration of all things, Satan included. The general plan of the work is defective, and does not provide for an adequate treatment of Christology, Soteriology, and Ecclesiology.

2. AUGUSTINE'S ENCHIRIDION AD LAURENTIUM: DE FIDE, SPE, ET CARITATE. As the subtitle indicates, the plan of this work is derived from the three Pauline virtues, faith, hope, and love. Under the first heading the author discusses the main articles of faith; under the second, the doctrine of prayer, following the order of the six petitions of the Lord's prayer; and under the third all kinds of moral questions. Though this arrangement is by no means ideal and

the work is not always self-consistent, it gives evidence of deep thought and of an earnest attempt to construe the whole of Christian doctrine from a strictly theological point of view. The author contemplates the entire world with all its rich variety *sub specie aeternitatis,* making the whole universe subservient to God. Through this and his many other dogmatical treatises Augustine exercised a tremendous influence, which is potent, especially in Reformed circles, even down to the present day. He did more than any other scholar of pre-Reformation times to develop the Scriptural doctrine of sin and grace.

Mention should be made in this connection also of the *Commonitorium* of Vincentius Lerinensis, which gives a representation of the doctrine of the Old Catholic Church, but can hardly be regarded as a systematic exposition of dogmatical truth. It served, however, to give definite form to the teachings of the Fathers. The author's ideal was to give an exposition of doctrine in harmony with the tradition of the Church, which he defined as *quod ubique, quod semper, quod ab omnibus creditum est.* The work has a Semi-Pelagian flavor.

3. John of Damascus' EKDOSIS AKRIBES TES ORTHODOXOU PISTEOS (An Accurate Exposition of the Orthodox Faith), 700-760. This work represents by far the most important attempt in the Eastern Church to give a systematic exposition of dogmatic theology, at once speculative and ecclesiastical. It is divided into four books, dealing with (a) God and the Trinity; (b) creation and the nature of man; (c) Christ's incarnation, death, and descent into hades; and (d) the resurrection and the reign of Christ, and further such subjects as faith, baptism, image-worship, and so on. The order of the last book is very defective. Yet the work is of great importance, and is, from a formal point of view, certainly the best systematic presentation of the truth in this period. It is on the whole conservative and in harmony with the teachings of the Church as they had come down to the author.

B. The Period of the Middle Ages.

The period following John of Damascus was characterized by a remarkable dialectical activity, especially in theology. The first centuries were rather barren, but towards the end of the tenth century there was a scientific awakening. In the eleventh century Scholasticism arose; in the twelfth Mysticism appeared alongside of it; and in the thirteenth century the former, in league with the latter, gained complete ascendancy, and reached its highest glory. Scholasticism represented an attempt to deal with the doctrinal material found in Scripture according to the strictly scientific method of the schools. On the whole it accepted the contents of the Bible with childlike faith, but it attempted at the same time to represent the various doctrines of Scripture in their inner unity, so as to promote a deeper knowledge of the truth. In course of time it became subject to the controlling influence of philosophy, Platonic and Aristotelian, Nominalistic and Realistic, and developed in a rather precarious direction. It derived from philosophy, not only its dialectical method, but also many problems and questions of a purely philosophical kind. As a result Dogmatics gradually degenerated into a philosophical system. The interrogatory form, in which the material was often cast, frequently promoted doubt, and in many instances had the result of placing authority and reason in antithetical relation to each other. Among the dogmatical treatises of this period the following are outstanding.

1. WORKS OF ANSELM. The first name of more than ordinary importance is that of Anselm of Canterbury (1033-1109). He was characterized at once by deep piety and great intellectual acuteness and penetration. While he did not produce a comprehensive systematic exposition of theology, he wrote several works of great dogmatical value, such as his Monologium and Proslogium, in which he discusses the nature of God and develops his ontological proof for the existence of God; his *de fide Trinitatis et de incarnatione Verbi,* which, as the title indicates, deals with the doctrine of the Trinity and of the incarnation; and his *de Concordia,* devoted to a discussion of predestination in the spirit of Augustine. Surpassing all these in importance, however, his *Cur Deus Homo?* offers a classical exposition of the satisfaction theory of the atonement. Anselm was the first to deal with this important subject in a thorough and systematic way. His great opponent was Abelard with his moral influence theory.

2. THE SENTENCES OF PETER THE LOMBARD. The first important systematic work of the Scholastic period, which aims at covering the whole field, is Peter the Lombard's *Sententiarum libri IV,* consisting of four books: the first on God, the second on His creatures, the third on redemption, and the fourth on the sacraments and the last things. On the whole the work simply reproduces the teachings of the Fathers, though, in distinction from many other works of this period, it also contains a good deal of original material. For several centuries it was widely used as a handbook of theology, and regarded as the most authoritative exposition of the truth. Many scholars followed the example of Peter the Lombard in writing *Sentences.*

3. THE SUMMA OF ALEXANDER OF HALES. Alongside of the Sentences *Summae theologiae* gradually made their appearance. Alexander of Hales, a man of great learning, wrote a *Summa universae theologiae,* which is really a commentary on the work of Lombardus. His work is cast in a strict dialectical and syllogistic form, and served to establish the scholastic method. It treats of God, of the creature, of the Redeemer and His work, and of the sacraments. From a formal point of view this work is somewhat similar to modern works on Dogmatics. Alexander presents both sides of a question, states what can be said in favor of each, and then gives his own conclusion. Bonaventura, his disciple, added to the dialectical acuteness of his master the mystical element, which was coming to the foreground at this time.

4. THE SUMMA OF THOMAS AQUINAS. Thomas Aquinas is undoubtedly the greatest of the Schoolmen. His *Summa totius theologiae* covers in three

volumes nearly the whole field of Dogmatics. The first book deals with God and His works; the second with man as the image of God, finding in God the highest end of his existence; and the third with Christ and the means of grace. The work remained incomplete, but the material for the doctrine of the sacraments and of the last things was culled from some of his other works and added to the *Summa*. Formally, the work is controlled by the Aristotelian philosophy; and materially, by the work of Augustine, though the work of this early Church Father is modified in important points and brought into greater agreement with the doctrine of the Church. Thomas Aquinas is the great authority of the Roman Catholic Church, and Thomism is its standard theology. Duns Scotus was the great opponent of Thomas Aquinas, but his work was critical and destructive rather than systematic and constructive. It marks the decline of Scholasticism.

C. The Period of the Reformation.

The theology of the Reformation is characterized by the special prominence given to the absolute normative authority of Scripture, and by the strong emphasis on the doctrine of justification by faith only. Luther was far more practical and polemical than scientific and dogmatical in his writings. The only doctrinal treatise with which he enriched the theological world, is his *De Servo Arbitrio,* which contains a clear exposition of the Augustinian doctrine of predestination. The period of the Reformation produced especially three works of a systematic character that were of more than ordinary significance.

1. MELANCHTON'S LOCI COMMUNES. This work of Melanchton was the first Protestant handbook of Dogmatics. It follows the order of the Epistle to the Romans in its exposition of the truth. In the first edition of the work the author was in entire agreement with Luther, but in the later editions he made concessions to several opponents and thus parted company with Luther on more than one point. In distinction from Luther, Melanchton stressed the ethical element in Christianity and preferred to place special emphasis on faith as the moral activity of the redeemed. In course of time he revealed an inclination also to soft-pedal the doctrine of predestination, and to sponsor the doctrine of the free will of man. In these points he yielded to the powerful influence of Erasmus. At the same time he also made concessions to Calvin in his Christology and in the doctrine of the Lord's Supper. His final position was somewhat of a half-way position between Luther and Calvin.

2. ZWINGLI'S COMMENTARIUS DE VERA ET FALSA RELIGIONE. Schaff speaks of this work of the great Swiss Reformer as the first systematic exposition of the Reformed faith. But, while it does contain the fundamental thoughts of the Reformed faith, it can hardly be called a well-rounded, systematic whole. The author does not, like Luther, stress the doctrine of justification by faith above all others, but rather the absolute sovereignty of God and the utter dependence of man. He speaks in stronger and less guarded terms than

Calvin about the doctrine of predestination. And in the doctrine of the Lord's Supper he approaches, but yet falls short of, the spiritual view of Calvin.

3. CALVIN'S INSTITUTIO CHRISTIANAE RELIGIONIS. The Institutes of Calvin is so far superior to the *Commentarius* of Zwingli as to be a truly epoch-making work. It consists of four books, of which the first three follow the trinitarian order, and the fourth treats of the Church and the Sacraments. The central thought, controlling the whole work, is that of the absolute sovereignty of God. Throughout the whole exposition of the truth doctrine and ethics are closely interwoven, and the practical side of the Christian life is made very prominent. This work of Calvin is rightly lauded for its conciseness, for its clarity of thought, for its well-proportioned parts, and for its warmth of expression. It forms quite a contrast with the later, more scholastic, productions of Protestant theology, and is easily the most important work of the Reformation. As another very important work of the Reformation period Ursinus' Commentary on the Heidelberg Catechism may be mentioned.

D. The Period of Protestant Scholasticism.

It is not surprising that the theology of the seventeenth century is on the whole, strongly polemical. The Reformation had to break with the immediate past with an appeal to the remoter past. It had to show that the hierarchical Church of the Middle Ages had wandered far from the path indicated by the theology of the early Church. Moreover, with its defense of the right of private judgment it had disturbed traditional foundations. As a result divergent opinions soon made their appearance in the Churches of the Reformation and were embodied in separate Confessions. There was a great deal of hair-splitting discussion, and in course of time a spirit of formalism and intellectualism gained the upper hand with chilling effect, and led to the introduction of the scholastic method in the study of theology.

1. DOGMATICAL STUDY AMONG THE LUTHERANS. The vacillating position of Melanchton soon led to reaction. Towards the end of the sixteenth and in the earlier years of the seventeenth century a party arose, which manifested a strong, and sometimes rather fanatical, attachment to the early Lutheran faith, the faith of Luther himself and of the first edition of the Augsburg Confession. This party found able spokesmen in Hutterus and, especially, John Gerhardo (1582-1637), lauded as "the greatest of all Lutheran theologians." His *Loci communes theologici* is a work of primary importance, noted for the philosophical development and the systematic arrangement of its subject-matter. Calixtus opposed the attitude of the strict Lutherans and insisted on going back to the Apostles' Creed and to the doctrine of the first five centuries. He was of an irenical turn of mind and sought to continue the theology of Melanchton. The Calixtine movement met with violent opposition, however, in the person of Calovius, a man of great learning and ardently devoted to the strict Lutheran position. In his *Systema locorum theologicorum*, consisting of twelve volumes,

he gives a careful exposition of the orthodox Lutheran faith. The works of two other noted and influential Lutheran theologians, namely, Quenstedt and Hollaz, move along the same lines.

2. DOGMATICAL STUDY AMONG THE REFORMED. Differences of opinion were not limited to the Lutherans, but also made their appearance among the Reformed. Some of these were of a purely formal, and others of a more material, nature. There were theologians who were perfectly loyal to the truth, but went far beyond Calvin in its schematic arrangement and in all kinds of logical distinctions; and there were others who minimized and even explained away fundamental truths. Some were unduly influenced in their doctrinal expositions by the philosophical tenets of the age, and especially by the philosophy of Cartesius.

a. *The original type of doctrine.* Theodore Beza, Calvin's successor at Geneva, was more scholastic than Calvin and more extreme in his supralapsarian view of predestination. He did not write any dogmatical treatise of importance, but nevertheless exercised great influence on the dogmaticians of the seventeenth century. Wollebius and Wendelinus both wrote works of great learning, strictly Calvinistic, but greatly affected by the conflict with Lutheranism, and therefore scholastic in form. Besides these, Polanus and Pictet also each produced a systematic exposition of the Reformed faith. After Beza, Wm. Twisse, the prolocutor of the Westminster Assembly, was one of the earliest to develop the doctrine of predestination with great logical precision and in a rather extreme supralapsarian form. His works give evidence of great speculative power, and furnish one of the best examples of the inexorable application of the basic thought of Supralapsarianism in Reformed doctrine. Three of the very best Calvinistic works of this period are the *Synopsis Purioris Theologiae* by the four professors of Leyden the elaborate work of Petrus Mastricht on *Beschouwende en Practicale Godgeleerdheit,* in which he takes issue with the position of Coccejus; and Turretin's *Institutio Theologiae Elencticae,* a very complete exposition of Reformed doctrine, and one that has exercised great influence on American Reformed theology. In England and Scotland the works of Perkins, Owen, Goodwin, and Boston were of great importance.

b. *The Federal Modification of Reformed doctrine.* With Coccejus a reaction set in against the speculative and scholastic method of some of the thorough-going Calvinists. He substituted a purely Biblical method, distributing his material according to the scheme of the covenants. However, his position represented not only a formal divergence, but also a material departure, from traditional Reformed theology, and entered ever increasingly into league with Cartesianism. Its really new thing was not the covenant doctrine, for this is already found in the works of Zwingli, Bullenger, Olevianus, Snecanus, Gomarus, Trelcatius, and Cloppenburg, but its federalistic method. It virtually changed Dogmatics into Biblical Theology, thus making it a historical discipline. Its method was anthropological rather than theological. Two of the best representatives of this school, are Burmannus and Witsius. The *Synopsis Theologiae* of the former is by far the best of the two, and is free from that forced exegesis which so often characterizes the work of the Cocceian school. The work of the latter, *Over de Verbonden* (Eng. tr. On the Covenants), is inferior to it, but is better known in this country. It represents a laudable but futile attempt to reconcile the more scholastic and the federal trend in theology. Other representatives of this school are Leydekker, Van Til, C. Vitringa, Lampe, d'Outrein, and the Van der Honerts. This type of theology gradually gained the ascendancy at this time in the Netherlands, though it was strongly opposed by Voetius, and though the more scholastic type of theology still continued to appear in à Marck's *Merch der Christene Godgeleertheit* and in Brakel's *Redelijke Godsdienst*.

c. *The more radical modifications.* The Arminians or Remonstrants represented a radical departure from Calvinism. They opposed its doctrines of predestination, total depravity, irresistible grace, particular atonement, and the perseverance of the saints. Arminius himself did not go to the extremes that were defended by his followers. Episcopius gave a clear and complete exposition of Arminian theology in his *Institutiones theologicae*, while Grotius in his *Defensio fidei catholicae de satisfactione Christi* developed the governmental theory of the atonement. With Limborgh's elaborate work entitled *Theologia Christiana*, this party turns in the direction of Rationalism. Maccovius and Voetius were among its strongest opponents.

The school of Saumur represents another attempt to modify strict Calvinism. Amyraldus taught a hypothetical universalism, and Placaeus, the doctrine of mediate imputation. These errors were combatted by Heidegger and Turretin, two of the authors of the *Formula Consensus Helvetica*.

3. DOGMATICAL STUDY AMONG THE ROMAN CATHOLICS. During this period, remarkable for the development of Protestant Dogmatics, there were also a few noted Roman Catholic dogmaticians. Bellarmin (1542-1621) is recognized as a prince among them. His great work, entitled *Disputationes de controversiis christianae fidei* marks him as a man of literary elegance and as a skilful controversilist. It contains a rather complete exposition of Roman Catholic Dogmatics, and represents the ultramontane standpoint of the Jesuits, which is Semi-Pelagian in its doctrine of sin and grace. Another distinguished scholar was Petavius, who published an elaborate, though incomplete work, under the title *De theologicis dogmatibus* (1644-1650). This work of great erudition is primarily a history of dogma, and is favorably known also among Reformed theologians. Finally, mention should also be made of Jansen's *Augustinus*, published in 1640, which contains a defense of the Augustinian doctrine of grace, as opposed to the Semi-Pelagian doctrine of the Jesuits. Jansenism was condemned by the Pope in 1713.

E. The Period of Rationalism and Supranaturalism.

The Dogmatics of this period are of a somewhat reactionary character. On the one hand there was reaction against the formalism and the cold intellectualism of the current study of theology, against what was called "dead orthodoxy," and an attempt to inject new life into the study of theology and to make it more directly subservient to a living and practical faith. And on the other hand there was a particularly strong and persistent reaction to the dominating influence of Scripture and of ecclesiastical tradition in Dogmatics, and to the doctrines that were taught in the historical Creeds of the Church; and a widespread movement to strike out on new paths, untrammeled by authority, under the guidance of human reason. Old barriers were broken down, and a Rationalistic apostasy became alarmingly prevalent in the Church.

1. PIETISTIC DOGMATICS. The close of the seventeenth century and the beginning of the eighteenth century saw the rise of Pietism, especially in the Lutheran Church. Its principal representatives were Spener, Francke, Freylinghausen, J. Lange, Rambach, and Oetinger. They desired to release Dogmatics from scholastic formalism, and insisted on a return to Biblical simplicity. From this point of view some of them made real contributions to Dogmatics, as, for instance, Spener, Francke, Freylinghausen, and Oetinger, though none of them produced an outstanding systematic exposition of the truth. Current orthodoxy at first opposed it, but finally yielded to its spirit. Consequently, a new tendency developed in the study of theology, which emphasized practical piety, was inimical to all scholastic subtlety, and showed great moderation in polemics.

2. RATIONALISTIC DOGMATICS. The principal influence that militated against Pietism appeared in the form of Rationalism, in the rigid method introduced by Wolff, whose ambition it was to reduce all theological statements to mathematical formulae. According to him anything that could not be made perfectly plain by actual demonstration, was not fit to be taught. Carpzovious essayed to demonstrate the truth of the teachings of the Church according to this method. Baumgarten and Mosheim moved along the same line. In the main these men were still orthodox, but had no proper appreciation of the *religious* value of the truth. For them the dogma of the Church was primarily an object of historical learning and intellectual demonstration. But the influence of Wolff also marked the inception of a thoroughly rationalistic tendency in the study of theology. The light of reason induced many theologians to adopt a position that was partly Socinian and partly Arminian. This tendency is seen especially in the writings of Toellner and Semler. In England the rationalistic movement appeared more particularly in the form of Deism, which denied supernatural revelation and aimed at the development of a system of natural religion. The English Deists, however, furnish little material for the history of Dogmatics. Of greater importance is the Unitarian movement, which continues the Socinian element in theology. Priestly constructed a

system of pure Naturalism in his *Institutes of Natural and Revealed Religion*. In Germany Kant was the first to oppose successfully the superficial Rationalism that gloried in its intellectual enlightenment; but his *Religion innerhalb der Grenzen der blossen Vernunft* is still purely rationalistic. Tieftrunk elaborated Dogmatics in the Kantian spirit, and Wegscheider still assumed an advanced rationalistic position.

3. SUPRANATURALISTIC DOGMATICS. Orthodoxy reacted against Rationalism in the weak form of Supranaturalism. This acknowledged a supernatural revelation and honored Scripture as the norm of religious truth, but nevertheless allowed reason to determine in various ways what is and what is not essential in the Bible. Thus it reduced the contents of revelation and by all kinds of concessions sought to make it square with reason. It was really a compromise between reason and revelation. This weak position is represented by Doederlein, Knapp, and Storr. A reconciliation between Rationalism and Supranaturalism was attempted especially by Bretschneider, who exercised great influence by means of his two works: *Systematische Entwickelung aller in der Dogmatik vorkommenden Begriffe*, and *Handbuch der Dogmatik der evangelischen Kirche*. A somewhat similar position is taken by De Wette in his *Lehrbuch der christliche Dogmatik*, and his *Ueber Religion und Theologie*. He rises above the superficiality and want of spirituality which characterized the illumination, seeks to do justice to the religious feelings, and explains the fundamental truths of Dogmatics as the symbolical expression of the subjective truths of personal experience.

F. The Period of Modern Theology.

In the nineteenth century the theological currents multiply, so that it will be necessary to call attention to several schools, though they can hardly be called schools in the strict sense of the word. Some of them simply represent a general tendency which, however, expresses itself in a variety of ways, and may even reveal sharp differences.

1. SCHLEIERMACHER AND HIS SCHOOL. Schleiermacher stands as an intellectual giant at the beginning of the theological development of the nineteenth century. He united in himself the various theological currents of his day, and sought to fuse them into a religious unity. This resulted in a syncretism of Rationalism, Supranaturalism, and Pietism. He had learned by experience that Christianity had introduced a new and higher life into the world, and was convinced that this life had to incorporate all possible religious currents. His big heart caused him to take a sympathetic attitude with respect to all schools of thought, and to assimilate the good elements in each. But when he attempted to transform his religious experiences into intellectual concepts, and to combine these into a coherent dogmatic system, he did not succeed. His theology became in fact a confirmation of all kinds of opinions. This accounts for the fact that both Roman Catholics and Protestants, both Rationalists

and Mystics, appeal to him. However great a religious thinker he was, his scientific theology was not a success. It is composed of all kinds of heterogeneous elements, and is therefore full of contradictions. In his *Reden ueber die Religion* and his Monologen (Monologues) he is entirely under the influence of Romanticism, an initial phase of German idealism, which served as a transition from Kant to Hegel. Religion is the sense of God, of the Infinite, and of the Universe, for the Universe is God. Schleiermacher speaks of it as a "Hinneigung zum Weltall." And God is not an object of thought, but only an object to be enjoyed in the depths of one's feelings. That enjoyment of God is religion. His *Glaubenslehre* contains the same philosophical principles with this difference, however, that religious feeling is now described as a feeling of complete dependence, that God is represented as absolute causality, and that Christianity is characterized as an ethical religion, in which everything is related to the redemption through Christ. According to Schleiermacher dogmas are descriptions of subjective states of consciousness or feeling, more particularly, of such states of consciousness as are determined by the Christian community, or by the Person of Jesus. With him Dogmatics leaves the solid foundation of the Word of God and is made to rest on the shifting sands of human experiences.

No one adopted the Dogmatics of Schleiermacher as a whole, and yet he had a controlling influence on the whole theological development after him. Among the immediate disciples of Schleiermacher none was so true to his dogmatic principles as A. Schweizer. His most important works are: *Die Glaubenslehre der reformirten Kirche*; *Die Protestantischen Centraldogmen innerhalb der reformirten Kirche*, and *Die christliche Glaubenslehre*. In the first of these works he combines Schleiermacher's feeling of dependence with the Reformed doctrine of predestination; and in his later works he stresses the fact that Dogmatics must go to the living Christian consciousness for its material. His representation of Reformed doctrine is open to several objections. Somewhat similar to his works are those of J. H. Scholten, *De Leer der Hervormde Kerk*, and Schenkel, *Die christliche Dogmatik vom Standpunkte des Gewissens*. Lipsius assumed a standpoint essentially distinct from that of Schleiermacher, but yet has this in common with the latter, that he seeks to build up his system from the standpoint of the Christian consciousness. For him religion is not only a feeling dependence, but also a sense of freedom. He denies the unique significance of the incarnation and makes Christ the typical Son of Man, in whom man first realizes his spiritual communion with God. Rothe may also be mentioned in this connection. Like Schleiermacher, he took his starting point in the Christian consciousness, the consciousness of communion with God and of redemption through Christ, and considered Dogmatics as a historical discipline.

2. THE SPECULATIVE SCHOOL. The philosophical movement from Kant to Hegel had a determining influence on the historical and scientific development of theology. The influence of Hegel was the most far-reaching. Like

Schleiermacher, he did a great deal to brush aside the old vulgar Rationalism, and to show the untenableness of Supranaturalism. But while Schleiermacher sought to deliver theology from the domination of philosophy, Hegel encouraged the study of theology in the very terms of philosophy. The theologians who accept and apply his principles are rightly called speculative theologians. Their theology is *essentially* and *in principle* speculative.

Daub has been called "the founder of Protestant speculative theology." He came successively under the influence of Kant, Fichte, Schelling, and Hegel. Together with Marheineke and Rosenkranz, he thought it was quite possible to harmonize the principles of Hegel with the truths of the Christian religion, and made use of those principles in the formulation of the truth. These theologians were on the whole comparatively conservative, and constitute what is generally called "the right wing" of the Hegelian school, of which Marheineke was the recognized leader. In his *System der christlichen Dogmatik* he applied the principles of Hegel and follows the trinitarian method. The work of John Caird on *The Fundamental Ideas of Christianity* is also strongly influenced by the Hegelian philosophy.

The "left wing" of the Hegelian school is represented especially by Strauss and Biedermann. It sacrifices the old content of the Christian truth to the new speculative form. The *Christliche Glaubenslehre* of Strauss is purely critical and destructive. The various dogmas are tested by the demands of modern science and found wanting. In the *Christliche Dogmatik* of Biedermann the principles of Hegel are worked out in a purely pantheistic way. The authority of the Bible is not acknowledged, and the personality of God and personal immortality are both denied. Pfleiderer discarded the Hegelian terminology, but is entirely in harmony with the fundamental principles of Hegel.

3. THE NEO-LUTHERAN SCHOOL. The negative position of the Hegelian school naturally evoked reaction. Some reiterated the confessional doctrine of the Lutheran Church, and others sought a *via media*. At present we are concerned with the former only. The so-called Neo-Lutherans made an earnest attempt to restore the old confessional truth on the basis of Scripture. Thomasius of Erlangen in his work on *Christi Person und Werk* presents an evangelical type of Lutheran Dogmatics, in which he makes Christology central. His kenosis doctrine, however, is scarcely compatible with the Lutheran doctrine of Christ's ubiquity. He maintains the satisfaction theory of the atonement, but in the doctrine of the Trinity hardly escapes a certain type of subordinationism. A second representative, Kahnis, maintains a somewhat freer attitude toward Lutheran orthodoxy. He follows the trinitarian method in his *Lutherische Dogmatik*. His doctrine of the Trinity is more or less Sabellian, and his Christology is marked by a certain subordinationism and by a kenosis doctrine similar to that of Thomasius.

Frank of Erlangen also departs in several points from pure Lutheranism. In his *System der christlichen Wahrheit* he postulates two *principia cognoscendi* in theology, namely, Scripture and the believing subject, held in unity by the *principium essendi,* which is God. The idea of God becoming man is the central thought of his theology, and from it he derives his *principium divisionis.* In its broad features his theology is in harmony with the doctrine of the Church. The work of Kaehler of Halle shows some resemblance to that of Frank. He also proceeds from the standpoint of Christian experience, and postulates a special kind of knowledge in the Christian. Philippi is the best representative of pure Lutheranism in Germany. His *Kirchliche Glaubenslehre* is a clear and well arranged exposition of the doctrine of the Church from a strictly confessional point of view. According to him Dogmatics seeks to elaborate the thought of the restoration of man in communion with God, and it is from this point that he derives his principle of division. In our own country strict Lutheranism finds expression in Schmid's *Doctrinal Theology of the Evangelical Lutheran Church,* Pieper's *Christliche Dogmatik,* and Mueller's *Christian Dogmatics.*

4. THE MEDIATING SCHOOL. There were many theologians who did not go as far as the Neo-Lutherans in their reaction against the speculative movement in theology. They preferred to steer a middle course and to seek a compromise. Hence they are called "mediating theologians." On the whole these scholars are clearly dependent on Schleiermacher, and with him take their starting point, not in the objective revelation of God, but in the subjective religious consciousness. But with this Schleiermacherian starting point they combine Hegelian speculation. What is first accepted as the content of experience, is next set forth speculatively as a necessity of thought, and thus justified before the bar of philosophy. Only a few names can be mentioned here. The greatest of the mediating theologians is Dorner, who on the one hand assumes a sympathetic attitude towards the confession of the Church, but on the other hand freely criticizes it and incorporates in his system all kinds of speculative elements, which cannot be harmonized with the orthodox, Scriptural position. This is quite evident in his attempt to explain the Trinity, and in his conception of Christ as the ideal man, with whom the Logos is progressively united. His *System der christlichen Glaubenslehre* contains a wealth of dogmatical and historical material, and is noted for its elaborate and acute criticism.

Alongside of Dorner mention should be made of Julius Mueller, a man of great moral earnestness and of deep insight into the truth. His *Die christliche Lehre von der Suende* is still the greatest monograph on the subject of sin. He revived the ancient idea of a pre-temporal self-determination of each man to sin, in order to maintain the voluntary origin of sin in the life of each individual despite the fact that man is sinful from the time of his birth. Nitzsch and Martensen also belong to this class of theologians. The *Christliche Dogmatik* of the latter, written in a very attractive style, reveals a syncretistic tendency. On the whole he is true to the Lutheran doctrine, but connects with it a mystical and a speculative element. He follows the trinitarian division in Dogmatics, and in his Christology defends a certain type of kenosis doctrine.

5. THE SCHOOL OF RITSCHL. Another German theologian who formed a school is Albrecht Ritschl; and even of him this cannot be asserted without qualification. It is difficult to say what constitutes the unity of the Ritschlian school. His followers scarcely agree in any point, except in their gratitude for the inspiration derived from their common master, and in their conviction that the characteristic feature of Christianity as a historical religion is found in Christ as its Founder. Ritschl gave the most complete exposition of his system in his *Die christliche Lehre von der Rechtfertigung und Versoehnung*. He claims to be in harmony with Protestantism in general and, more particularly, with the doctrine of the Lutheran Church. While he desires to banish metaphysics (especially ontology) from theology, he is himself controlled by a purely speculative theory of knowledge. Strictly speaking, his scientific position is that of an agnostic. In his doctrine of God he is really a Unitarian, and in connection with the atonement he accepts the moral influence theory as the only tenable one. He distinguishes between scientific and religious truth. The latter is based, not on judgments of being, but exclusively on judgments of value. The truth of a religious idea is determined by the value which it has for the Christian life. We honor Christ as God, not because we consider Him to be very God, but because He has for us the value of a God. In the doctrine of sin and redemption he deviates from the confession of the Church. He largely ignores the work of the Holy Spirit, and professes ignorance respecting the future life. The doctrine of the Kingdom of God is central in his system. Christ is its Founder, and all those who come under His influence are its citizens, and are controlled by the principle of love to God.

Hermann accepts the principles of Ritschl in general. By means of his work on *Der Verkehr des Christen mit Gott* he did a great deal to popularize the leading principles of the Ritschlian theology. He is more subjective and even less Biblical than Ritschl, and reveals a tendency to exchange the rationalistic element of Ritschl for a certain religious mysticism. The most prominent dogmatician of the school is Julius Kaftan. He modifies the dogmatic positions of Ritschl in more than one respect, asserts that judgments of value cannot be dissociated from judgments of being, and denies the distinction between scientific and religious truth as it is usually represented by the critics of Ritschl. His work on *Die Wahrheit der christlichen Religion* is important for the introduction to Dogmatics, and his *Dogmatik* is a clear systematic presentation of the truth. He seems to be inclined to make important concessions to orthodox theology in the doctrine of sin, of redemption, and of the Person of Christ. Of all the followers of Ritschl no one has returned in greater measure to the doctrines of the Church than Haering in his work on *The Christian Faith*.

6. REFORMED THEOLOGY. Reformed dogmatic theology had several distinguished representatives during this period, who were absolutely opposed alike to vulgar Rationalism and Supranaturalism, to the speculative movement and to the theology of experience with its subjectivism. It was indeed in a

sad state of decline at the opening of the nineteenth century and during its first decennia. Supranaturalism had made large inroads in the circles of Reformed theologians; and this, according to the words of Dr. Bavinck, "wanted to be Biblical, but was anti-confessional, anti-philosophical, anti-calvinistic; it produced a dogmatics which was deistic in theology, Pelagian in anthropology, moralistic in Christology, collegialistic in ecclesiology, and eudaemonistic in eschatology."[1] But there has been a repristination of Reformed theology, especially in the Netherlands, through the labors of Kuyper, Bavinck, and many others. It is regrettable that their works are not better known in our country. In Scotland a great deal was done in the field of Dogmatics by such men as Hill, Dick, Cunningham, Bannerman, Crawford, Candlish, and others. And for our own country we need only to mention the names of Breckenridge, Thornwell, Dabney, Ch. Hodge, A. A. Hodge, Shedd, H. B. Smith, Warfield, and Girardeau. Mention may also be made of the Barthian theology, though its Reformed character is of a rather dubious nature.

REFERENCES: Bavinck, *Geref. Dogm.* I, pp. 104-206; McPherson, *Chr. Dogm.*, pp. 43-97; Van Oosterzee, *Chr. Dogm.* I, pp. 42-84; Briggs, *History of the Study of Theology*, 2 vols.; Workman, *Christian Thought to the Reformation*; McGiffert, *Christian Thought Before Kant*; Moore, *Christian Thought Since Kant*; Heppe, *Dogmatik des deutschen Protestantismus im zechzehnten Jahrhundert*, 3 vols.; Gruetzmacher, *Textbuch zur systematischen Theol.*; Lichtenberger, *Hist. of German Theol. in the Nineteenth Century*; Hurst, *History of Rationalism*; Pfleiderer, *The Development of Theol. in Germany since Kant*; Storr, *The Development of English Theol. in the Nineteenth Century*; Walker, *Scottish Theology and Theologians*; Aubrey, *Present Theological Tendencies*; Burtt, *Types of Religious Philosophy*; Mackintosh, *Types of Modern Theology*; Horton, *Contemporary English Theology*; and *Types of Continental Theology*; W. A. Brown, *The Essence of Christianity*.

1. *Geref. Dogm.* I, p. 191.

THE PRINCIPIA OF DOGMATICS

THE PRINCIPIA OF DOGMATICS

I. PRINCIPIA IN GENERAL

A. Principia in Non-Theological Sciences

1. DEFINITION OF 'PRINCIPIUM.' In a discussion of principia it is naturally of the greatest importance to know exactly what the term denotes. 'Principium' is a term that is widely used in science and philosophy. It is the Latin rendering of the Greek word *arche*, beginning, a term which Aristotle used to denote the primary source of all being, actuality, or knowledge. The English word 'principle' is derived from it, and corresponds with it in meaning, especially when it denotes a source or cause from which a thing proceeds. The term first principle is an even closer approximation to it. After giving several meanings of the word *arche*, Aristotle says: "What is common to all first principles, is that *they are the primary source from which anything is, becomes, or is known.*" Eisler in his *Handwoerterbuch der Philosophie* gives the following definition: "Prinzip ist also sowohl das, woraus ein Seiendes hervorgegangen ist oder was den Dingen zugrunde liegt (Realprinzip, Seinsprinzip), als das, warauf sich das Denken und Erkennen notwendig stuetzt (Denkprinzip, Erkenntnisprinzip, Idealprinzip formaler unde materialer Art), als auch ein oberster Gesichtspunkt, eine Norm des Handelns (praktisches Prinzip)." The statement of Fleming in Krauth-Fleming's *Vocabulary of the Philosophical Sciences* is in perfect agreement with this: "The word is applied equally to thought and to being; and hence principles have been divided into those of being and those of knowledge, or *principia essendi* and *principia cognoscendi* . . . . *Principia essendi* may also be *principia cognoscendi* for the fact that things exist is the ground or reason of their being known. But the converse does not hold; for the existence of things is in no way dependent on our knowledge of them." In ancient philosophy *principia essendi*, and in modern philosophy *principia cognoscendi*, receive the greater amount of attention. There is on the one hand a remarkable similarity between the principia that apply in the non-theological sciences and those that are pertinent to theology; but on the other hand there is also a difference that should not be disregarded. The former bear a natural and therefore general character. They are given with creation itself, are as such adapted to man as man, and have a controlling influence in all non-theological sciences.

2. PRINCIPIA OF THE NON-THEOLOGICAL SCIENCES. These are the following three:

a. *God is the principium essendi.* God is the source and fountain of all our knowledge. He possesses an archetypal knowledge of all created things, embracing all the ideas that are expressed in the works of His creation. This knowledge of God is quite different from that of man. While we derive our knowledge from the objects we perceive, He knows them in virtue of the fact that He has from eternity determined their being and form. While we attain to a scientific insight into things and relations only by a laborious process of discursive thought, He has an immediate knowledge of all things, and knows them not only in their relations but also in their very essence. And even so our knowledge is imperfect, while His knowledge is all-comprehensive and perfect in every way. We are only partly conscious of what we know, while He is always perfectly conscious of all His knowledge. The fulness of the divine knowledge is the inexhaustible source of all our knowledge, and therefore God is the *principium essendi* of all scientific knowledge. Naturally, Pantheism with its impersonal and unconscious Absolute cannot admit this, for a God, who has no knowledge Himself, can never be the principle or source of our knowledge. In fact, all absolute Idealism would seem to involve a denial of this principle, since it makes man an autonomous source of knowledge. The origin of knowledge is sought in the subject; the human mind is no more a mere instrument, but is regarded as a real *fons* or source.

b. *The world as God's creation is the principium cognoscendi externum.* Instead of "the world as God's creation" we might also say "God's revelation in nature." Of His archetypal knowledge God has conveyed an ectypal knowledge to man in the works of His hands, a knowledge adapted to the finite human consciousness. This ectypal knowledge is but a faint reproduction of the archetypal knowledge found in God. It is on the one hand real and true knowledge, because it is an imprint, a reproduction, though in temporal and therefore limited forms, of the knowledge of God. On the other hand it is, just because it is ectypal, no complete knowledge, and since sin put its stamp on creation, no perfectly clear nor absolutely true knowledge. God conveyed this knowledge to man by employing the Logos, the Word, as the agent of creation. The idea that finds expression in the world is out of the Logos. Thus the whole world is an embodiment of the thoughts of God or, as Bavinck puts it, "a book in which He has written with large and small letters, and therefore not a writing-book in which we, as the Idealists think, must fill in the words." God's beautiful creation, replete with divine wisdom, is the *principium cognoscendi externum* of all non-theologial sciences. It is the external means, by which the knowledge that flows from God is conveyed to man. This view of the matter is, of course absolutely opposed to the principle of Idealism, that the thinking man creates and construes his own world: not only the form of the world of thought (Kant), but also its material and contents (Fichte), and even the world of being (Hegel).[1]

c. Human reason is the *principium cognoscendi internum.* The objective revelation of God would be of no avail, if there were no subjective receptivity for it, a correspondence between subject and object. Dr. Bavinck correctly

---
1. *Bavinck, Geref. Dogm. I.* p. 215.

says: "Science always consists in a logical relation between subject and object." It is only when the subject is adapted to the object that science can result. And God has also provided for this. The same Logos that reveals the wisdom of God in the world is also the true light, "which lighteth every man coming into the world." Human reason with its capacity for knowledge is the fruit of the Logos, enables man to discover the divine wisdom in the world round about him, and is therefore the *principium cognoscendi internum* of science. By means of it man appropriates the truth revealed in creation. It is not satisfied with an aphoristic knowledge of details, but seeks to understand the unity of all things. In a world of phenomena which are many and varied, it goes in quest of that which is general, necessary, and eternal,—the underlying fundamental idea. It desires to understand the cause, the essential being, and the final purpose of things. And in its intellectual activity the human mind is never purely passive, or even merely receptive, but always more or less active. It brings with it certain general and necessary truths, which are of fundamental significance for science and cannot be derived from experience. This thought is denied by Empiricism in two different ways: (1) by regarding the human spirit as a *tabula rasa* and denying the existence of general and necessary truths; and (2) by emphasizing analytical experience rather than synthetic reason. Dr. Bavinck points out that it ended in Materialism. Says he: "First the thought-content, then the faculty, and finally also the substance of the spirit is derived from the material world."[1]

B. Principia in Religion or Theology

Religion and theology are closely related to each other. They are both effects of the same cause, that is, of the facts respecting God in His relation to the universe. Religion is the effect which these facts produce in the sphere of the individual and collective life of man, while theology is the effect which they produce in the sphere of systematic thought. The principia of the one are also the principia of the other. These principia are not of a natural and general, but of a spiritual and special character. They do not belong to the realm of creation as such, but to the sphere of redemption. Notwithstanding this fact, however, they are also of inestimable value for the Christian pursuit of scientific knowledge in general.

1. GOD IS THE PRINCIPIUM ESSENDI. This is equivalent to saying that all our knowledge of God has its origin in God Himself. God possesses a complete and in every way perfect knowledge of Himself. He knows Himself in the absolute sense of the word, not only as He is related to His creatures, nor merely in His diversified activities and their controlling motives, but also in the unfathomable depths of His essential Being. His self-consciousness is perfect and infinite; there is no sub-conscious life in Him, no subliminal region of unconscious mentality. And of that absolute, perfectly conscious self-knowledge of God, the knowledge which man has of the divine Being is but a faint

---

1. *op. cit.,* p. 221.

and creaturely copy or imprint. All human knowledge of God is derived from Him, Matt. 11:27; I Cor. 2:10 f. And because there can be no knowledge of God in man apart from self-consciousness in God, Pantheism spells death for all theology. It is impossible to deduce a conscious creature from an unconscious God, a creature that knows God from a God that does not know Himself. We can find the principium of our theology only in a personal God, perfect in self-consciousness, as He freely, consciously, and truly reveals Himself.

2. THE PRINCIPIUM COGNOSCENDI EXTERNUM IS GOD'S SPECIAL REVELATION. The knowledge which God desires that we should have of Him is conveyed to us by means of the revelation that is now embraced in Scripture. Originally God revealed Himself in creation, but through the blight of sin that original revelation was obscured. Moreover, it was entirely insufficient in the condition of things that obtained after the fall. Only God's self-revelation in the Bible can now be considered adequate. It only conveys a knowledge of God that is pure, that is, free from error and superstition, and that answers to the spiritual needs of fallen man. Because it has pleased God to embody His special revelation in Scripture for the time being, this, in the words of Bavinck, has the character of a *"causa efficiens instrumentalis* of theology." It is now the *principium unicum*, from which the theologian must derive his theological knowledge. Some are inclined to speak of God's general revelation as a second source; but this is hardly correct in view of the fact that nature can come into consideration here only as interpreted in the light of Scripture. Kuyper warns against speaking of Scripture, or God's special revelation, as the *fons theologiae*, since the word *fons* has a rather definite meaning in scientific study. It denotes in general a certain object of study which is in itself passive, but which embodies certain ideas, and from which man must, by means of scientific study, extract or elicit knowledge. The use of that word in this connection is apt to give the impression that man must place himself above Scripture, in order to discover or elicit from these the knowledge of God, while as a matter of fact this is not the case. God does not leave it to man to discover the knowledge of Him and of divine things, but actively and explicitly conveys this to man by means of His self-revelation. This same idea was later on also stressed by Schaeder and Barth, namely, that in the study of theology God is never the object of some human subject, but is always Himself the subject. We should bear in mind that the word 'principium,' as we use it in theology, has a casual signification, just as the corresponding Hebrew and Greek words do in the Bible, when it speaks of the fear of the Lord as the principle (reshith) of wisdom (Ps. 111:10) or knowledge (Prov. 1:7), and of Christ as the principle (arche) of creation and of the resurrection (Col. 1:18; Rev. 3:14). By means of His self-revelation God communicates the requisite knowledge of Himself and of divine things to man. Man can know God only because and in so far as God actively reveals Himself. And if we do speak of Scripture as the fountain-head of theology, we shall have to remember that it is a living foun-

tain, from which God causes the streams of knowledge to flow, and that we have but to appropriate these. The same point should be borne in mind, when we follow the common custom in speaking of God's special revelation as the source of theology. Man cannot place himself above his object in theology; he cannot investigate God.

3. THE PRINCIPIUM COGNOSCENDI INTERNUM IS FAITH. As in the non-theological sciences, so also in theology there must be a *principium cognoscendi internum* that answers to the *principium cognoscendi externum*. Scripture sometimes represents regeneration (I Cor. 2:14), purity of heart (Matt. 5:8), doing the will of God (John 7:17), and the anointing of the Holy Spirit (I John 2:20) as such. But it most frequently points to faith as the principium internum of the knowledge of God (Rom. 10:17; Gal. 3:3, 5; Heb. 11:1, 3), and this name undoubtedly deserves preference. The self-communication of God aims at conveying the knowledge of God to man, in order that God may receive honor and glory through man. Therefore it may not terminate outside of man, but must continue right on into the mind and heart of man. By faith man accepts the self-revelation of God as divine truth, by faith he appropriates it in an ever increasing measure, and by faith he responds to it as he subjects his thoughts to the thoughts of God. The *principium internum*, says Bavinck, is sometimes called the *verbum internum* or even the *verbum principale*, because it brings the knowledge of God into man, which is after all the aim of all theology and of the whole self-revelation of God. Barth stresses the fact that it is only by faith that the knowledge of God becomes possible.[1] These three principia, while distinct, yet constitute a unity. The Father communicates Himself to His creatures through the Son as the Logos and in the Holy Spirit.

QUESTIONS FOR FURTHER STUDY: Has the doctrine of the principia always received adequate attention in Reformed theology? What took the place of it under the influence of Rationalism? What was the nature of the so-called 'Prolegomena,' 'Prinzipienlehre,' or 'Fundamentaldogmatik,' which came into vogue under the influence of Schleiermacher? Should theology derive its principia from other sciences or from philosophy? Which are the fundamental objections of modern theology to the doctrine of the principia, as it was stated in the preceding? Does Barth also regard Scripture as the *principium cognoscendi externum* of theology?

REFERENCES: Bavinck, *Geref. Dogm. I*, pp. 207-237; Kuyper, *Enc. der Heil. Godgel.* II, pp. 291-346; Girardeau, *Discussions of Theological Questions*, pp. 72-272; Thornwell, *Collected Writings* I, pp. 43-52; Strong, *Syst. Theol.*, pp. 1-15; Miley, *Syst. Theol.*, pp. 7-47; McPherson, *Chr. Dogm.*, pp. 18-37.

---

1. *The Doctrine of the Word of God*, p. 260 ff.

II. RELIGION

A brief discussion of religion at this point will have a double advantage. It will enable us to see the rationality of the principia to which attention was called in the preceding, and will prepare us for a more detailed discussion of God's special revelation, the necessary corollary of religion, and the *principium cognoscendi externum* of theology. There is a very close relation between religion and theology. This is evident from the very fact that many regard theology as the science of religion. While this is certainly a mistake, the fact remains that the two are inseparably connected. There is no such thing as theology apart from religion. Religion consists in a real, living, and conscious relationship between a man and his God, determined by the self-revelation of God, and expressing itself in a life of worship, fellowship and service. It presupposes that God exists, that He has revealed Himself, and that He has enabled man to appropriate this revelation. And where man does appropriate the revealed knowledge of God, reflects on it and unifies it, there the structure of theology arises on the basis of God's revelation. We do not proceed on the assumption, so common among modern students of religion, that the essential nature of religion can be determined only in the light of its origin and history, and therefore do not begin this discussion with a historical study of the religions of the world. Since our conception of religion is frankly determined by Scripture, it seems more desirable to follow the logical order in its discussion, and to consider first of all the essence of religion.

A. The Essence of Religion

1. THE DERIVATION OF THE WORD 'RELIGION'. The derivation of the word 'religion' is still uncertain, and even if it were certain, would only yield a historical, and not a normative, definition of religion. It would only shed some light on the conception of religion that gave rise to the use of this particular word. Several derivations of it have been suggested in course of time. The earliest of these is that of Cicero, who derived it from *re-legere*, to re-read, to repeat, to observe carefully. In the light of this derivation religion was regarded as a constant and diligent observance of all that pertains to the knowledge of the gods. One of the influential Church Fathers of the fourth century, Lactantius, held that the word was derived from *religare*, to attach, to establish firmly, to bind together, and therefore pointed to religion as the bond between God and man. Gellius suggested the derivation from *relinquere* in the sense of to separate oneself from someone or something. The word 'religion' would then indicate that which by reason of its holiness is separated from all that is profane. Finally, Leidenroth assumed that it was derived from a supposed

root *ligere*, meaning *to see*. Religere would then mean, to look back, and religion, to look back with fear. The derivation of Gellius found no favor whatsoever. That of Lactantius was generally accepted for a long time, but was gradually relinquished when Latin scholars pointed out that it was linguistically impossible to derive 'religion' from 'religare'. Some admit the possibility of the derivation suggested by Leidenroth, but the derivation of Cicero is now preferred by most theologians. Calvin also gave preference to this, though he did not share Cicero's explanation of the term. Says he: "Cicero truly and shrewdly derives the name *religion* from *relego*, and yet the reason which he asigns is forced and far-fetched, namely, that honest worshippers *read and read again*, and ponder what is true. I rather think the name is used in opposition to vagrant license—the greater part of mankind rashly taking up whatever first comes their way, whereas piety, that it may stand with a firm step, confines itself within due bounds."[1]

2. SCRIPTURAL TERMS FOR RELIGION. The Bible contains no definition of religion, nor even a general term descriptive of this phenomenon. It has become customary in Reformed theology to distinguish between objective and subjective religion. The word 'religion' is clearly used in a two-fold sense. When we speak of the Christian religion in distinction from other religions, we mean one thing; and when we say that a man's religion is too intellectual or too emotional, we have something different in mind. In the one case we refer to something that has objective existence outside of man, and in the other, to a subjective phenomenon in the inner life of man, which finds expression in a variety of ways. The term '*religio objectiva*' is used to denote that which determines the nature of man's religion, its regulative norm, namely, the knowledge of God and of man's relation to Him, as this is prescribed by the Word of God. It is sometimes practically equivalent to 'the divine revelation.' And the term '*religio subjectiva*' serves to designate the life that is so regulated or determined by the Word of God, and that expresses itself in worship, fellowship, and service. Now the Bible uses different terms for each of these aspects of religion.

The *religio objectiva* is, as was said, practically identical with God's revelation, and is indicated in the Old Testament by such terms as 'law,' 'commandments', 'precepts', 'judgments', 'ordinances', and so on. In the New Testament the revelation of God is embodied, not primarily in a set of laws, but in the Person of Christ, in His redemptive work, and in the apostolic *kerugma*, which centers about Christ, and is merely an interpretation of the facts of redemption. Such terms as 'the gospel', 'the faith', and 'the kerugma' serve to designate the *religio objectiva*.

The *religio subjectiva* corresponds to the *religio objectiva*, and is described in the Old Testament as "the fear of the Lord," which is repeatedly called "the beginning of wisdom." The term is expressive of the inner disposition of the pious Israelite with reference to the law of God. This fear of

---
1. *Inst.* I. xii, 1.

God should be distinguished, however, from that anxious solicitude, accompanied with dread, that is so characteristic of heathen religions. The really God-fearing Israelite was not controlled by the distrust, the dread anxiety, and slavish fear, with which the Gentiles thought of their gods. In his case the fear of the Lord was accompanied with other religious dispositions, such as faith, hope, love, trust, taking refuge in, leaning on, and clinging to, God, and therefore was perfectly consistent with joy and peace, childlike confidence and blessedness, in communion with God.

The New Testament rarely employs the terms that are most prominent in classical Greek as designations of religion, such as *deisidaimonia* (fear or reverence for the gods), Acts 25:19, *theosebeia* (reverence towards God), I Tim. 2:10, and *eulabeia* (circumspection in religious matters, fear of God, reverence, piety), Heb. 5:7; 12:28. The only word that occurs with some frequency is *eusebeia* (piety towards God, godliness), which is found fifteen times. These words do not express the characteristic element of New Testament religion. The fear of the Lord is indeed mentioned here as an element in religion, Luke 18:2; Acts 9:31; II Cor. 5:11; 7:1, but is far less prominent than in the Old Testament. The usual New Testament term for the *religio subjectiva* in the New Testament is *pistis*, faith. In classical Greek this word is used to denote: (a) a conviction based on the testimony of another; and (b) trust in a person whose testimony is accepted. It does not stand out as a designation of trust in the gods, though it is occasionally so used. And it is exactly this element that is brought to the foreground in the New Testament. To the glorious message of salvation, there is an answering faith on the part of man, a faith consisting in childlike trust in the grace of God, and becoming at the same time a fountain of love to God and of devotion to His service. This faith is not the natural expression of any so-called inborn religious disposition of man, but is the fruit of the supernatural operation of the Holy Spirit. The words *latreia*, Rom. 9:4; 12:1; Heb. 9:1, 6, and *threskeia*, Acts 26:5; Col. 2:18; Jas. 1:27, are used to denote the service of God that springs from the principle of faith.

3. HISTORICAL CONCEPTIONS OF THE ESSENCE OF RELIGION. Religion is one of the most universal phenomena of human life. Man has sometimes been described as "incurably religious." This need not surprise us in view of the fact that man was created in the image of God, and was destined to live in communion with Him. And while it is true that man fell away from God, his fall did not involve a complete loss of the image of God. The Belgic Confession states in Art. XIV that man "lost all his excellent gifts which he had received from God, and only retained a few remains thereof, which, however, are sufficient to leave man with excuse." And according to the Canons of Dort III and IV, Art IV: "There remain, however, in man since the fall, the glimmerings of natural light, whereby he retains some knowledge of God, of natural things, and of the difference between good and evil, and discovers some regard for virtue, good order in society, and for maintaining an orderly de-

portment." This remaining light, however, does not avail unto salvation, and is even abused by man in natural and civil things. At the same time it does serve to explain the presence of some form of religion even among the lowest and most barbaric tribes of the earth. But however general this phenomenon may be among the nations of the world, this does not mean that there is general agreement as to the essential nature of it. Even the history of the Christian Church reveals considerable difference of opinion on this point. The following are the most important conceptions that come into consideration here:

a. *The conception of the early Church.* The Bible does not furnish us with a definition of religion, nor even with a description of it, though it contains in its entire compass a clear revelation of what God requires of man. There are a few passages, however, which contain some specific indications. Thus Paul says in Rom. 12:1; "I beseech you therefore, brethren, by the mercies of God, to present your bodies a living sacrifice, holy, acceptable to God, which is your spiritual (or: reasonable) service (*latreia*)." The Epistle to the Hebrews contains this admonition: "Wherefore receiving a kingdom that cannot be shaken, let us have grace, whereby we may offer service well-pleasing to God with reverence and awe," 12:28. In this passage the words *latreio* and *eulabeia* are both used. James adds a specific element in the words: "Pure religion (*threskeia*) and undefiled before our God and Father is this, to visit the fatherless and widows in their affliction, and to keep oneself unspotted from the world," 1:27.

In the early Church Christians enjoyed religious experiences and engaged in consecrated service and in reverential worship long before they began to reflect on the exact nature of religion. One of the earliest definitions of it was that of Lactantius in the beginning of the fourth century. He defined religion as *recta verum Deum cognoscendi et colendi ratio* (the right manner of knowing and serving the true God). This definition has always met with considerable favor, and is even now found in some works on dogmatic theology. During the previous century, however, it was criticized as favoring an external conception of religion, in which the heart is not concerned. But this criticism is hardly justified, since the definition does not pretend to specify what is the right manner of knowing and serving God. There is nothing in it to prevent anyone from assuming that the author had in mind a knowledge, which is not only intellectual, but also experiential, and a service which springs from the heart and is truly spiritual. The right manner of knowing and serving God is after all determined by the Word of God, which is not satisfied with a purely intellectual knowledge, nor with a merely external service. It is true, however, that the definition applies to the *religio objectiva*, the religion as prescribed by God in His Word, rather than to the *religio subjectiva*, religion as experienced and practiced by men; and that it does not indicate the connection between the right knowledge and the right service of God.

b. *The conception of the Middle Ages.* It is a well known fact that during the Middle Ages, under the influence of the Church of Rome, religious life was gradually externalized. The one-sided emphasis on the Church as an external organization brought with it a similar emphasis on the performance of external rites and ceremonies, to the neglect of the inner disposition of the heart. And this undue attention to mere ritual punctuality reached its culmination in the scholastic period. Moreover, since the authority of the Church and of tradition gradually surpassed, if it did not supersede, that of Scripture, and the Bible was excluded from the hands of the laity, the element of knowledge was reduced to a minimum in the religious life of the people. The conception of religion, which was then present, finds its best expression in Thomas Aquinas' definition of it as "the virtue by which men render to God the required service and honor." Thus religion takes its place among the human virtues, and is practically identified with the single element of *latreia*. Thomas Aquinas distinguishes between the theological virtues, faith, hope, and charity, which have God for their object, and the moral virtues, justice, fortitude, prudence, and temperance, which find their object in the things that lead us to God. He looks upon religion as a part of the virtue of justice, because in it man renders to God what is His due. While this definition does indeed stress the *religio subjectiva*, it contemplates this one-sidedly as service. Religion is not merely service and worship; it is primarily a disposition of the heart, which expresses itself in service and worship. The definition of Thomas Aquinas is even now found in some Roman Catholic works. Spirago voices the same external conception of religion, when he says: "Religion is not a matter of feeling; it is a matter of the will and of action, and consists in following out the principles that God has laid down."[1]

c. *The conception of the Reformers*. The Reformers broke with the externalism of the Church of Rome in general, and also with its external conception of religion. They could not conceive of religion as being merely one of the moral virtues. In fact they did not regard it as a human virtue at all, but rather as spiritual communion with God, coupled with reverential fear, and expressing itself in grateful worship and loving service. Says Calvin: "Such is pure and genuine religion, namely, confidence in God coupled with serious fear—fear, which both includes in it willing reverence, and brings along with it such legitimate worship as is prescribed by the law."[2] Moreover, he adds: "And it ought to be more carefully considered, that all men promiscuously do homage God, but very few reverence Him. On all hands there is abundance of ostentatious ceremonies, but sincerity of heart is rare."

Since the Reformers regarded religion as a conscious and voluntary spiritual relation to God, which expresses itself in life as a whole but particularly in certain acts of worship, they distinguished between *pietas* as the principle and *cultus* as the action of religion. And even this cultus they regarded as twofold. They drew a clear line of distinction between a *cultus internus*, which manifests itself primarily in faith, hope and love, and a *cultus externus*, which finds expression in the worship of the Church and in a life of service. Further-

1. *The Catechism Explained*, p. 75.
2. *Inst.* I. ii, 3.

more they spoke of a *religio subjectiva* and a *religio objectiva,* and indicated the relation between the two. The *religio subjectiva,* which is primarily a disposition of the heart, disturbed, degenerated, and falsified by sin, but restored by the operation of the Holy Spirit, is determined, directed, and fructified by, and passes into action under the influence of, the *religio objectiva,* consisting in the revealed truth of God, in which God Himself determines the adoration, worship, and service that is acceptable to Him. All will-worship, such as the detailed ritualism of the Roman Catholic Church, and the individualism of the Anabaptists, was regarded a contraband.

The question may be raised at this point, what should be regarded as the really characteristic disposition of the soul in religion. There has been no general agreement on this point. It has been found in piety, fear, reverence, faith, a feeling of dependence, and so on; but these are all emotions or affections which are also felt with reference to man. Otto in his psychological study of religion seems to have hit upon the right idea. He feels that, while Schleiermacher suggested an important idea, when he spoke of "a feeling of dependence," yet this can hardly be regarded as an adequate statement of what is felt in religion. He finds something more, for instance, in the words of Abraham, when he undertakes to plead for the men of Sodom: "Behold now, I have taken upon me to speak unto the Lord, which am but dust and ashes." Gen. 18:27. Says he: "There you have a self-confessed 'feeling of dependence,' which is yet at the same time far more, and something other than, *merely* a feeling of dependence. Desiring to give it a name of its own, I propose to call it 'creature-consciousness' or 'creature-feeling.' It is the emotion of a creature, abased and overwhelmed by its own nothingness in contrast to that which is supreme above all creatures."[1] The really characteristic thing is this, that in religion the absolute majesty and infinite power of God and the utter insignificance and absolute helplessness of man come into consideration. This does not mean, however, that religion is merely a matter of the emotions, nor that man's absolute subjection to the infinite God is simply a necessity imposed on man. The relation of man to God in religion is a conscious and voluntary one, and instead of enslaving man leads him into the enjoyment of the highest liberty. In religion man knows God on the one hand as a holy Power on which he is absolutely dependent, and on the other hand, as the highest Good, the source of all natural and spiritual blessings. In it he entrusts himself voluntarily to God with all his interests for time and eternity, and thus acknowledges his dependence on Him. And it is exactly by this acknowledgment that the moral life of man gains the highest victory through the grace of God and enters upon the enjoyment of true liberty.

d. *The modern conception of religion.* In more recent times the conception of religion handed down by the Reformers, was changed considerably. The Reformers maintained the right of private judgment, and this soon resulted in a rather considerable number of Churches and Confessions. Conse-

---
1. *The Idea of the Holy,* p. 9 f.

quently a tendency manifested itself in course of time to seek the essence of the *religio objectiva* in that which all Churches had in common. Some found this in the truth as it is expressed in the Apostolic Confession. Quite a different note, however, was sounded by Rationalism, which broke with the Word of God and limited religion in the objective sense to the familiar triad of God, virtue, and immortality. Thus the *religio objectiva* was reduced to a minimum. Kant and Schleiermacher went still farther by transferring the center of gravity from the object to the subject, and divorcing the *religio subjectiva* from the *religio objectiva*. The former regarded religion simply as a form of moral action, in which man recognizes his duties as divine commandments. According to him, says Moore, "morality becomes religion when that which the former shows to be the end of man is conceived also to be the end of the supreme law giver, God."[1] And Schleiermacher considered religion to be merely a condition of devout feeling, a feeling of dependence, a "Hinneigung zum Weltall." In the system of Hegel religion becomes a matter of knowledge. He speaks of it as "the knowledge possessed by the finite mind of its nature as absolute mind"; or, regarded from the divine side, as "the divine Spirit's knowledge of itself through the mediation of the finite spirit." This makes God, not only the object, but also the subject of religion. Thus, in the words of van Oosterzee, religion becomes "a play of God with Himself." Ever since the days of Schleiermacher religion has come to be regarded as something purely subjective, and in modern theology it is generally represented as man's search for God, as if it were possible to discover God apart from divine revelation, and as if God did not first have to find man before men could really find Him. In fact the idea of religion as a conscious and voluntary relation of man to his God, a relation determined by God Himself, was gradually lost. It is now often defined without any reference to God whatsoever, as may be seen from the following examples: Religion is "morality touched with emotion" (Matthew Arnold), "a sum of scruples which impede the free exercise of our faculties" (Reinach), "faith in the conservation of values" (Hoeffding), or "the belief that there is an unseen order and that our supreme good lies in harmoniously adjusting ourselves thereto" (James).

e. *The Barthian conception.* Modern theology turned from the objective to the subjective; it relegated the idea of revelation to the background, and brought the idea of religion prominently to the fore. Moreover, it contemplated religion as something native to man, as the highest achievement of man in the life of the human race, and as a prized possession, on the basis of which man can rise to the heights of God. It saw in religion the manifestation of the divine in man, which makes him continuous with God, enables him to scale the heavens, and makes him entirely fit to dwell in the presence of God. Over against this modern subjectivism, Barth again stresses the objective in religion, and centers attention once more on the divine revelation, on the Word of God. He never wearies of dinning it into the ears of the

---

[1] *History of Christian Thought Since Kant*, p. 49.

present generation that there is no way from man to God, not even in religion, but only a way from God to man. He points out that the Bible has nothing commendable to say about the kind of religion of which the Modernists boast, but repeatedly spurns and condemns it. It is like the religion of the Pharisees in the days of Jesus, and of the Judaists in the days of Paul. He even shocked and horrified his modernist contemporaries by stigmatizing this religion as the greatest sin against God. According to him the history of religion, which became so prominent during the last decennia, is really the history of what is untrue in religion. "For," says he, "at the moment when religion becomes conscious of religion, when it becomes psychologically and historically conceivable, it falls away from its inner character, from its truth, to idols. Its truth is its other-worldliness, its refusal of the idea of sacredness, its non historicity."[1] It is his desire to break the strangle-hold which Schleiermacher had for so long a time on modern theology. Says he: "With all due respect for the genius shown in his work, I can *not* consider Schleiermacher a good teacher in the realm of theology because, so far as I can see, he is disastrously dim sighted in regard to the fact that man as man is not only in *need*, but beyond all hope of saving himself; that the whole of so-called religion, and not least the Christian religion, shares in this need; and that one can *not* speak of God simply by speaking of man in a loud voice."[2] Barth does not regard religion as a possession of man, something which man has, and which is therefore something historical rather than something that comes to man from above. It is not something by which man can improve himself and thus become fit for heaven, since this loses sight of the qualitative difference between this world and the world to come. It is not a historical quantum, on the possession of which man can base his hope for the future, but rather an attitude, a frame of mind, a disposition, into which man is brought when he is confronted with the divine revelation. The truly religious man is the man who despairs of himself and of all that is purely human, the man who cries out with Isaiah, "Woe is me! for I am undone," or with Paul, "Wretched man that I am! who shall deliver me out of the body of this death?" In his Roemerbrief (2nd ed. p. 241) Barth expresses himself as follows: "It (religion) gives him no solution of his life's problems, but rather makes him an insoluble enigma to himself. It is neither his salvation, nor a discovery of it; it is rather the discovery that he is not saved . . . . It is a misfortune which falls with fatal necessity upon some men, and from them is carried to others. It is the misfortune under the weight of which John the Baptist goes into the wilderness to preach repentance and the judgment to come; under the weight of which such a deeply moving long drawn-out sigh as the second Epistle to the Corinthians was put on paper; under the uncanny weight of which a physiognomy like that of Calvin becomes what it finally was." While all this is by no means

---

1. *The Word of God and the Word of Man.* p. 68.
2. *op. cit.,* p. 195.

a complete statement of what Barth has to say about religion, it does indicate sufficiently what he regards as the essence of it.[1]

B. The Seat of Religion

A brief consideration of the question as to the real seat of religion in the human soul will undoubtedly promote a proper understanding of its essential nature. The question has been raised in the course of history, whether it has its seat in, and therefore operates through, just one of the faculties of the soul—to speak in the language of the old faculty psychology—, or occupies a central place in the life of man and functions through all the powers of the soul. It has been erroneously represented as a function, now of this, and then of that, faculty, while it should undoubtedly be regarded as something in which the soul of man as whole, with all its psychical powers, is operative. Its place in life is fundamental and central, and consequently it affects all the manifestations of life. The following views come into consideration here and call for a brief discussion.

1. IT HAS ITS SEAT IN THE INTELLECT. There is an intellectual conception, which seeks the essence of religion in knowledge, and therefore locates its psychical basis in the intellect. It was especially Hegel that sponsored the intellectual view and brought it to the foreground. According to him the whole life of man is merely a process of thought, and religion is simply a part of the process. In the finite spirit of man the Absolute becomes conscious of itself, and this self-consciousness of the Absolute in the human spirit is religion. According to this view religion is neither feeling nor action—though these are not entirely excluded—, but essentially knowledge. At the same time it is not the highest form of knowledge, but a knowledge clothed in symbols, from which only philosophy can extract that which is ideal and permanent. Religion never gets beyond the stage of apprehending reality in concrete and imaginative terms, while philosophy makes the attempt to discover the pure idea that lies behind the image. This view is certainly a very serious misconception of the essence of religion, since it reduces this to a sort of imperfect philosophy. This virtually means that one's knowledge determines the measure of one's piety. Certainly, there is also knowledge in religion, but it is knowledge of a specific kind; and the attainment of knowledge does not constitute the real end in religion. Science aims at knowledge, but religion seeks comfort, peace, salvation. Moreover, religious knowledge is not purely intellectual, but above all experiential, a knowledge accompanied with emotions and resulting in action. Religion is not merely a matter of the intellect, but also of the will and of the affections. This consideration should also serve as a warning to all those in the Christian Church who speak and act as if true religion were only a matter of a proper conception of the truth, of sound doctrine and of an orthodox profession of the verities of the Christian religion;

---

1. Cf. further his *Roemerbrief*, pp. 161, 162, 241, 252; his *Dogmatik* (1st Ed.) p. 305ff; Lowrie, *Our Concern with the Theology of Crisis*, pp. 191-201; Hoyle, *The Teaching of Karl Barth*, p. 115.

and as if Christian experience and the Christian life in all its varied manifestations were matters of comparative insignificance. Cold intellectualism would never have made Christianity the power it proved to be in the world.

2. IT HAS ITS SEAT IN THE WILL. Some have simply defined religion as moral action and sought its seat in the will. The way for this view was paved by Pelagianism in its various forms, such as Semi-Pelagianism, Arminianism, Socinianism, Deism, and Rationalism, all of which represent Christianity as a *nova lex*, and stress the fact that faith is a new obedience. Doctrine is made subordinate as a means to a higher end, and that end is practical piety. It was especially Kant that gave prominence to this moralistic type of religion. He stressed the fact that the supernatural is beyond the reach of pure reason, and that the great concepts of God, virtue, and immortality, are but the necessary postulates of the practical reason. In this view faith becomes a knowledge resting on practical grounds, and religion is reduced to moral action determined by the categorical imperative. Moral duties are fundamental in the life of man, and religion begins at the point where man recognizes these duties as divine commands, that is, where he comes to the discovery that God requires those duties of him. Thus the intimate relation between religion and morality is indeed maintained, but the order of the two is reversed. Morality loses its foundation in religion, and in turn itself becomes the foundation of religion. Man becomes morally autonomous, and religion loses its objective character. But a morality that is not rooted in religion cannot itself be religious. Moreover, religion is never mere moral action. There is also knowledge in religion, and a far greater measure of knowledge than that for which the system of Kant made allowance. And in addition to that there is in religion also a self-surrender of man to God, by which he is delivered from guilt and pollution, and becomes a participant in all the blessings of salvation as the reward of the faithful. This moralistic conception of religion has become very popular in the American religious world. This is undoubtedly due in part to the influence of Ritschl, who adopted the fundamental principles of Kant and found many followers in our country, but also in part to the practical temper of the American people and to Pragmatism, in which that temper found philosophical expression. There is a one-sided emphasis on religious action in our country. Many concern themselves very little about religious experience, and even less about religious knowledge. 'Service' is the great watchword of the day, and service only is the mark of true Christianity. There is little concern about the question whether this action springs from true religious principles. It is no wonder that the term 'Activism' is used to characterize American Christianity.

3. IT HAS ITS SEAT IN THE FEELINGS. There have been those who defined religion as feeling, especially in mystical and pietistic circles. Romanticism, which was a reaction of the free emotional life against a rather formal and inflexible classicism, was in no small measure conducive to this view. Schleiermacher was its great apostle. According to him religion is essentially

a sense of the infinite, a feeling of dependence, not so much on a personal God as on the universe conceived as a unity. Hence he spoke of religion as a *"Hinneigung zum Weltall."* In religion man feels himself one with the Absolute. Religion is pure feeling, disconnected from thought on the one hand, and from morality or action on the other. It is, to use the words of Edwards, "a warm, intimate, immediate awareness of the Infinite in the finite, the Eternal in the temporal, a sense of dependence on the Whole."[1] Now it is undoubtedly true that feeling has an important place in religion, but it is a mistake to regard it as the exclusive seat of religion. And it is even more incorrect to regard it as the source of religion, as Schleiermacher does. His conception of religion makes it entirely subjective, a product of human factors, and ignores its relation to absolute truth. In human feeling the great question is, whether a sensation or perception is pleasant or unpleasant, and not whether it is true or false; and yet this is the all-important question in religion. This view of religion is just as one-sided as the other two. True religion is not merely, and is not even fundamentally, a matter of feeling, but also of knowledge, and of volition or moral action. Moreover, this conception easily leads to a confusion of religious and aesthetic feeling, and to an identification of religion and art. And also in connection with this philosophical view it is necessary to remark that it is not a mere abstract theory, but one that reverberates in practical life. Many regard religion purely as a matter of emotional enjoyment, good enough for women, but hardly fit for men. According to them it is something apart from the life of man in general. It really means little or nothing for the serious business of life. It has no controlling influence on the thoughts of man, neither does it determine his action in any way. One can be a Christian with his heart (feeling), and a heathen with his head. He can say, "Lord, Lord" in private or public worship, and at the same time refuse to do the Lord's bidding in daily life. This is not only an un-Scriptural, but also an unpsychological view of religion, and one that has done a great deal of harm to the cause of God in the past.

4. IT HAS ITS SEAT IN THE HEART. The only correct view is that religion has its seat in the heart. Some might be inclined to regard this position as identical with the preceding one, since the word 'heart' may denote the seat of the affections and passions in the life of man, in distinction from the intellect and the will. In that case it is really a designation of the emotional nature, that is, of the feelings. It is used in that sense, when it is said that a man's heart is better than his head. But the word 'heart' is also used in a far more general sense, and may denote even the entire personality of man as capable of being influenced or moved. It is so employed, when it is said that a man loves with all his heart. It is in a somewhat related sense, a sense that is derived from Biblical psychology, that the word is used here. The word is not always used in the same sense even in the Bible, but in some cases has a general, and in others a more specific meaning. And when it is said

---
1. *The Philosophy of Religion*, p. 140.

that religion has its seat in the heart, it is employed in its most general sense. To the question what is meant with the 'heart,' we may answer with Laidlaw that the 'heart' in the language of Biblical psychology means "the focus of the personal and moral life. It never denotes the personal subject, always the personal organ. All the soul's motions of life proceed from it, and react upon it."[1] It is the central organ of the soul, and has sometimes been called "the workshop of the soul." Religion is rooted in the image of God in man, and that image is central. It reveals itself in the whole man with all his talents and powers. Consequently, man's relation to God is central and involves the whole man. Man must love God with all his heart, and with all his soul, and with all his mind. He must consecrate himself to his God entirely, body and soul, with all his gifts and talents, and in all relations of life. Thus religion embraces the entire man with all his thoughts and feeling and volitions. It has its seat in the heart, where all the faculties of the human soul are seen in their unity. In view of this fact we can readily understand the Scriptural emphasis on the heart as that which we must give unto the Lord, Deut. 30:6; Prov. 23:26; Jer. 24:7; 29:13. Out of the heart are the issues of life, Prov. 4:23. And in religion the heart takes possession of the intellect, Rom. 10:13, 14; Heb. 11:6, of the feelings, Ps. 28:7; 30:12, and of the will, Rom. 2:10, 13; Jas. 1:27; I John 1:5-7. The whole man is made subservient to God in every sphere of life. "In de religie," says Dr. J. H. Bavinck, "dalen wij af tot het wezen van den mensch. Daar waar de waarlijk religieuze krachten in den mensch tot ontwaking komen hebben wij het meest met hemzelf te doen. Daar klopt de ziel zelve in, de mensch, in de wereld gevangen, staat op en zegt tot zichzelven: ik zal naar mijnen Vader gaan."[2]

C. The Origin of Religion

Different methods have been applied in the study of the origin of religion. During the last century persistent attempts have been made to explain it as a purely natural phenomenon. This was the inevitable result of the application of the philosophy of evolution. Both the historical and the psychological methods were the fruit of this tendency. It may be said that in these naturalism is largely pitted against supernaturalism. In this chapter little more than a bare indication of these methods can be given.

1. THE HISTORICAL METHOD. The historical method aims at discovering the origin of religion by studying the history of mankind, with special attention to its primitive religions. According to Edwards this method seeks to answer such questions as the following: "How did religion first appear in time

---

1. *The Bible Doctrine of Man*, p. 225.
2. *Inleiding in de Zielkunde*, p. 277.

---

2. Translation: "In religion we descend to the essential being of man. There where the really religious powers of man are awakened we mostly deal with man himself. The soul itself beats in it; man, captive in the world, arises and says to himself: I shall go to my Father."

and place? In what way did the religious nature of man first express itself? What was the most rudimentary form of religion, from which all other forms may be said to have developed?"[1] But these are questions which no historian can answer with any degree of assurance. He cannot go back far enough in history to observe man *in the process of becoming religious*, for man is already religious at the very dawn of history. Moreover, there are no records of the oldest forms of religion, either in written documents or in trustworthy traditions. And if this is so, then the question naturally arises, How can the historian ever find a satisfactory answer to the questions which present themselves here? Edwards says that "by a sympathetic study of the mind and ways of modern savages and of children, and by constructive imagination on the basis of such study, the anthropologist may rebuild for us the religion of the primitive man. His reconstruction must necessarily be purely hypothetical."[2] All this means that the historian who would investigate the origin of religion must take his stand on pre-historical ground, and that as a result he can only suggest theories, which may be shrewd guesses but do not carry conviction. Moreover, the advocates of the historical method make a fundamental mistake, when they proceed on the assumption, based on the theory of evolution, that the religious life of the most primitive peoples reflects religion in its earliest and original form. This is, of course, merely a bare assumption rather than an established fact, and does not take into account the possibility that the earliest known forms may be corruptions of a far earlier form. It has long been taken for granted that the original form of religion was polytheistic, but the investigations of Lang, Radin, Schmidt, and others have found traces of the recognition of "high gods," also called "creator gods," among peoples of very low culture, and regard these as evidences of an original monotheism.

We shall mention a few of the theories suggested to explain the origin of religion, not because of their inherent value, but mainly to illustrate the insufficiency of this method. Some anthropologists found the historical explanation of religion in *the cunning of priests or the craft of rulers*, who exploited the credulity and the fears of the ignorant masses, in order to gain control over them. This view is so superficial that it finds no support in scientific circles today. Others were of the opinion that the higher forms of religion developed out of *fetish-worship*. But while this may explain the origin of certain forms of religion, it does not explain the origin of religion as such, since this fetish-worship is already religion and therefore itself requires explanation. Moreover, wherever it is in vogue, there are generally also manifest traces of an earlier higher form of religion. The fetishes themselves are frequently mere symbols of religious objects. The theories of Tyler and Spencer are closely related. The former is of the opinion that the conception of a soul or other-self, located somewhere in the body and continuing after death, gradually developed among the earliest men; and that *animism* (from *anima,* soul), as the

1. *The Philosophy of Religion,* p. 34.
2. *op. cit.,* p. 35.

doctrine of souls, expanded in the course of time into the doctrine of spirits, whether gods or devils, as objects of worship. The theory of Spencer is related to that of Tyler but is more specific. It suggests *ancestorism*, the worship of the souls of departed ancestors, as the most fundamental form of religion. According to him primitive peoples ascribed great influence to the spirits of departed ancestors, and consequently acquired the habit of praying, and of offering sacrifices, to them. But these theories are also unsatisfactory. They fail to explain the very forms they assume, the *worship* of the spirits of the departed, and the universal underlying conviction that these spirits are gods highly exalted above men. Moreover, wherever this spirit-worship is found, there is also a separate and distinct worship of the gods. Durkheim criticized these theories of Tyler and Spencer, and offered instead a sociological theory of the origin of religion. He found the origin of religious belief in the idea of a mysterious impersonal force controlling life, a sense of power derived from the authority of society over the individual. The sense of the power of the social group develops into the consciousness of a mysterious power in the world. The totem is the visible emblem of this power; it is the emblem of the tribe; and in worshipping the totem man worships the tribe. Man's real god is society, and the power which he worships is the power of society. But this theory was also severely criticized by other scientists, and that from various points of view. It is no more satisfactory than the others as an explanation of the origin of religion. The theory of naturism was brought into the limelight especially by Pfleiderer. According to this theory religion was originally merely respect for the great and imposing phenomena of nature, in the presence of which man felt himself weak and helpless. This feeling of respect led to the worship, in some cases of these phenomena themselves, and in others of the invisible power(s) revealing itself in them. But the question naturally arises, How did man ever hit upon the idea of *worshipping* nature? May not this nature-worship, which is undoubtedly prevalent in some tribes, be the result of a decline from a purer stage of religious belief and practice? Like all the preceding hypotheses, this theory also fails to offer any explanation whatsoever of religion on its psychological side. In more recent times it was suggested that the origin of religion is connected with the belief in magic. Some think that the former in some way evolved out of the latter, but Frazer, who is the great authority on this subject, claims that the contribution of magic to religion was negative rather than positive. Man tried magic first, but was disappointed, and the despair of magic gave birth to religion. On the whole the result of this historical investigation is very disappointing *as an explanation of the origin of religion.*

2. THE PSYCHOLOGICAL METHOD. It was felt in the course of time that the historical method had to be supplemented by the psychological, and this is now regarded as the more important of the two. This method raises the question as to the source of religion in man's spiritual nature, not merely in the beginning, but everywhere and always. Edwards puts the questions thus:

What are the constant factors in the inner life of man which, in interplay with the environment, generate the attitude which we call religious? What are the impulses, promptings, motives, felt needs, which lead him to apprehend the supernatural and to adjust his life to it? What is there in his mental make-up that accounts for the fact that wherever man is found he has some form or other of religion?"[1] The psychological method seeks to derive religion from certain factors in man, which are not themselves religious, but which by combination and in cooperation with man's natural environment give rise to religion.

It will hardly do to say, as some have done, that man is religious because he has a *religious instinct*, for this supposed instinct is already religious, and is therefore the very thing to be explained. It is equally unsatisfactory to account for religion, as others have done, by holding that man has a *religious faculty*, for there is no proof for the existence of such a faculty, and if there were, this faculty itself would require explanation. Schleiermacher sought the explanation of religion in feeling, more particularly, in a feeling of dependence, but failed to explain how a mere feeling of dependence passed into a religious attitude. Some suggest that the transition may be found in a feeling of awe, which is akin to fear, in the presence of unknown but mighty powers. But fear is not yet religion and does not necessarily lead to worship. Moreover, religious emotion is far too complex to be explained in such a simple way. It includes not only awe, wonder, and admiration, but also gratitude, love, hope, and joy. Kant and Ritschl find the origin of religion in the desire of man to maintain himself as a free moral being over against the physical world. Man is conscious of the fact that he, as a spiritual being, is of far greater value than the whole natural world, and therefore ought to control this. At the same time he cannot help feeling that, as to the physical side of his being, he is simply a part of nature, and that in striving for ethical and spiritual ends he is repeatedly thwarted by natural conditions. This tension results in an attempt on the part of man to realize his destiny by believing and resting in a higher being that controls the natural order and makes it subservient to spiritual ends. On this view God becomes merely a helper in time of need. But seeking help with a higher being is not yet religious adoration. Moreover, this theory does not explain the origin of such religious phenomena as consciousness of guilt, penitence, desire for redemption, prayer for forgiveness, and so on. Neither does it account for the universality of the felt need of God, despite the fact that discoveries and inventions make it increasingly possible for man to maintain himself over against nature. Evolutionists made the attempt to demonstrate the development of religion out of such characteristics as a sense of dependence, fidelity, attachment, and love, as these are present in the animal world. But this attempted explanation can hardly be called successful. The so-called "doctrine" of evolution is still a mere hypothesis, and what is said about the inner "soul" life of the animals is largely conjectural. And the assumptions that seem to be warranted on this point still leave the most important elements of religion unexplained. Modern psychologists differ so greatly

---

1. *op. cit.*, p. 34.

in their suggested explanations of the origin of religion that we cannot begin to enumerate them. Nor do we consider it necessary to do this.

The psychological method labors under a difficulty similar to that with which the historical method is burdened. It must take its starting point in a hypothetical man, so undeveloped and barbarian that he has not even a spark of religion in him. Religion must be derived from factors that are not themselves religious. But Dr. Bavinck correctly says that such a man is a pure *Gedankending*, an empty abstraction. In reality such men do not exist. Moreover, this method makes religion dependent on an accidental concourse of circumstances. If the complex in which the explanation of religion is sought had been slightly different, religion would never have originated. This, of course, robs religion of its independent significance, of its universality and necessity, and of its incalculable worth. If it is purely accidental, it lacks the firm foundation on which it ought to rest. But this is not all: religion really becomes an absurdity, when it is explained without assuming the existence of a God. According to the psychological method man creates his own God, and determines how that God must be served. The relation between the *religio objectiva* and the *religio subjectiva* is reversed, and the latter becomes the source of the former. In principle this method conflicts with the essence of religion and virtually destroys the phenomenon which it ought to explain.

3. THE THEOLOGICAL METHOD. Speaking of the origin of religion, Edwards says that there are two views "which were once widely prevalent, but which are now obsolete or obsolescent. The first is the view that traced religion back to a primitive or a special Divine revelation."[1] He rejects this view as being, in its usual forms, too intellectual and mechanical, pre-scientific and crudely unpsychological. However, it is the Biblical view of the origin of religion, and is far more satisfying than any of the historical and psychological views that were offered to the world. In distinction from these, it alone contains a real explanation of the universal phenomenon of religion. Both the historical and the psychological method proceed on the assumption that religion, like science and art, must be explained in a purely naturalistic way, though some of their protagonists—Edwards being one of these—feel that it may be necessary in the last analysis to appeal to some sort of revelation. The theological method, on the other hand, maintains that religion can only find its explanation in God. Religion, being communion of the soul with God, naturally implies that God exists, that He has revealed Himself, and that He has so constituted man that the latter can know Him, is conscious of kinship with Him, and is even prompted by nature to seek after Him. While the historical and psychological methods are not even able to explain religion in its most primitive forms, the theological method offers us the key to the explanation, not only of the lowest, but also of the highest there is in religion. And of course a real explanation can be satisfied with nothing less than that. It is the only method that is in harmony with the real nature of religion. Scientists do not start out with a

---

1. *The Philosophy of Religion*, p. 30.

normative view of religion, and then undertake to explain the origin of it. They begin with a study of the phenomena of the religious life, and then adapt their views, their definitions, of religion to their findings. This gives rise to a great number of historical definitions which utterly fail to do justice to that which is essential in religion.

On the basis of God's revelation, the theological method posits the following truths:

a. *The existence of God.* If in religion we are concerned with the most intimate relationship between God and man, then it naturally involves the assumption that God exists. And we frankly proceed on the assumption that there is a personal God. It is true, many consider it unscientific to refer anything back to God. They admit that the Hebrews did this, but find the explanation for that in the fact that these people lived in a pre-scientific age. Consequently their explanations may meet with an indulgent smile, but cannot now be taken seriously. Over against this it may be said, however, that it is a poor science that may not rise above the visible and experimental, and is not permitted to take God into account. And this is doubly true of all scientific attempts to explain the origin of religion without any reference to God, for apart from Him religion is an absurdity. Religion is either an illusion, because God does not exist or cannot be known; or it is founded on reality, but then it presupposes the existence and the revelation of God.

b. *The Divine Revelation.* We also proceed on the assumption that God has revealed Himself. The idea of revelation is, in some form or other, found in all religions, and this proves quite sufficiently that it is a necessary corollary of religion. There is no religion in any real sense of the word apart from a divine revelation. If God had not revealed Himself in nature, in providence, and in experience, there would be no religion among the Gentile nations of the world; and there would be no *true religion* in any part of the world today, if God had not enriched man with His special revelation, enbodied in His divine Word, because it is exactly this revelation, as the *religio objectiva*, which determines the worship and service that is acceptable to Him. The *religio subjectiva* owes its inception, its development, and its proper regulation instrumentally to the *religio objectiva*. Divorced from its objective foundation, religion turns into a will-worship that is purely arbitrary.

c. *Man's creation in the image of God.* A third presupposition is that God so constituted man that he has the capacity to understand and to respond to the objective revelation. Religion is founded in the very nature of man, and was not imposed upon him from without in a somewhat mechanical way. It is a mistake to think that man first existed without religion, and was endowed with this later on as a sort of *superadditum*. The very idea of revelation presupposes the existence of a religious consciousness in man. Created in the image of God, man has a natural capacity for receiving and appreciating the self-communication of God. And in virtue of his original endowment man seeks communion with God, though under the influence of sin he now, as long as he is left to his unaided powers, seeks it in the wrong way. It is only under the influence of God's special revelation and of the illumination of the Holy Spirit, that the sinner can, at least in principle, render to God the service that is due to Him.

This view is not open to the criticism voiced by Edwards in the following words: "In its usual forms the doctrine of revelation has explained the origin of religion in far too intellectual and mechanical a fashion, as if religion began with the impartation to man of a set of ideas, ready-made and finished ideas poured into a mind conceived as a kind of empty vessel. This is a crudely unpsychological view."[1] He speaks of the view that must be traced back to a primitive or special revelation as "obsolete or obsolescent," but admits that the "category of revelation may be ultimately necessary in a statement of the objective ground of the validity of religious beliefs and in order to safeguard the place of the divine initiative in the religious life of man." He insists, however, that it should be the idea of a continuous and progressive revelation. But when he says this he has in mind the kind of revelation which, from another point of view, may also be called human discovery.

QUESTIONS FOR FURTHER STUDY: Does the present emphasis on the immanence of God in any way affect the current conceptions of religion? Can the psychology of religion be of great assistance in the study of the essential nature of religion? How does the philosophy of the psychologists affect their investigations in the field of religion? Is it proper to speak of man as having a religious instinct or a religious faculty? Is it correct to say that affections are more fundamental in religion than either the intellect or the will? Why is it wrong to study merely the lowest forms of the religious life of man, in order to explain the origin of religion? Are there conclusive proofs that the higher forms of religion developed out of the lower? What can be said in favor of the idea that the historical process in religion was one of deterioration rather than of development?

REFERENCES: Bavinck, *Geref. Dogm.* I, pp. 207-290; Kuyper, *Enc. der Heil. Godgel.* II, pp. 291-369; Wisse, *Religie en Christendom*, pp. 25-57; J. H. Bavinck, *Inleiding in de Zielkunde*, pp. 265-277; Galloway, *The Philosophy of Religion*, pp. 54-187; Edwards, *The Philosophy of Religion*, pp. 29-178; Wright, *A Student's Philosophy of Religion*; Leuba, *A Psychological Study of Religion*; Jevons, *Introduction to the Study of Comparative Religion*; Kirkpatrick, *Religion in Human Affairs*, pp. 1-166; Lidgett, *The Christian Religion*, pp. 138-224; Beattie, *Apologetics*, pp. 139-247; Bruce, *Apologetics*, pp. 71-163; Patton, *Fundamental Christianity*, pp. 1-208; Clark, *Ten Great Religions*; Menzies, *History of Religion*; Aalders, *De Heilige Schrift en de Verelijkende Godsdiens Twentenschap*; Sabatier, *Outlines of a Philosophy of Religion*, pp. 3-117; Brown, *The Essence of Christianity*; Pratt, *The Religious Consciousness*; Hughes, *The New Psychology and Religious Experience;* Moore, E. C., *The Nature of Religion*.

---

1. *The Philosophy of Religion*, p. 30 f.

III. THE PRINCIPIUM COGNOSCENDI EXTERNUM (Revelation)

A. Name and Concept of Revelation

1. CONNECTION BETWEEN RELIGION AND REVELATION. The idea of religion naturally leads on to that of revelation as its necessary corollary. In the study of comparative religion it is recognized ever increasingly that all religion is based on revelation of some kind, and that there is no purely "natural," as distinguished from "revealed," religion. Dr. Orr says: "In a wider respect, there is probably no proposition on which the higher religious philosophy of the past hundred years is more agreed than this—that *all religion originates in revelation.*"[1] The study of the *History of Religions* yields abundant evidence of the fact that belief in revelation is quite general among the nations of the world, and that every religion of any importance appeals to some form of revelation. Buddhism has sometimes been regarded as an exception to the rule, but in reality it is no exception, for when it became a religion it regarded Buddha as its god. Not only conservative, but also liberal scholars, grant explicitly that the knowledge of God, and therefore also religion, rests on revelation, though their conception of revelation varies a great deal.[2] To quite an extent the term 'natural theology' has fallen into disuse, and even when it is still used, it is often with the distinct understanding that it should not be regarded as the designation of a theology which is the opposite of 'revealed theology.' W. Fulton finds fault with this old mediaeval distinction, which is still tacitly accepted by J. G. Frazer in his Gifford Lectures, and says: "the knowledge of God derived from the consideration of nature, or from the light of reason, is as much entitled to be called revealed knowledge as the knowledge of God mediated through the Scriptures and the Church."[3] John Caird declares: "There is therefore, we repeat, no such thing as a natural religion or religion of reason distinct from revealed religion."[4] McPherson was perfectly justified in saying: "In the idea and fact of religion, therefore, revelation as the operation of God is the necessary correlate of faith as the spiritual act of man."[4] This could not be otherwise, because religion brings man in contact with an invisible Power, inaccessible to human investigation. If man is ever to know and serve God, the latter must reveal Himself. This is all the more true in view of the fact that in religion man is seeking something which he cannot find in science

---

1. *Revelation and Inspiration,* p. 2.
2. *Cf.* Bavinck, *Geref. Dogm. I,* p. 291 ff.
3. *Nature and God,* p. 18.
4. *The Fundamental Ideas of Christianity I,* p. 23
5. *Chr. Dogm.,* p. 19.

and art, in commerce and industry, in sensual pleasures and worldly riches, namely, redemption from sin and death, and life in communion with God. He can obtain these blessings only if God reveals Himself in relation to man and points out the way of salvation.

2. THE GENERAL IDEA OF REVELATION. The word 'revelation' is derived from the Latin *'revelatio,'* which denotes an unveiling, a revealing. In its active sense it denotes the act of God by which He communicates to man the truth concerning Himself in relation to His creatures, and conveys to him the knowledge of His will: and in the passive sense it is a designation of the resulting product of this activity of God. It should be observed that in theology it never denotes a mere passive, perhaps unconscious, becoming manifest, but always a conscious, voluntary, and intentional deed of God, by which He reveals or communicates divine truth. The idea of revelation assumes (a) that there is a personal God who actively communicates knowledge; (b) that there are truths, facts, and events which would not be known without divine revelation; and (c) that there are rational beings to whom the revelation is made and who are capable of appropriating it. The words more particularly used in Scripture for revelation are the common words for 'disclose,' 'make known,' or 'reveal,' with a deepened meaning as applied to supernatural communications, or the effect of these. In the Old Testament the outstanding word is *'galah,'* the original meaning of which is 'to be naked.' As applied to revelation, it points to the removal of a covering which obstructs the view. There is no noun derived from this verb, which denotes the concept of revelation. The corresponding New Testament term is *'apokalupto,'* which also signifies the removal of a veil or covering, in order that what is back of it or under it may be seen. The noun *'apokalupsis'* denotes an uncovering, a revelation. Another word that is frequently used is *'phaneroo'* (noun, *'phanerosis'*), to make manifest, to expose to view. The classical passage concerning the revelation of God to man is Heb. 1:1, 2: "God, having of old time spoken unto the fathers in the prophets by divers portions and in divers manners, hath at the end of these days spoken to us in his Son."

3. HISTORICAL CONCEPTIONS OF REVELATION. The idea of revelation has had a rather checkered history. There was no general agreement as to just what constituted divine revelation. Baillie distinguishes five periods in the history of human thought on this subject, and a brief characterization of these periods will serve to indicate the conflicting opinions that gained currency in the course of time.

a. *In the earliest times.* Primitive peoples found the final court of appeal in all religious matters in the mass of tribal traditions that were handed down conscientiously from one generation to another. They regarded the knowledge of the gods and of divine things, contained in these traditions, as perfectly reliable, because it had been acquired by the inspired men of the race by divination, that is, by signs provided by the gods in the entrails of animals, the flight and cries of birds, the constellations, and so on. These signs were interpreted by those who were skilled in such matters (artificial divination), or by communications which were directly clear to the mind, and which were made during sleep or in a waking state of ecstacy or frenzy (natural divination). The traditions which originated in this fashion were sometimes embodied in sacred books.

b. *In the philosophy of the Greeks.* The Greeks virtually set aside the idea that the gods revealed themselves to man, and substituted for it the idea that man gradually discovered the gods. They did not deny the reality of divination altogether, but did not consider this sufficient to explain the whole body of religious knowledge. In their opinion the truth about the gods was not suddenly acquired in dreams or visions, but by means of calm and persevering thought. The prevailing opinion was that God and nature were one, and that the study of nature would therefore yield religious knowledge. The philosophy of Socrates and Plato represented, at least to a certain extent a protest against this idea. In a measure they rose above the polytheism of their day.

c. *In the Christian era up to the latter half of the seventeenth century.* Under the influence of the Semitic and the Christian religion a distinction was made between a revelation of God in nature and a special revelation, finally embodied in Scripture. This idea of a twofold revelation prevailed for more than sixteen hundred years without being seriously questioned. The only point in dispute was that of the exact line of demarcation. This was not always stated in the same way. Thomas Aquinas held that natural revelation could lead to the knowledge of God as a unity, and furnished an adequate basis for a scientific theology, but that only special revelation could acquaint man with God as triune and as incarnate in Jesus Christ, and conveyed to man a knowledge of the mysteries of faith.

d. *In the latter half of the seventeenth century and the eighteenth century.* During this period there was a growing tendency to emphasize the revelation of God in nature at the expense of His special revelation in Scripture. The idea, fostered especially by Deism and Rationalism, was that the light of nature is quite sufficient for man, and that the Christian revelation really adds nothing to it, but is merely a "republication" of the truths of nature for the benefit of those who cannot discover or reason out things for themselves. By the "light of nature" they meant "partly certain intuitive or self-evident religious beliefs, and partly certain discursive proofs based on scientific and metaphysical speculation."

e. *Since the beginning of the nineteenth century.* Under the influence of Kant, and especially of Schleiermacher, the difference between the light of nature and the light of God's special revelation was supposedly transcended. They are no more regarded in modern liberal theology as two different avenues to the knowledge of God, but only as two distinct ways of conceiving of the only avenue there is. The doctrine of the immanence of God is beginning to play an important part. Both Kant and Schleiermacher are "convinced that the only argument capable of reaching Deity is one that starts not from external, but from human, nature; and they believe, too, that it is in human nature, and not in its abeyance in trance or dream or frenzy, that God characteristically reveals Himself." They represent neither the doctrine of the light of nature nor that of special revelation in its old form, but resolve both in a higher unity. This new representation is in a measure a return to that of Greek philosophy, and it is especially this view of revelation that is strongly opposed by the Theology of Crisis.

4. THE IDEA OF REVELATION IN MODERN THEOLOGY.

a. *The Deistic conception.* Eighteenth century Deism believed in a personal God and in a general revelation in nature and history, but denied the necessity, the possibility, and the reality of a supernatural revelation. It denied the *necessity* of such a revelation in view of the fact that human reason can discover, in the general revelation of God, all that a special revelation might convey to man. The only conceivable advantage of a special revelation is that it might facilitate the acquirement of the necessary knowledge. Lessing, though not himself a Deist, agreed with them in asserting the all-sufficiency of natural revelation. According to him special revelation offers man nothing "worauf die menschliche Vernunft, sich sellbst ueberlassen, nicht auch kommen wuerde; sondern sie gab und gibt ihm die wichtigsten dieser Dinge nur fruehrer." Deism also considered a supernatural revelation as *impossible,* that is, *metaphysically inconceivable and morally unworthy of God.* Such a revelation would imply that the existing world is defective and, consequently, that the Creator, when He called it into being, was wanting, either in the necessary wisdom to plan a better world, or in the requisite power to create a superior world. The one is just as inconceivable as the other, and both involve an unworthy conception of God. Finally, it also boldly denied the *existence* of any supernatural revelation, since it considered such a revelation as absolutely contrary to the fact that God always works according to the established laws of nature. The world is under the control of an iron-clad system of laws, and therefore necessarily excludes the intrusion of supernatural elements. Prophecy and miracles do not prove the existence of a revelation transcending the bounds of reason, since they admit of a natural explanation. The Deist, then, ruled out the supernatural, and retained only the natural revelation of God, and he was followed in that respect by the philosophy of the Enlightenment. Even Kant did not transcend this view, but argued just as Lessing did before him. His religion was a religion within the bounds of reason.[1]

b. *The modern Idealistic conception.* While Deism placed God at a distance from the world and allowed no point of contact, the idealistic philosophy of the beginning of the previous century stressed the immanence of God in the world, and thereby gave rise to a new conception of revela-

---
1. *Cf.* Moore, *Christian Thought Since Kant,* p. 50.

tion. That philosophy was essentially pantheistic and therefore excluded revelation in the sense in which it was always understood by the Church. The fundamental principle of Pantheism is that God and the world are one. God has no independent existence apart from the world; neither does the world exist in distinction from God. A distinction is usually made between the monistic, infinite, and self-sufficient ground of all things, and the temporal, finite, and constantly changing phenomena that necessarily flow from it. These phenomenal forms are only modifications of the unknown something that lies back of them, and that has been variously designated as Brahm (in Indian philosophy), Pure Being (Greeks), Substance (Spinoza), or Pure Thought (Hegel). These are all pure abstractions which, as Bavinck remarks, may mean everything or nothing. Opinions differed as to the way in which the world of phenomena comes forth out of this hidden background. The Indian philosophers spoke of *emanation*, the Greeks, of *manifestation*, Spinoza, of *modification*, and Hegel, of *a process of idealistic evolution*. But this process, of whatever kind it may be, does not, strictly speaking, reveal the Absolute; this remains an unknown quantity. Moreover, on this standpoint one can at best speak of a becoming manifest, and not at all of a conscious, voluntary, and active self-communication. And, finally, this pantheistic view knows no object, to which knowledge could be communicated. Subject and object are one. Moore correctly says that, according to Hegel, "God is revealer, recipient, and revelation all in one."[1]

Through Schleiermacher and his followers the one-sided emphasis of the Idealists on the immanence of God also became popular in theological circles, and was often stressed to the point of Pantheism. The whole of nature was not only regarded as a manifestation of the immanent God, but often identified with Him. The divinity of man was emphasized in view of the fact that the most important revelation of God was found in the inner life of man, in which, according to Hegel, the Infinite comes to self-consciousness. And since Christ was regarded as the purest flower of the human race, the highest revelation of God was also found in Him, primarily in His inner life, but secondarily also in His historical appearance. Thus the continuity of God and man was made emphatic, and the idea of the distance separating the two was minimized and often completely ignored. McGiffert, speaking of the influence of the doctrine of immanence on the idea of revelation, says: "As God is immanent in the life of man divine revelation comes from within, not from without. The religious man looks into his own experience for the disclosure of divine truth, and if he also turns to the pages of a sacred book, it is simply because it is a record of the religious experiences of others who have found God in their own souls and have learned from Him there."[2]

This Idealism also rules out the supernatural revelation of God. It is true that, while Deism denies the supernatural, Idealism in a formal sense denies the natural, since it regards all thoughts, facts, and events in the natural

---
1. *Christian Thought Since Kant*, p. 69.
2. *The Rise of Modern Religious Ideas*, p. 204 f.

THE PRINCIPIUM COGNOSCENDI EXTERNUM (REVELATION)

world as the direct products of the immanent God. All that Deism called natural is denominated supernatural by Idealism. In its estimation the supernatural is, in the last analysis, not distinct from the natural, but finds expression in the common laws of nature and in the ordinary course of events. All the natural is supernatural, and all the supernatural is natural. In view of this fact it is no wonder that present day liberalism sometimes speaks of a "natural supernaturalism" and of a "supernatural naturalism." It might seem therefore that, in this idealistic view, they who contend for a supernatural revelation receive even more than they are asking for; but the gain is merely apparent. It only means that all revelation is regarded as supernatural *in origin,* that is, as coming from God. Hence the question remains, whether there is a revelation of God, which transcends all that man can learn by his natural powers, a revelation, which not only flows from a supernatural source, *but is also mediated and brought to man in a supernatural way.* And at this point Idealism, in spite of all its pretended belief in the supernatural, joins Deism in its denial. Over against it, we must emphasize the fact that there is a revelation of God, *which was mediated and brought to man in a supernatural way.*

There is another point that deserves particular attention here, namely, that concerning the content of the divine revelation. The Church has always regarded the revelation of God as a communication of knowledge to man: knowledge of the nature and of the will of God. But in modern liberal theology, which is dominated by Idealism with its doctrine of the divine immanence, we repeatedly meet with the assertion that revelation is not a communication of divine truth, but assumes the form of experience or of a historical person, namely, Jesus Christ. Sometimes it is said that God reveals Himself in acts rather than in words. This is entirely in line with the common view that Christianity is not a doctrine but a life. G. B. Foster says that the Christian concept of revelation differs from that "of the orthodox ecclesiastical dogmatics. The latter rests on the equivalence of *revelatio specialis* with Sacred Scriptures. In consequence of this, revelation is conceived (a) as communication of doctrine; (b) as internally authoritative and statutory; (c) as miraculous in the sense that main stress is placed on the absence of natural mediations; (d) as historyless."[1] According to Gerald Birney Smith "revelation is more and more being considered as exceptional spiritual insight rather than as a non-human communication of truth."[2] Edwards admits that the category of revelation may be ultimately necessary, but "it must be a revelation of God in terms of the whole life of man and not in terms of mere intellectual knowledge or ideas, conveyed to the mind of man from above."[3] Modesty does not permit the modern liberals to pretend that they are in possession of the truth, and therefore they assume the humble attitude of being seekers after truth. At the same time they have enough confidence in man to think that he can discover the truth, and has even discovered God. And even if they do still

---
1. *Christianity in Its Modern Expression,* p. 49.
2. *A Dictionary of Religion and Ethics,* Art. *Revelation.*
3. *The Philosophy of Religion,* p. 31.

believe in divine revelation, they must insist that human discovery goes hand in hand with it.

c. *The conception of the Theology of Crisis.* The Theology of Crisis, represented by such men as Karl Barth, Emil Brunner, E. Thurneysen, F. Gogarten, and A. Bultmann, represents in no small measure a reaction against the modern idealistic view of revelation. Several of its interpreters have already suggested that it might appropriately be called "The Theology of the Word of God." This would be quite in harmony with the title of Barth's Prolegomena, "*Die Lehre vom Worte Gottes.*" In this theology the "infinite qualitative difference between time and eternity" is stressed, and with it as its necessary corollary the discontinuity between God and man. By taking this position it at once cut the ground from under the modern subjective conception of revelation, in which human discovery plays so great a part. It rebukes the pride of those who imagine that they can build a tower high enough to reach heaven, and places great and repeated emphasis on the fact that there is no way from man to God, but only a way from God to man. God is a hidden God, and man in his spiritual blindness can never find Him. It is a God who finds man and thereby puts him in a crisis. Revelation, according to this theology, has no concrete historical existence, not even in the Bible, and therefore it would not be correct to say, This is the Word of God. It would involve bringing the Word of God down to the level of the historical and relative, and putting it in the power of man to make God an object of study, while, as a matter of fact, God is never object, but always subject. In revelation all the emphasis falls on the free act of God. It is God in the act of speaking, and speaking now to this and then to that man, and bringing the word home to the soul in faith.

The Theology of Crisis speaks of a revelation given once for all. And if the question is raised, when this revelation was given, the answer is, in the incarnation, in which God actually came to man to perform a great all-decisive deed in order to constitute afresh our humanity. However, it is not in the historical life of Jesus that the supreme revelation of God was given, as the modern liberals claim, but only in that which is absolutely new in Him, that in which the eternal comes vertically down from above and penetrates into the horizontal line of history. Camfield says in his Barthian study: "Christ makes the entrance into history of something that is new. In that which makes Him Christ, the revelation of God, he is not continuous with history but discontinuous. In Him, history is lifted out of its temporal sequential setting and set in the light of the divine event of revelation."[1] Brunner speaks in a similar vein: "Jesus Christ means eternity in time, the Absolute within relativity, the fulfilment of time, the beginning of that which is above all temporal change, the *aion mellon,* the coming of the word of God and salvation."[2] The revelation of God came to man therefore in a great central fact rather than in a communication of knowledge. In it God approaches man, not with a teaching that must be believed, but with a challenge that must be met, with a behest or a

---
1. *Revelation and the Holy Spirit,* p. 96.
2. *The Word and the World,* p. 36.

command that must be obeyed. There is no revelation, even in Christ, however, until there is faith. Faith is not, strictly speaking, to be understood as a spiritual activity of man, by which he accepts the divine revelation, for this would make man subject and put him in possession of the revelation. It is rather the negation of man as subject. It is the creative work of God, and particularly of the Holy Spirit, by which, and by which alone, the revelation finally becomes an accomplished fact. Faith is a miracle, the deed and gift of God; it is revelation on its subjective side. Camfield says: "In faith man becomes the subject of a great aggression upon his life, a great approach of God, which disqualifies his consciousness, his thought-world for purposes of revelation."[1] It is true that Barth sometimes speaks of faith as the response of man to the divine revelation, but this must be understood in the light of the preceding. He says that it is the Word of God in Christ, the revelation therefore, which itself creates the apprehension of it.

Barth also speaks of the Word of God that came to the prophets and the apostles as the original revelation; and the question naturally arises, how this Word is connected with the revelation in Christ. In his work on *God in Action* Barth represents God as having gone forth as a warrior to meet the hosts of sinful men in a terrible contest, and then says: "This event is God's revelation to man; and whoever fails to understand it in this manner does not know what he is saying when he takes the word 'revelation' on his lips."[2] He points out that the great central revelation came in Jesus Christ, and that the men who bore the brunt of the attack were the men of the first line, that is the prophets and the apostles. To them the revelation of God in Christ came first of all; and since there is no revelation apart from the apprehension of it, the revelation that came to them may be called the original revelation.

They in turn bear witness to the revelation in the Bible, so that the Bible may be called a witness to, or a token of, the divine revelation, and can only in so far be called the Word of God. It is not itself the revelation, for this always comes as an act of God. Says Barth: "Holy Scripture as such is not the revelation. And yet Holy Scripture *is* the revelation, if and in so far as *Jesus Christ* speaks to us through the witness of His prophets and apostles."[3] And again: "The prophetic apostolic Word is the word, the witness, the proclamation and the preaching of Jesus Christ. The promise given to the Church in this word is the promise of God's mercy—expressed in the person of Him who is true God and true man—which takes to itself us who, because of our enmity towards God, could literally never have helped ourselves."[4] The word of Scripture may and does become for man the Word of God, the revelation, when it comes to him with the creative force that engenders faith. Barth speaks of the Bible as the second, and of the preaching of the Word, as the third, form of the Word of God. Church proclamation is the gospel of Jesus Christ, *preached with the*

---
1. *op. cit.*, p. 103.
2. p. 4.
3. *Revelation*, p. 67.
4. *The Doctrine of the Word of God*, p. 121.

expectation that it will become for some the Word of God. It becomes this only in those cases in which it is brought home to the heart in faith, and it is recognized as a divine revelation through the operation of the Holy Spirit,— a testimony of the Holy Spirit in each particular case.

The characteristic thing of the revelation of God is not that it communicates truth to man, but that it comes to him as a challenge, as a command, as a behest, which calls for obedience on the part of man, an obedience which is again wrought in faith. It is factual rather than verbal, that is, it comes to man as an act rather than as a word or, to speak in the words of Forsyth, who has been called "a Barthian before Barth," as "a word in the form of an act." Moreover, it is not merely something that took place in the past, but is also something actual and contemporaneous. This is correctly stressed by Walter Lowrie in the following words: "When we say that revelation is not a question of fact but of actuality, we completely alter the statement of the problem as it was conceived by Protestant as well as by Catholic orthodoxy. The question now is not first of all whether God *spoke*—some time in the past, more or less remote—and by what criterion we can determine that the record of this speech, a word recorded in Holy Scripture, was really a Word of God. Instead it is a question whether God actually speaks, now, at this moment and to *me*. And whether I hear. For *if* I hear a word addressed to me in God's voice, the question cannot arise *how* I am to recognize it as God's Word. And if I do not thus hear it, I can have no interest in asking such a question. The doctrine of the Reformers that the Word of God authenticates itself, or is authenticated to the individual by the testimony of the Holy Ghost, is much more evidently applicable here than in the connection in which they used it. Regarded as *actual* the Word of God is either heard as the Word of God, or it is not heard at all."[1]

5. THE PROPER CONCEPTION OF THE NATURE OF REVELATION. The existing variety of opinions respecting the idea of revelation naturally gives rise to the question, how we can arrive at a proper conception of revelation. Is it possible to determine precisely what constitutes a genuine divine revelation, and to define it in a way that will meet with general approval? And if it is possible to arrive at a proper conception of revelation, what method should be pursued in quest of it?

a. *The historical method*. Many are of the opinion that the answer to the question under consideration should be sought by the study of the history of religions. The investigator should approach the study of the subject with an unbiased mind, place himself, as it were, outside of all religions and their supposed revelations, take careful notice of the claims which they present, and then finally draw his conclusions. They regard this as the only scientific way in which the essential elements of a divine revelation can be discovered, and in which a unitary view of revelation can be obtained. But this method

---

1. *Our Concern with the Theology of Crisis*, p. 154 f.

is bound to disappoint for various reasons. (1) It is pure self-deception to think that anyone can ever take his stand outside of history, study the various beliefs respecting revelation in the different religions of the world without any presuppositions, and thus reach a purely objective conclusion as to its nature. We are all historically conditioned, and cannot possibly take our stand outside of history. Moreover, we cannot set ourselves aside in our investigations, nor the religious content of our consciousness, and usually reach a conclusion which was in principle determined beforehand. (2) On the supposition that one does succeed in approaching one's subject in an entirely unbiased manner, without any presuppositions on the subject, one, for that very reason, enters upon the study of the subject without a standard by which to determine the genuineness of a revelation. Approaching the matter in such a fashion, it is simply impossible to reach a sound judgment. And if on the other hand one comes to the study with a rather definite standard in mind, one is no more unbiased and is guilty of *petitio principii,* a begging of the question. (3) No science, however, objective, will ever be able to remove the differences of opinion respecting the idea of revelation, and to unify all nations and individuals in the deepest convictions of the heart. Only unity of religion can lead to such a spiritual unity. It cannot be said that the study of the history of religions has led to very gratifying results in this field.

b. *The theological method.* In the study and evaluation of the idea of revelation we must have a standard of judgment. And the all-important question is, Whence shall we derive it? Certainly not from philosophy, for this has no right to determine *a priorily* what constitutes genuine revelation. The Christian can derive the real concept of revelation only from what he recognizes as the special revelation of God. This means that we must turn to what we consider to be the divine revelation itself, in order to learn what revelation really is. It will of course be said that in following this method of procedure we are also reasoning in a circle, and we frankly admit this; but it is the same kind of circle as that in which the scientist moves when he turns to the earth, in order to learn what really constitutes it. Edwards feels constrained to resort to the same kind of reasoning, when he seeks to determine the norm of religion in a historical way. Says he: "In pursuing this inquiry it will be difficult for us to avoid reasoning in a circle—i. e., to avoid using our norm to guide us in our description of the common element as well as using the common element to guide us in our search for the norm .... It may be doubted whether in our actual reasoning we ever quite avoid the 'circles,' except when our reasoning is purely formal, sterile, and pedantic."[1] The situation is this: If no revelation has ever taken place, all efforts to reflect on the nature of it will be in vain; but if there is a revelation, then this itself must shed light on its essential nature and thus supply us with a standard of judgment. The many so-called revelations constitute no reason why the Christian in his scientific study should set aside his convictions respecting the truth of

---

1. *The Philosophy of Religion,* p. 136 f.

God's special revelation in Scripture. If it did, then the contention of many in our day that the true, the good, and the beautiful are relative concepts, would also have to constrain us to abandon our convictions concerning the laws of logic, of morals, and of aesthetics. It is perfectly true that people of other religions may argue in the same way, but this makes no essential difference. In the last analysis each one standeth and falleth to his own Lord. It is true that this method does not lead to a unitary view of revelation, but neither does any other method. And it is quite possible that we can do more to heal the existing breach by adhering to our Christian faith also in our scientific study than in any other way. Bavinck says that a science which seeks refuge in indifference does not know what to do with religion and revelation, and finally classes both as superstition.

6. DISTINCTIONS APPLIED TO THE IDEA OF REVELATION. In course of time two different distinctions were applied to the idea of revelation. The earliest of these is that between *natural* and *supernatural* revelation. Later on many abandoned this in favor of the distinction between *general* and *special* revelation. Each one of these modes of distinguishing between different kinds of revelation has its own peculiar fitness and describes a real difference between the two in their essential nature, in their comprehensiveness, and in the purpose which they serve.

a. *Natural and supernatural revelation.* Scripture does not make the distinction between natural and supernatural revelation, though it does afford a basis for it. Neander mistakenly regarded *phaneroun* and *apokaluptein* as being respectively designations of natural and supernatural revelation.. In a certain sense it may be said that, according to Scripture, all revelation of God is supernatural, since it comes from God and reveals God, who possesses a life distinct from that of nature. As a rule the Bible does not trace the phenomena of nature to secondary causes, but to their primary cause, which is God or the will of God. The distinction was made rather early in history, however, but was not intended as a designation of a two-fold origin of revelation. It was clearly understood that all revelation of God is supernatural in origin, since it comes from God. It served rather to discriminate between two different modes of revelation. Natural revelation is communicated through the media of natural phenomena, while supernatural revelation implies a divine intervention in the natural course of events; it is supernatural not only in origin, but also in mode. The distinction between natural and supernatural revelation became very prominent in the Middle Ages, and occupied an important place in the discussions of the Scholastics. It was especially the problem of the relation between the two that engaged the attention of several of the most prominent Schoolmen. In their minds the question was really that of the relationship between reason and revelation. Some ascribed the primacy to revelation and expressed their conviction in the words "Credo ut intelligam," while others regarded reason as primary. Toward the end of the scholastic period, however, the distinction took the form of an antithesis, particularly in the teachings of Thomas Aquinas. He considered it necessary to keep the truth of philosophy and the truth of revelation each in its own place, and to handle the problems of philosophy as a philosopher, and those of theology, as a theologian. Of the two methods to be followed the one leads to scientific knowledge, and the other to faith, that is, to an acceptance of the truth, which is not based on intellectual insight. He considered it possible to construct a science on the basis of reason, but not on the basis of faith, though he recognized the possibility of proving some of the propositions of faith or revelation by means of rational argumentation. Revelation, it was thought, added to the knowledge obtained by reason specifically the knowledge of the *mysteria* (Trinity, incarnation, etc.), and these, as resting exclusively on authority, remain a matter of faith. This view led to a dualism, involving an over-valuation of natural, and an under-valuation of supernatural, revelation.

The Reformers retained the distinction, but sought to get away from the dualism of Thomas Aquinas. They denied the possibility of arriving at a strictly scientific knowledge of God from natural revelation, and held that through the entrance of sin into the world God's natural revelation was corrupted and obscured, and man's understanding was so darkened that he was unable to read and interpret correctly God's handwriting in nature. As a result of the fall two things became necessary: (1) that in a supernatural revelation God should re-publish, correct, and interpret the truths which man could originally learn from nature; and (2) that He should so illumine man by the operation of the Holy Spirit as to enable him to see God once more in the works of His hands. Consequently natural theology, which had been emphasized by Scholasticism, lost its independence on the basis of reason, and was incorporated in the Christian system of doctrine. This does not mean, however, that the Churches of the Reformation attached little or no value to natural revelation. Both the Lutherans and the Reformed continued to maintain its great significance. Several Reformed scholars defended it against the Socinians, who regarded all knowledge of God as the fruit of an external communication. It may be said that even the Churches of the Reformation did not entirely escape the dualistic representation of the Scholastics. Reformed scholars have sometimes given the impression—and do this occasionally even now—that there is still a sphere, however small, where human reason reigns supreme and does not need the guidance of faith. Under the influence of the Cartesian philosophy, with its emphasis on reason as the source of all knowledge, some of them published separate works on natural theology. In the eighteenth century English Deism and German Rationalism gave such prominence to the *theologia naturalis* that the *theologia revelata* was made to appear as altogether superfluous. This culminated in the philosophy of Wolff, who considered it possible to prove everything by a rationalistic procedure and a deductive method, and to present it in a clear way. Kant overthrew this position entirely by pointing out that the supersensual and supernatural lies beyond the reach of human reason. Moreover, the history of the study of religions proved that none of these are based on a purely natural revelation.

b. *General and special revelation.* Alongside of the distinction between natural and supernatural revelation, another distinction arose, namely, that between general and special revelation. The former was considered faulty, since it was found that even heathen religions are based, not exclusively on the revelation of God in nature, but in part also on elements of a supernatural revelation, handed down by tradition and to a great extent perverted. The distinction between general and special revelation runs to a certain degree parallel to the preceding one, though it is not entirely the same. It contemplates the extent and purpose of the revelation rather than its origin and mode. There is, however, a certain overlapping. General revelation rests on the basis of creation, is addressed to all intelligent creatures as such, and is therefore accessible to all men; though as the result of sin they are no more able to read and interpret it aright. Special revelation on the other hand rests on the basis of re-creation, is addressed to men *as sinners* with a view to their redemption, and can be properly understood only by the spiritual man. General revelation is not exclusively natural, but also contains supernatural elements; and special revelation also comprises elements which assume a perfectly natural character. The revelation of the covenant of works before the fall was supernatural and at the same time general. And when the sphere of special revelation was limited to Israel, God repeatedly gave supernatural revelations to non-Israelites, and therefore outside of the sphere of special revelation, Gen. 20:40, 41; Judg. 7:13; Dan. 2; 5:5. And on the other hand, when God reveals Himself in the history of Israel, in the providential vicissitudes of that ancient people, and in the ritual worship in tabernacle and temple, He is clothing His special revelation in natural forms. Of course, in so far as these elements are now embodied in the inspired Word of God, they come to us as a part of God's supernatural revelation. In view of the preceding it can hardly be said that natural and general revelation on the one hand, and supernatural and special revelation on the other hand, are in all respects identical. Roman Catholics still give preference to the older distinction, while Reformed theologians prefer the later one, though they do not use it exclusively.

B. General Revelation

General revelation, as we know it, does not come to man in a verbal form. It is a revelation in *res* rather than in *verba*. It consists in those active manifestations to the perception and consciousness of man which come to him in the constitution of the human mind, in the whole framework of nature, and in the course of God's providential government. Divine thoughts are embodied in the phenomena of nature, in the human consciousness, and in the facts of experience or history. As was pointed out in the preceding, this general revelation has sometimes also included elements of supernatural revelation. The existence of such a general revelation was taught in Reformed theology from the very beginning. In Calvin's Institutes we read: "That there exists in the human mind, and indeed by natural instinct, some sense of Deity, we hold

THE PRINCIPIUM COGNOSCENDI EXTERNUM (REVELATION)

to be beyond dispute, since God himself, to prevent any man from pretending ignorance, has endued all men with some idea of his Godhead, the memory of which He constantly renews and occasionally enlarges, that all to a man being aware that there is a God, and that He is their Maker, may be condemned by their own conscience when they neither worship him nor consecrate their lives to his service."[1] In a following chapter he points out that God has not only been pleased "to deposit in our minds the seed of religion of which we have already spoken, but so to manifest his perfections in the whole structure of the universe, and daily place himself in our view, that we cannot open our eyes without being compelled to behold him."[2] Still farther on he speaks of God's revelation in the providential guidance of the world. At the same time he stresses the fact that man does not derive great benefit from this revelation. Says he: "Bright, however, as is the manifestation which God gives both of himself and his immortal kingdom in the mirror of his works, so great is our stupidity, so dull are we in regard to these bright manifestations, that we derive no benefit from them."[3]

In answer to the question by what means God is known to us, the Belgic Confession says: "We know Him by two means: First by the creation, preservation, and government of the universe; which is before our eyes as a most elegant book, wherein all creatures, great and small, are as so many characters leading us to *see clearly the invisible things of God, even His everlasting power and divinity*, as the apostle Paul says (Rom. 1:20). All which things are sufficient to convince men and leave them without excuse." These words contain a clear recognition of the general revelation of God, as it is taught in Scripture, and a statement of its significance for man.[4] A further recognition of this general revelation is found in Art. XIV, which speaks of the creation of man in the image of God, of his fall in sin, whereby he lost all his excellent gifts, and of the fact that he "retained only small remains thereof, which, however, are sufficient to leave man without excuse."

Liberal theology greatly over-emphasized the general revelation of God. In distinction from Deism, it found this revelation primarily in man and in his religious experiences, and supremely in the man Christ Jesus, in whom the divine element that is in every man, reached its highest manifestation. The Bible, and particularly the New Testament, was regarded merely as a record of the religious experiences of men who enjoyed special privileges in their close contact with Christ, the source of their deep God-consciousness. In this way it was robbed of its supernatural character and made to differ only in degree from other parts of God's general revelation. The self-disclosure of God in human experience became the all-sufficient revelation of God unto salvation. The immanent God is present in every man and saves all those who heed His promptings.

---

1. *op. cit., I. iii.* 1.
2. *op. cit. I. v.* 1.
3. *op. cit. I. v.* II.
4. *Art.* II.

Over against this view the Theology of Crisis once more places all emphasis on special revelation. In fact, Barth goes to the extreme of denying all natural revelation, whether it be in nature round about us, in the human consciousness, or in the course of historical events. That is, he denies that there is in the work of creation a revelation, from which the natural man can learn to know God, and on the basis of which he can construct a theology, and rejects absolutely the *analogia entis* of the Roman Catholic Church. He is willing to admit that the invisible things of God are visible in the world, but only to seeing eyes, and the natural man is blind. There would be a revelation for him in these things, only if he could see them. But the subjective condition of revelation is utterly wanting in his case. There is no point of contact in him, since the image of God was utterly destroyed by sin. Right here an important difference emerges between Barth and Brunner. The latter does believe in natural revelation, and denies that the image of God was utterly defaced, so that not a trace of it is left. He holds that the image of God was utterly destroyed *materially* but not *formally*, and that there is still an *Anknuepfungspunkt* in the natural man to which revelation can link itself. In this respect he certainly comes closer to the historical position of Reformed theology. Barth takes issue with him on this point in his pamphlet entitled *"Nein."*[1]

1. THE VALUE AND SIGNIFICANCE OF GENERAL REVELATION. The fact that after the fall the general revelation of God was superseded by a special revelation, is apt to lead to an under-valuation of the former. But we may not neglect the data of Scripture on this point. The Gospel of John speaks of a light that lighteth every man (John 1:9). Paul says that the invisible things of God "since the creation of the world are clearly seen, being perceived through the things that are made, even His everlasting power and divinity; that they may be without excuse," and speaks of the Gentiles as "knowing God" (Rom. 1:20, 21). In the following chapter he says that "they show the work of the law written in their hearts, their consciences bearing witness therewith, and their thoughts one with another accusing or else excusing them (Rom. 2:15). God did not leave Himself without a witness among them (Acts 14:17). There is therefore a general revelation of God, for which the natural man has a certain susceptibility, for it renders him without excuse. And while they who enjoy only this general revelation never live up to the light, and many deliberately go contrary to it, there are also some who do by nature the things of the law. In spite of the fact that God has now revealed Himself in a superior manner, His original revelation remains of great importance.

a. *In connection with the Gentile world.* Though there is no purely natural religion, yet the general revelation of God in nature and history furnishes the firm and lasting foundation for the Gentile religions. It is in

---

1. Cf. further on this subject: McConnachie, *The Significance of Karl Barth*, p. 142 f.; Lowrie, *Our Concern with the Theology of Crisis*, pp. 114, 122 f.; Mackintosh, *Types of Modern Theology*, 277 f.; Baillie, *Our Knowledge of God*, p. 18 ff.; Barth, *Roemerbrief*, comments on the first chapter; *The Doctrine of the Word of God* p. 147.

virtue of this general revelation that even the Gentiles feel themselves to be the offspring of God, Acts 17:28, that they seek God, if haply they might find Him, Acts 17:27, that they see God's everlasting power and divinity, Rom. 1:19, 20, and that they do by nature the things of the law, Rom. 2:14. In spite of that fact, however, Scripture does not regard their religions as true religions, differing from the Christian religion only in degree, as so many students of religion do at the present time, but ascribes them to a wilful perversion of the truth. It passes a severe judgment on them, and describes the condition of the Gentile world, devoid of the light of God's special revelation, as one of darkness, Isa. 9:1 f.; 60:2; Luke 1:79; Eph. 4:18, ignorance, Acts 17:30; Rom. 1:18 f.; I Pet. 1:14, folly, I Cor. 1:18 ff.; 2:6; 3:19 f.; and of sin and unrighteousness, Rom. 1:24 f.; 3:9 f. The heathen gods are no gods, but idols which have no real existence and are really lies and vanity, Isa. 41:29; 42:17; Jer. 2:28; Acts 14:15; 19:26; Gal. 4:8; I Cor. 8:4; and the heathen religions even give evidence of the operation of demoniacal power, Deut. 32:17; I Cor. 10:20 f.; Rev. 9:20.

But though Scripture passes a severe judgment on the religions of the Gentiles, and represents them as false religions over against Christianity as the only true religion, it also recognizes true elements in them. There is also among the heathen a revelation of God, an illumination of the Logos, and an operation of the Holy Spirit, Gen. 6:3; Job. 32:8; John 1:9; Rom. 1:18 ff.; 2:14, 15; 14:16, 17; 17:22-30. Nevertheless, it beholds in the Gentile world only a caricature of the living original which is seen in Christianity. What is mere appearance in the former, is real in the latter, and what is sought in the former is found in the latter.

Philosophy has not been satisfied with the explanation which Scripture gives of the religions of the Gentiles, and substituted for it another under the influence of the doctrine of evolution. According to this, mankind gradually developed out of an irreligious condition, through the stages of fetishism, animism, nature-worship, and henotheism, into ethical monotheism. But in recent years some renowned scientists, engaged in archaeological researches, such as Langdon, Marston, and Schmidt, declared themselves in favor of an original Monotheism as the primary form of religion.

b. *In connection with the Christian religion.* General revelation also has a certain value for the Christian religion. Not that it provides us with a *religio naturalis*, which is quite sufficient in itself and therefore renders all supernatural revelation superfluous. Such a natural religion does not exist, and is in fact impossible. Neither can it be said that the Christian derives his knowledge of God first of all from general revelation, and then supplements this with the knowledge of Christ. He derives his theological knowledge of God from special revelation only; this is his *principium unicum*. Yet there is a close relation between the two. Special revelation has incorporated, corrected, and interpreted general revelation. And now the Christian theologian takes his stand on the Word of God, and from that point of vantage also contemplates nature and history. He reads God's general revelation with the eye of faith and in the light of God's Word, and for that very reason is able to see God's hand in nature, and His footsteps in history. He sees God in everything round about him, and is thereby led to a proper appreciation of the world. Moreover, general revelation offers the Christian a basis, on which he can meet and argue with unbelievers. The light of the Logos that lighteth every man is also a bond that unites all men. The whole creation testifies with many voices that man is created in the image of God, and therefore cannot find rest except in God. Finally, it is also due to God's general revelation that His special revelation is not, as it were, suspended in the air, but touches the life of the world at every point. It maintains the connection between nature and grace, between the world and the kingdom of God, between the natural and the moral order, between creation and re-creation.

2. THE INSUFFICIENCY OF GENERAL REVELATION. Pelagians taught the sufficiency of general revelation and of the *religio naturalis* founded on it. They spoke of three different ways of salvation, the very names of which point to *autosoterism*, the doctrine that man saves himself. These three ways were called: (a) the *lex naturae*, (b) the *lex Mosis*, and (c) the *lex Christi*. At the time of the Reformation both the Roman Catholics and the Protestants regarded general revelation as insufficient. But in the eighteenth century Deists and Rationalists again followed the Pelagians in their over-estimation of general revelation. And under the influence of Schleiermacher and of the idealistic philosophy of the nineteenth century, with its one-sided emphasis on the immanence of God, many began to regard the revelation of God in man as quite sufficient for the spiritual needs of man, and this was tantamount to an admission of the sufficiency of general revelation. Over against this modern tendency it is necessary to stress its insufficiency. There are especially three reasons why it cannot be considered adequate.

a. *It does not acquaint man with the only way of salvation.* By general revelation we receive some knowledge of God, of His power, goodness, and wisdom, but we do not learn to know Christ, the highest revelation of God, in His redemptive work and in His transforming power. And yet an experimental knowledge of Him is the only way of salvation, Matt. 11:27; John 14:6; 17:3; Acts 4:2. Since general revelation knows nothing about grace and forgiveness, it is entirely insufficient for sinners. Moreover, while it teaches certain truths, it changes nothing in the sphere of being. And yet it is absolutely necessary that the sinner should be changed, that a new element should be introduced into history, and that a new process should be set in motion, if the divine purpose is to be realized in the life of mankind.

b. *It does not convey to man any absolutely reliable knowledge of God and spiritual things.* The knowledge of God and of spiritual and eternal things derived from general revelation is altogether too uncertain to form a trustworthy basis, on which to build for eternity; and man cannot afford to pin his hopes for the future on uncertainties. The history of philosophy clearly shows that general revelation is no safe and certain guide. Even the best of philosophers did not escape the power of error. And though some rose to a height of knowledge that compels admiration, they proved quite inadequate to present that knowledge in such a form that it became the common property of the masses. As a rule it was of such a nature that only the limited number of intellectuals could really share it. Paul tells us that the world through its wisdom knew not God.

c. *It does not furnish an adequate basis for religion.* The history of religions proves that not a single nation or tribe has been satisfied with a purely natural religion. Through the devastating influence of sin God's revelation in nature was obscured and corrupted, and man was deprived of the ability to read it aright. This noetic effect of sin remains, and general revelation itself makes no provision for its removal, but leaves the spiritual condition of man as it is. Therefore it cannot serve as a basis for true religion. The so-called natural religion of the Deists and the *Vernunftreligion* of Kant are pure abstractions, which never had any real existence. It has become increasingly evident that such a religion does not, and cannot exist. It is generally admitted at present that all religions are positive and appeal to a greater or less degree to a supposed or real positive revelation.

C. Special Revelation

1. THE SCRIPTURAL IDEA OF REVELATION. Alongside of the general revelation in nature and history, we have a special revelation, which is now embodied in Scripture. The Bible is the book of the *revelatio specialis,* and is in the last analysis the only *principium cognoscendi externum* of theology. It is therefore to this source that we also turn for our knowledge of special revelation. Several words are used in Scripture to express the idea of revelation, such as certain forms of the Hebrew words *galah, ra'ah,* and *yada',* and the Greek words *epiphanein* (*epiphaneia*), *emphanizein, gnorizein, deloun, deiknunai, lalein,* and especially *phaneroun* and *apokaluptein.* These words do not denote a passive becoming manifest, but designate a free, conscious, and deliberate act of God, by which He makes Himself and His will known unto man. Barth stresses the fact that God is absolutely free and sovereign in revealing Himself to man. Scholten had the mistaken notion that *apokaluptein* refers to subjective internal illumination, and *phaneroun,* to objective manifestation or revelation. The former is also used to denote objective revelation, Luke 17:30; Rom. 1:7, 18; 8:18; Eph. 3:5; II Thess. 2:3, 6, 8, etc. Neander was equally mistaken, when he regarded *phaneroun* as a designation of God's general revelation in nature, and *apokaluptein* as a denomination of the special revelation of grace. The former is also used of special revelation, John 17:6; Rom. 16:26; Col. 1:26; I Tim. 3:16; II Tim. 1:10, etc., and the latter serves, at least in one passage, to denote general revelation, Rom. 1:18.

It is difficult, if not impossible, to make a distinction between the two that will hold in all cases. Etymologically, *apokaluptein* refers to the removal of a covering by which an object was hidden, and *phaneroun*, to the manifestation or publication of the matter that was hidden or unknown. *Apokalupsis* removes the instrumental cause of concealment, and *phanerosis* makes the matter itself manifest. This also accounts for the fact that phanerosis is always used of objective, and *apokalupsis* of both subjective and objective, revelation; and that *phanerosis* is repeatedly used to denote either general or special revelation, while *apokalupsis* is, with a single exception, always used of special revelation. There is also a characteristic difference between these two words and the words *gnorizein* and *deloun*. The former stress the fact that matters are brought to light, so that they fall under our observation; and the latter indicate that these matters, by virtue of that revelation, now also become the object of our conscious thought.

2. THE MEANS OF SPECIAL REVELATION. The Christian religion is not only like the heathen religions in its appeal to revelation; even in the means of revelation a certain similarity can be seen. In general these can be reduced to three forms.

a. *Theophanies*. Gentile religions are frequently associated with traditions respecting appearances of the gods. The gods are not considered to be like man and to be living with him on a footing of equality, but are nevertheless represented as coming to man occasionally and bestowing rich blessings upon him. In this respect these religions are somewhat like the Christian religion, which also has, not only a God afar off, but also a God at hand. Scripture teaches us that God dwelt among the cherubim in the days of old, Ps. 80:1; 99:1, etc. His presence was seen in clouds of fire and smoke, Gen. 15:17; Ex. 3:2; 19:9, 16 f.; 33:9; Ps. 78:14; 99:7, in stormy winds, Job 38:1; 40:6; Ps. 18:10-16, and in the gentle zephyr, I Kings 19:12. These appearances were tokens of God's presence, in which He revealed something of His glory. Among the Old Testament appearances that of "the Angel of the Lord" occupies a special place. This Angel was not a mere symbol, nor a created angel, but a personal revelation, an appearance of God among men. On the one hand He is distinguished from God, Ex. 23:20-23; Isa. 63:8, 9, but on the other hand He is also identified with Him, Gen. 16:13; 31:11, 13; 32:28, and other passages. The prevailing opinion is that He was the second Person of the Trinity, an opinion that finds support in Mal. 3:1. Theophany reached its highest point in the incarnation of the Son of God, in Jesus Christ, in whom the fulness of the Godhead dwelt bodily, Col. 1:19; 2:9. Through Him and the Spirit which He sent, God's dwelling among men is now a true spiritual reality. The Church is the temple of the Holy Spirit, I Cor. 3:16; 6:19; Eph. 2:21. But an even fuller revelation of this will follow, when the new Jerusalem descends out of heaven from God and the tabernacle of God is pitched among men, Rev. 21:2, 3.

b. *Communications*. In all religions we meet with the idea that the gods reveal their thoughts and will in some way. The usual representation is that

THE PRINCIPIUM COGNOSCENDI EXTERNUM (REVELATION)

they do this by means of natural phenomena, such as the constellation of the stars, the flight of birds, the intestines of sacrificial animals, and so on. But alongside of this there is another, according to which they do it through the mediation of men in the capacity of soothsayers, visionaries, interpreters of dreams, diviners, consulters with familiar spirits and others claiming special powers. In a parallel line of thought Scripture teaches us that God revealed His thoughts and His will in various ways. Sometimes He spoke with an audible voice and in human language, Gen. 2:16; 3:8-19; 4:6-15; 6:13; 9:1, 8. 12; 32:26; Ex. 19:9 f.; Deut. 5:4, 5; I Sam. 3:4. In other cases He adapted Himself to the use of forms that were rather common among the nations, as the lot and Urim and Thummim.[1] The dream was a very common means of revelation, Num. 12:6; Deut. 13:1-6; I Sam. 28:6; Joel 2:28, and was used repeatedly in revelations to non-Israelites, Gen. 20:3-6; 31:24; 40:5; 41:1-7; Judg. 7:13; Dan. 2; 4:4 ff; Matt. 2:12. A closely related but higher form of revelation was the vision. It was in this form that the Lord often revealed Himself to the prophets. As a rule they did not receive these visions while they were in a state of ecstasy, in which their own mental life was held in abeyance, but in a state in which their intelligence was fully alert. In some cases the visions seem to have been objective, but in others they were clearly subjective, though not the products of their own minds, but of a supernatural factor. In distinction from the true prophets, the false prophets brought messages out of their own hearts. The following are some of the passages that speak of this form of revelation, Isa. 1:1; 2:1; 6:1; Jer. 1:11; Ezek. 8:2; Dan. 7:2, 7; 8:1, 2; Amos 7:1; 8:1; 9:1; Zech. 1:8, 18; 2:1; 3:1. Most generally, however, God revealed Himself to the prophets by some inner communication of the truth, of which the method is not designated. After the prophets received their revelations of God, they in turn communicated them to the people, and habitually designate their message to the people as *debhar Yahweh*, the Word of God. In the New Testament Christ appears as the true, the highest, and, in a sense, the only prophet. As the Logos He is the perfect revelation of God, Himself the source of all prophecy, and as the Mediator He receives the fulness of the Spirit in preparation for His prophetic work, John 3:34. He communicated the Spirit to His disciples, not only as the Spirit of regeneration and sanctification, but also as the Spirit of revelation and illumination, Mark 13:11; Luke 12:12; John 14:17; 15:26; 16:13; 20:22; Acts 6:10; 8:29.

c. *Miracles*. Finally, we also find in all religions a belief in the special intervention of the gods in times of need. The practice of magic is widespread, in which men seek to make the divine power subservient to them by the use of mysterious means, such as sacred words, magic formulas, amulets, and so on. Little understood powers of the human soul were often applied to the performance of so-called miracles. At the present day we often see the operation of these occult powers in spiritualism, theosophy, telepathy, and hypnotism. Scripture clearly testifies to the fact that God also revealed Himself in

---
1. Cf. Article on *Lapidaria* in the *Enc. of Rel. and Ethics*, IV, 813.

miracles. That miracles are also regarded in Scripture as means of revelation, is evident from the following passages: Deut. 4:32-35; Ps. 106:8; John 2:11; 5:36; 10:37, 38; Acts 4:10. Word-and fact-revelation go hand in hand in the Bible, the former explaining the latter, and the latter giving concrete embodiment to the former. It is especially from this point of view that the miracles of Scripture should be studied. They are designated by various names. Sometimes they are called *niphla'oth, mophthim,* Gr. *terata*, names which point to the unusual in the miracle, that which fills men with amazement. Again, they are called *gebhuroth, ma'asim,* Gr. *dunameis*, to indicate that they are revelations of a special power of God. Finally, they are also designated as *'othoth,* Gr. *semeia,* since they are signs of a special presence of God and often symbolize spiritual truths. The miracles are founded in the creation and preservation of all things, which is a perpetual miracle of God. At the same time they are made subservient to the work of redemption. They serve repeatedly to punish the wicked and to help or deliver the people of God. They confirm the words of prophecy and point to the new order that is being established by God. The miracles of Scripture culminated in the incarnation, which is the greatest and most central miracle of all. Christ Himself is the miracle in the most absolute sense of the word. In Him creation is again brought back to its pristine beauty, for His work results in the *apokatastasis* or restoration of all things, Acts 3:21.

3. THE CONTENTS OF SPECIAL REVELATION. It goes without saying that the knowledge of God forms the content of special revelation. In the nature of the case all revelation of God is self-revelation. God reveals Himself in nature and history, but the study of these is not necessarily theology, since both can be studied simply as they are in themselves, apart from their revelational implications. It is only when they are contemplated in relation to God and considered *sub specie aeternitatis*, that they assume the character of a revelation and enable us to know something of God. God is also the content of special revelation. The difference between general and special revelation does not primarily consist in this that the latter, in distinction from the former, is in all its parts and in every way strictly supernatural, but more particularly in this that it is a revelation of the *gratia specialis*, and therefore gives rise to the Christian religion of redemption. It is a revelation of the way of salvation. While general revelation gives prominence to the *theiotes* (Rom. 1:20), the divine greatness of God, His absolute power and infinite wisdom, special revelation reveals with increasing clearness the triune God in His personal distinctions, and the divine economy of redemption. It reveals a God who is on the one hand holy and righteous, but on the other hand also merciful and gracious. Three points deserve particular attention in connection with special revelation.

a. *It is a historical revelation.* The content of special revelation was gradually unfolded in the course of the centuries. This is clearly demonstrated in the *historia revelationis,* sometimes called Biblical Theology. This study shows that special revelation is controlled by a single thought, namely, that

God graciously seeks and restores fallen man to His blessed communion. There is a constant coming of God to man in theophany, prophecy, and miracle, and this coming reaches its highest point in the incarnation of the Son of God, which in turn leads to the indwelling of the Holy Spirit in the Church. The divine *telos*, towards which the whole of revelation moves, is described in Rev. 21:3: "Behold, the tabernacle of God is with men, and He shall dwell with them, and they shall be His peoples, and God Himself shall be with them and be their God."

b. *It is both word and fact-revelation.* The Socinians were undoubtedly wrong in holding that special revelation merely serves the purpose of furnishing man complete information respecting God and the duty of man; but Barth is equally wrong when he speaks as if the revelation of God is factual rather then verbal, and consists in redemptive acts rather than in a communication of knowledge. Special revelation does not consist exclusively in word and doctrine, and does not merely address itself to the intellect. This is more clearly understood at present than it was formerly. The Old Testament revelation is not found in the law and the prophets only, but also in theophany and miracle, and in the whole history of Israel. And in the New Testament Christ is not only prophet, but also priest and king. He is not merely the Word, but also the appearance and servant of God. He is the personal revelation of God's righteousness and holiness on the one hand, and of His mercy and grace on the other. And when the apostles enter the world with their message of redemption, not only their words, but also their charismatic gifts and miracles were revelations of God. The view, once widely held, that revelation consists exclusively in a communication of doctrine, was clearly one sided. At present, however, some go to the other extreme, equally one-sided, that revelation consists only in a communication of power and life. It finds expression in the familiar slogan, that "Christianity is not a doctrine, but a life."

c. *It is a soteriological revelation.* Special revelation is a revelation of salvation, and aims at the redemption of the entire man, both in his being and in his consciousness. This must be maintained over against a false intellectualism, which connects salvation with historical faith, as if the only thing that is necessary is the correction of the error, and the removal of the darkness, of the understanding. But in combatting this view, we should not go to the other extreme. Though God's special revelation is thoroughly soteriological, this does not mean that it consists only in a communication of life. The entire man is corrupted by sin and needs redemption. Sin also includes the lie, the power of error, and the darkness of the understanding, and therefore revelation must also be a communication of truth. Not only grace, but also truth came by Jesus Christ, John 1:17. He is the way, because He is the truth and the life, John 14:6.

4. THE PURPOSE OF SPECIAL REVELATION. In speaking of the purpose of revelation we may distinguish between its final end and its proximate aim. The final end can only be found in God. God reveals Himself, in order to rejoice in the manifestation of His virtues, especially as these shine forth in the

work of redemption and in redeemed humanity. The proximate aim of revelation, however, is found in the complete renewal of sinners, in order that they may mirror the virtues and perfections of God. If we bear in mind that revelation aims at the renewal of the entire man, we shall realize that it cannot seek the realization of its aim merely by teaching man and enlightening the understanding (Rationalism), or by prompting man to lead a virtuous life (Moralism), or by awakening the religious emotions of man (Mysticism). The purpose of revelation is far more comprehensive than any one of these, and even more inclusive than all of them taken together. It seeks to deliver from the power of sin, of the devil, and of death, the entire man, body and soul, with all his talents and powers, and to renew him spiritually, morally, and ultimately also physically, to the glory of God; and not only the individual man, but mankind as an organic whole; and mankind not apart from the rest of creation, but in connection with that whole creation, of which it forms an organic part. This purpose also determines the limits of special revelation. The historical process of revelation may be said to reach its end in a measure in Christ. Yet it does not end with the ascension of Christ. This is followed by the outpouring of the Holy Spirit and the special operation of gifts and powers under the guidance of the apostolate. Such a continued revelation was necessary, in order to ensure special revelation a permanent place in the midst of the world, and that not only in Scripture, but also in the life of the Church. But after the revelation in Christ, appropriated and made effective in the Church, has thus been introduced into the world, a new dispensation begins. Then special revelation ceases and no new constitutive elements are added. The work of Christ in furnishing the world with an objective revelation of God is finished. But the redemption wrought by Christ must still be applied, and this requires a constant operation of the Holy Spirit, always in connection with the objective revelation, for the renewal of man in his being and consciousness. By the Spirit of Christ man is led to accept the truth revealed in Scripture, and becomes a new creature in Christ Jesus, making God's revelation the rule of his life, and thus aiming at the glorification of God. This representation is not in harmony with that of the Theology of Crisis, except in that which is said respecting the purpose of revelation. Says Barth: "The revelation, Jesus Christ, is the work in which God Himself *restores* the shattered *order* of the relation between Himself and man. We must always apprehend the revelation as this work of restoration, whether we seek to apprehend it relatively to its essence or its tokens. A shattered relation between God and man has to be restored; hence the work of God, if it is not to consist in abandoning man or in annihilating what He has created, must consist in revelation."[1] Neither Barth nor Brunner believe in a completed, and now objectively existing, revelation. They stress the fact that revelation is simply God speaking, and at the same time, creatively, eliciting from man the desired response. The response is wrought in man by the Holy Spirit through the word of revelation itself. Without it there is no revelation, though there are tokens of it. The

---

1. *Revelation*, p. 75.

word of revelation was addressed to prophets and apostles in the days of old, and is still addressed to men up to the present time, and may in that sense be called continuous, or, perhaps better, frequentative. The revelation is never completed and never becomes an object on which man can lay hold. This refusal to ascribe to the divine revelation an objective character seems to be based fundamentally on an idealistic conception of an object. "An object," says Brunner, "is what I can think myself; a subject is what I cannot think. In my thinking it becomes an object."[1] To regard revelation as an object would seem to put man in control of it. The question may be raised, whether on this view God's revelation is not in the last analysis simply equivalent to the calling of God in Christ Jesus, made effective by the Holy Spirit. If this is really what is meant, it naturally follows that is continues up to the present time.

QUESTIONS FOR FURTHER STUDY: What is the relation between religion and revelation? In how far can we maintain that all religion originates in revelation? Why is it better to speak of general and special, than of natural and supernatural, revelation? Can the *necessary* manifestations of God as the ground of all existing things, or as the indwelling spirit in all creation, properly be called revelation? What is included in what is generally called natural revelation? Is this revelation static or progressive? Is there any such thing as a pure mind, which may serve as an undimmed mirror of natural revelation? How do they who apply the doctrine of evolution to the history of revelation conceive of what we call special revelation? How do the Gentiles testify to the need of special revelation? Does the existence of revelation depend on its subjective apprehension?

REFERENCES: Bavinck, *Geref. Dogm.* I, pp. 291-369; Kuyper, *Enc. der Heil. Godgel.*, II, pp. 205-241; Warfield, *Revelation and Inspiration*, pp. 3-49; Orr, *Revelation and Inspiration*, pp. 1-154; Mead, *Supernatural Revelation*, pp. 1-278; Fisher, *Nature and Method of Revelation*, pp. 1-86; Ladd, *The Doctrine of Sacred Scriptures* II, pp. 302-451; Smith, *Introduction to Chr. Theol.*, pp. 84-187; Ewald, *Revelation, Its Nature and Record*, pp. 1-299; Given, *Revelation, Inspiration, and the Canon*, pp. 9-103; McGregor, *The Revelation and the Record*; Sabatier, *Outlines of a Philosophy of Religion*, pp. 32-66; Baillie, *The Interpretation of Religion*, pp. 71-76, 449-470; id., *Our Knowledge of God*, pp. 3-43; Dickie, *Revelation and Response*; Lewis, *A Philosophy of the Christian Revelation*; Camfield, *Revelation and the Holy Spirit* (Barthian); Barth, *The Doctrine of the Word of God*; Brunner, *The Word and the World*; *Revelation* (edited by Baillie and Martin); Gilson, *Reason and Revelation in the Middle Ages. The Word of God and the Reformed Faith*. pp. 51-79, 102-111.

D. Special Revelation and Scripture

1. HISTORICAL VIEWS OF THE RELATION BETWEEN THE TWO.

a. *In the patristic period.* The Gnostics and Marcion had erroneous views respecting the Bible, but the early Church Fathers regarded it in all its parts as the revealed Word of God. They frankly spoke of it as inspired, but did not yet have a clear conception of its inspiration. Justin and Athenagoras clearly thought of the writers as passive under the divine influence, and compared them to a lyre in the hands of a player. Clement of Alexandria and Tertullian asserted that both the Old and the New Testament were equally inspired, and as such constituted the infallible Word of God. Eusebius regarded it as presumptious to admit the possibility of error in the sacred books; and Augustine said that the apostles wrote what Christ dictated. Chrysostom called the prophets "the mouth of God," and Gregory the Great spoke of the Holy

---

1. *The Word and the World*, p. 24.

Spirit as the real author of Scripture. All this goes to show that these Church Fathers regarded the Bible as the Word of God, and therefore identified it with the divine revelation.

    b. *During the Middle Ages.* The firm belief in the Bible as the Word of God was not shaken during the Middle Ages. At the same time the thought was developed that there is not only a *written,* but also an *oral,* revelation of God. The idea of an apostolic tradition, handed down from generation to generation, gradually gained currency. This tradition was considered necessary for the establishment of the authority of Scripture, and for the determination of its proper meaning. It was said that without the guidance of tradition Scripture could be made to speak in so many discordant ways that its authority was destroyed altogether. The development of this theory was detrimental to the proper conception of Scripture. It is true, the Bible was still regarded as the infallible Word of God, but its authority and proper meaning was made dependent on tradition, and that means, on the Church. The importance ascribed to so-called apostolic tradition even involved a denial of the absolute necessity, the sufficiency, and the perspicuity of the Bible.

    c. *At the time of the Reformation.* The Reformers took position over against the Roman Catholic Church on this point. When they spoke of the Word of God, they had the Bible, and the Bible only, in mind. They rejected the authority of what was called apostolic tradition, and acknowledged the Bible only as the final authority and the absolute norm in all matters of faith and conduct. Instead of admitting its dependence on the testimony of the Church, they boldly declared its *autopistia.* Though they did not yet develop the doctrine of inspiration as fully as it was developed by seventeenth century theologians, it is quite evident from their writings that they regarded the whole Bible as the inspired Word of God in the strictest sense of the word. Though it has often been said by liberal theologians that they drew a distinction between the divine revelation and Scripture, and conceived of the former, not as identical with, but as contained in, the former; and though this view is now echoed by the representatives of the Theology of Crisis in a slightly different way,—this contention cannot bear close scrutiny. On the basis of their writings it must be maintained that the Reformers identified the divine revelation and Scripture. It was especially in the seventeenth century that the doctrine of the perfections of Scripture was developed.

    d. *In modern theology.* Under the influence of Rationalism strong opposition arose to the strict conception of the Bible as the infallible Word of God. Various philosophical and scientific, critical and historical, studies served to undermine the prevalent belief in the supernatural, and therefore also the doctrine of the divine inspiration of Scripture. The old conception of the Bible as the infallible Word of God was brushed aside as untenable, and several other views of it were suggested as alternatives, but not a single one of them has been able to entrench itself in the hearts and minds of Christian people in general. For a time the idea was rather popular that the Bible is partly human and partly divine, and it became rather popular to say that the divine revelation is *contained* in the Bible, and that parts of the Bible are therefore inspired. But it soon became evident that it was impossible to say where the divine ended and the human began, or what parts of the Bible were, and what parts were not, inspired. Others discarded the idea of inspiration and simply regarded the Bible as the human record of a divine revelation. Idealistic philosophy, with its doctrine of the divine immanence, and the subjectivism of Schleiermacher, led to a new conception of both revelation and inspiration. Inspiration came to be regarded as a special divine illumination, differing only in degree from the spiritual illumination of Christians in general; and revelation, as the resulting heightened insight into the nature of things. This in course of time led on to a certain identification of revelation and human discovery. On this view the Bible becomes a record of rather exceptional human experiences,—a record which is purely human. The Theology of Crisis is an attempt to restore the idea of revelation as a supernatural act on the part of God to its rightful place. But it also disowns the doctrine of the infallible inspiration of Scripture, and therefore does not identify the revelation of God and the Bible. The Bible is merely a human witness to the divine revelation, which may, just because it witnesses to the revelation, be called the Word of God in a secondary sense[1].

2. THE REFORMED CONCEPTION OF THE RELATION BETWEEN THE TWO. According to the great Reformers of the sixteenth century the special revelation of God was given permanent form in Scripture. This idea is not in itself anything out of the ordinary. Among all cultured nations we find magical formulas, liturgical texts, ritual tracts, ceremonial laws, and historical and mythological literature, connected with their religious life. Several religions have holy books, to which divine authority is ascribed, and which serve as rules of doctrine and practice. Every prominent religion possesses a dogma which is expressed in language and assumes a permanent form in writing. Christianity forms no exception to the rule in that respect. It was of the utmost importance for the special revelation of God that it should be embodied in writing, because it was given in the course of many centuries and comprises deeds and events that are not repeated, but belong to the past, so that the knowledge of them would soon be lost in oblivion, if they were not recorded and thus preserved for posterity. And it was important that this knowledge should not be lost, since the divine revelation contains eternal truths, that are pregnant with meaning for all times, for all peoples, and under all circumstances. Therefore God provided for its inscripturation, so that His revelation now comes to us, not in the form of deeds and events, but as a description of these. In order to guard it against volatilization, corruption and falsification, He gave it permanent form in writing. From this it follows that there is a very close connection between special revelation and Scripture.

---

1. The Word of God and the Reformed Faith pp. 51-79; 102-111.

It should be pointed out, however, that the word 'revelation' is not always used in the same sense. It may serve to denote the direct, supernatural communications of God to man, which were far more frequent in the old dispensation than in the new, and culminated in the Word made flesh. If the word 'revelation' be understood in that sense, then it cannot be said that special revelation is identical with the Bible, but only that it is contained or recorded in the Bible. Scripture contains a great deal that was not so communicated by God. It should be borne in mind, however, that this does not justify the distinction, sometimes made in modern theology, between the Word of God as divine and its record as human. Neither does it warrant the unqualified statement that the Bible *is not*, but merely *contains* the Word of God. The terms 'Word of God' and 'special revelation' are also used in a sense in which they are identical with 'Scripture.' In most cases revelation or the direct self-communication of God preceded its inscripturation. The prophets usually received their communications some time before they committed them to writing, Jer. 25:13; 30:1, 2; 36:2. This is true of the apostles as well. When they received the highest revelation of God in Jesus Christ, they did not at once record it for future generations, but only after the lapse of several years, and even then they did not record everything that was revealed, John 20:30; 21:25. It may be that some things were revealed to them while they were writing. Moreover, in some cases men who received no direct revelations themselves yet recorded them for the future. In view of all this it may be said that there is a sense in which we must distinguish between special revelation and Scripture.

But the term 'revelation' may also be used in a broader sense. It can be applied to that whole complex of redemptive truths and facts, which is recorded in Scripture and has its guarantee as a divine revelation in the fact that the whole of Scripture is infallibly inspired by the Holy Spirit. In that sense the entire Bible from Genesis to Revelation, and it only, is for us God's special revelation. It is only through Scripture that we receive any knowledge of the direct revelations of God in the past. We know absolutely nothing about God's revelations among Israel through the prophets and finally in Christ, except from the Bible. If this is set aside, we abandon the whole of God's special revelation, including that in Christ. It is only through the word of the apostles that we can have communion with Christ. Consequently, it is unthinkable that God gave a special revelation and then took no measures to preserve it inviolate for coming generations. Scripture derives its significance exactly from the fact that it is the book of revelation. By means of Scripture God constantly carries His revelation into the world and makes its content effective in the thought and life of man. It is not merely a narrative of what happened years ago, but the perennial speech of God to man. Revelation lives on in Scripture and brings even now, just as it did when it was given, light, life, and holiness. By means of that revelation God continues to renew sinners in their being and consciousness. Scripture is the Holy Spirit's chief instrument for the extension and guidance of the Church, for the perfecting of the saints, and for the building up of the body of Jesus Christ. It forms a lasting bond of union between heaven and earth, between Christ and His Church, and between God and His people. In it we hear ever anew the voice of God, for it remains the inspired Word of God. And it will not have served its purpose fully until the new creation is completed, when all the children of God will be inspired and will all be fully taught of the Lord.

IV. THE INSPIRATION OF SCRIPTURE

A. The Doctrine of Inspiration in History

Revelation and inspiration stand in the closest possible relation to each other. As far as special revelation is concerned, it may be said that the one is inconceivable without the other. Peter tells us that "no prophecy ever came by the will of man: but men spake from God, being moved by the Holy Spirit." II Pet. 1:21. The recognition of the Bible as the special revelation of God depends on the conviction that its authors were inspired by the Holy Spirit. But, however closely related the two may be, they should not be identified. Dr. Hodge correctly calls attention to the fact that they differ both as to their object and in their effects. "The object or design of revelation is the communication of knowledge. The object or design of inspiration is to secure infallibility in teaching . . . . The effect of revelation was to render its recipient wiser. The effect of inspiration was to preserve him from error in teaching."[1] The doctrine of inspiration was not always held in the same form, and therefore a brief statement of its history would seem to be desirable.

1. BEFORE THE REFORMATION. In a sense it may be said that this doctrine had no history before the Reformation, because it remained essentially the same from the first century down to the sixteenth. Nevertheless it will serve a useful purpose to call specific attention to the fact that throughout all these centuries the Church stood firm in the conviction that the Bible is the inspired, and therefore infallible, Word of God. It is a well known fact that the Jews held the strictest view of inspiration. They regarded first of all the Law as divinely and infallibly inspired, and therefore ascribed to it absolute divine authority, and afterwards ascribed the same inviolable character and authority to the Prophets and the Holy Writings. This view passed right over into the Christian Church. Even liberal scholars, who reject that strict view of inspiration, feel constrained to admit that Jesus and the New Testament writers also held the same view. The early Church Fathers had the same exalted view of the Bible, as appears abundantly from their writings. Sanday admits that from the very first they are found using expressions, which even point to verbal inspiration.[2] Some of their expressions certainly seem to suggest that the writers of the books of the Bible were passive under the influence of the Holy Spirit, and therefore point to a mechanical conception of inspiration. But Dr. Orr calls attention to the fact that the general trend of their teaching shows that it was not their intention to teach a doctrine of inspiration, which involved

---

1. *Syst. Theol. I*, p. 155.
2. *Inspiration*, p. 34.

the suppression of the human consciousness, that Origen contended against such a view, and that Montanism, which held it, was condemned by the Church.[1] Between the time of the early Church Fathers and that of the Reformation the prevailing opinion in the Church did not differ essentially from that previously held. The Scholastics shared the common conviction of the Church, and merely tried to give a more precise definition of some of the details of the doctrine of inspiration. It must be admitted, however, that equal inspiration was ascribed to apostolic tradition, and that in practice this tended to weaken the consciousness of the absolute authority of the written Word of God. Moreover, there were some Mystics, who gloried in a special illumination and in revelations of the divine presence within, and manifested a tendency to undervalue the supernatural inspiration of the writers of the Bible, and to reduce it to the level of that gracious inner teaching which all Christians alike enjoyed. But their subjectivism did not seriously affect the view that was held in the Church at large.

2. AFTER THE REFORMATION. It has become quite the vogue with those who are opposed to what Dr. Warfield calls "the church-doctrine of inspiration," to saddle their own loose views on the great Reformers of the sixteenth century. They find in the works of Luther and Calvin a few expressions which seem to reflect a certain freedom in dealing with canonical questions, and then hastily conclude from this that these great men did not share the current doctrine of inspiration. But why should they rely on mere inferences, when these great Reformers use several expressions and make many plain statements, which are clearly indicative of the fact that they held the strictest view of inspiration, and that this view was not at all, as the opponents claim, an invention of Protestant Scholasticism in the seventeenth century. They even speak of the Holy Spirit as the author of every part of Scripture, and of the human writers as having written what was dictated to them. Such expressions had been common from the earliest times. At the same time it is quite evident from their teachings in general that inspiration, as they conceived of it, did not suppress the individuality and the intellectual activity of the human authors. Seeberg speaks of Calvin as the author of the strict, seventeenth century view of inspiration. The only difference on this point between the Reformers and the following generation of theologians is, that the latter made the subject of inspiration an object of special study and worked it out in details, and that some manifested a tendency to "reduce the inspired man, when under the influence of the Spirit, to the level of an unconscious and unintelligent instrument." (Bannerman) This tendency also found expression in one of the Confessions, namely, the *Formula Consensus Helvetica*, drawn up in 1675 in opposition to the loose views of the school of Saumur. This Confession never found wide acceptance as an ecclesiastical standard.

At a later date, however, when Rationalism made its influence felt, Le Clerc (1657-1736) impugned the strict infallibility of Scripture and asserted

---

1. *Revelation and Inspiration,* p. 207.

the existence of errors in the record, and many of the apologists, who took up the defense, admitted his contentions and felt constrained to have recourse to the theory of an inspiration, differing in degrees in various parts of the Bible, and thus allowing for imperfections and errors in some portions of Scripture. This was a theory that allowed of various modifications. One of these, which enjoyed considerable popularity for a while, was the theory of a *partial* inspiration, that is, an inspiration limited to parts of the Bible, but it soon became evident that it was impossible to reach a unanimous opinion as to the exact extent of inspiration. Since this view will be discussed later on, it is not necessary to enlarge upon it here.

A radically different theory owes its origin especially to Schleiermacher. In distinction from the theory of partial inspiration, which at least ascribed strict inspiration to some parts of Scripture, it altered the character of inspiration altogether by excluding the supernatural element. It held inspiration to be (to express it in the words of Bannerman) "the natural, or at most the gracious, agency of God illuminating the rational or the spiritual consciousness of a man, so that out of the fulness of his own Christian understanding and feelings he may speak or write the product of his own religious life and beliefs."[1] Here inspiration is changed to a divine illumination, differing only in degree from that of Christians in general. The special, supernatural and miraculous operation of the Holy Spirit, is superseded by one of His ordinary operations in the lives of believers. Many of the works on inspiration, written since the days of Schleiermacher are simply variations on this general theme. Some, such as Wegscheider and Parker, went even farther, and spoke of a purely natural operation, common to all men. Such works as those of Lee, Bannerman, McIntosh, Patton, Orr, Warfield, and others naturally form exceptions to the rule. Sad to say, Barth and Brunner also reject the doctrine of the infallible inspiration of Scripture, and regard it as a product of Protestant Scholasticism. Their own views still await clarification.

B. Scriptural Proof for the Inspiration of the Bible

The question arises, whether the record of the divine revelation, as well as the revelation itself, is from God, or whether God, after giving the revelation of redemption, simply left it to man to record this as best he could. Have we in Scripture a merely human or a divinely inspired record? And if God's special revelation was given by inspiration, how far does that inspiration extend? In seeking an answer to these and other similar questions, we turn to Scripture itself. This will not seem strange in view of the fact that for us the Bible is the only *principium cognoscendi externum* of theology. Just as the Bible contains a doctrine of God and man, of Christ and redemption, it also offers us a doctrine concerning itself; and we receive this in faith on the basis of the divine testimony. In saying this, we do not mean to intimate that Scripture contains a clear-cut and well formulated dogma of inspiration, but

---

1. *Inspiration of the Scriptures*, p. 142.

THE INSPIRATION OF SCRIPTURE

only that it supplies all the data that are necessary for the construction of such a dogma. We shall consider the Scriptural proof for the inspiration of the authors of Scripture under two headings: (1) proof for their inspiration considered apart from their writing; and (2) proof for their inspiration in writing the books of the Bible.

1. PROOFS FOR THE INSPIRATION OF THE SECONDARY AUTHORS OF SCRIPTURE CONSIDERED APART FROM THEIR WRITING. It may be well to point out first of all that the secondary authors of Scripture were inspired as the organs of divine revelation, even apart from their activity in recording the special revelation of God. Then it will appear that inspiration was deemed necessary for the immediate purpose of revelation. We derive our proof in this respect primarily from prophecy, or what may be called the prophetic inspiration, but also in part from the apostolic inspiration.

a. *Prophetic inspiration.* Several points deserve attention here: (1) *The nature of a prophet.* There are two classical passages in the Bible, which shed light on the Biblical conception of a prophet, namely, Ex. 7:1 and Deut. 18:18. According to these passages a prophet is simply the mouthpiece of God. He receives a message from God, and is in duty bound to transmit it to the people. In his capacity as a prophet of the Lord, he may not bring a message of his own, but only the message which he receives from the Lord. It is not left to his own discretion to determine what he shall say; this is determined for him by his Sender. For the message divinely entrusted to him He may not substitute another. (2) *The consciousness of the prophets.* The prophets of Israel knew that they were called of the Lord at a certain moment, sometimes contrary to their own desire, Ex. 3:1, ff.; I Sam. 3; Isa. 6; Jer. 1; Ezek. 1-3. They were conscious of the fact that the Lord had spoken to them, and in some cases even knew that He had put His words into their mouth, Num. 23:5; Deut. 18:18; Jer. 1:9; 5:14. This consciousness was so strong that they even designated the time and place when and where the Lord spoke to them, and distinguished between times in which He did, and times in which He did not, speak to them, Isa. 16:13, 14; Jer. 3:6; 13:3; 26:1; 27:1; 33:1; Ezek. 3:16; 8:1; 12:8. Hence they also made a sharp distinction between what the Lord revealed to them and what arose out of the depths of their own hearts, Num. 16:28; 24:13; I Kings 12:33; Neh. 6:8. They accused the false prophets of speaking out of their own hearts, without being sent of the Lord, Jer. 14:14; 23:16, 26; 29:9; Ezek. 13:2, 3, 6. When they addressed the people, they knew that they were not bringing their own word, but the word of the Lord, and this because the Lord demanded it of them, Jer. 20:7-9; Ezek. 3:4 ff.; Amos 3:8; Jonah 1:2. (3) *The prophetic formulae.* The prophetic formulae were also very significant in this respect. They were in themselves clear indications of the fact that the prophets were conscious of bringing a message that was inspired by the Lord. There is quite a variety of these formulae, but they all agree in ascribing the initiative to the Lord. The faithful watchmen on the walls of Zion were deeply impressed with the fact that they received the word, with which they came to the people, at the mouth of the Lord. They were ever mindful of the word of the Lord to Ezekiel: "Son of man, I have made thee a watchman unto the house of Israel: therefore hear the word at my mouth, and give them warning from me." Ezek. 3:17. Moreover, they clearly wanted the people to understand this. Such formulae as the following testify to this: "Thus saith the Lord," "Hear the word of the Lord," "The word that came to . . . from the Lord," "Thus the Lord showed me," "The burden of the word of the Lord." (4) *Failure to understand their own message.* The fact that the prophets sometimes failed to understand the message which they brought to the people, also goes to show that it came to them from without, and did not arise out of their own consciousness. Daniel brought a message which was entrusted to him, but declares that he did not understand it, Dan. 12:8, 9. Zechariah saw several visions, which contained messages for the people, but needed the help of an angel to interpret these for him, Zech. 1:9; 2:3; 4:4. And Peter informs us that the prophets, having brought their message respecting the sufferings and the following glory of Christ, often searched into the details of it, in order that they might understand it more clearly, I Pet. 1:10, 11.

b. *Apostolic inspiration.* The operation of the Holy Spirit after the day of Pentecost differed from that which the prophets in their official capacity enjoyed. The Holy Spirit came upon the prophets as a supernatural power and worked upon them from without. His action on them was frequently repeated, but was not continuous. The distinction between His activity and the mental activity of the prophets themselves was made to stand out rather clearly. On the day of Pentecost, however, He took up His abode in the hearts of the apostles and began to work upon them from within. Since He made their hearts His permanent abode, His action on them was no more intermittent but continuous, but even in their case the supernatural work of inspiration was limited to those occasions on which they served as organs of revelation. But because of the more inward character of all the Spirit's work, the distinction between His ordinary and His extraordinary work was not so perceptible. The supernatural does not stand out as clearly in the case of the apostles, as it did in the case of the prophets. Notwithstanding this fact, however, the New Testament contains several significant indications of the fact that the apostles were inspired in their positive oral teachings. Christ solemnly promised them the Holy Spirit in their teaching and preaching, Matt. 10:19, 20; Mark 13:11; Luke 12:11, 12; 21:14, 15; John 14:26; 15:26; 16:13. In the Acts of the Apostles we are told repeatedly that they taught "'being full of," or "filled with," the Holy Spirit. Moreover, it appears from the Epistles that in teaching the churches they conceived of their word as being in very deed the word of God, and therefore as authoritative, I Cor. 2:4, 13; I Thess. 2:13.

2. Proofs for the Inspiration of the Secondary Authors in Writing the Books of the Bible. The guidance of the Holy Spirit was not limited to the spoken word, but also extended to the written word. If God deemed it necessary to guide prophets and apostles in their oral teaching, which was

naturally limited to their contemporaries, it would seem to follow as a matter of course that He would consider it far more important to ensure them of divine guidance in committing His revelation to writing for all following generations. It is only in its written form that the Word of God is known in the world, and that His revelation is the continuous speech of God to man. And there are several indications in the New Testament that He did so guide the apostles. These are contained in certain general pehnomena, and in some direct assertions.

a. *Certain general phenomena.* (1) *Commands to write the word of the Lord.* Repeatedly the writers of the Old Testament are explicitly commanded to write what the Lord reveals unto them, Ex. 17:14; 34:27; Num. 33:2; Isa. 8:1; 30:8; Jer. 25:13; 30:2; 36:2, 27-32; Ezek. 24:1 f.; Dan. 12:4; Hab. 2:2. Some prophecies were evidently not intended to be spoken, but to be written for the careful consideration of the people, Jer. 29; 36:4ff., 27ff.; Ezek. 26; 27; 31; 32:39. In such cases the prophetic formulae naturally also refer to the written word. (2) *Suppression of the human factor.* In many of the prophecies the divine factor, as it were, overpowers the human. The prophetic word begins by speaking of God in the third person, and then, without any indication of a transition, continues in the first person. The opening words are words of the prophet, and then all at once, without any preparation of the reader for a change, the human author simply disappears from view, and the divine author speaks apparently without any intermediary, Isa. 10:12; 19:1, 2; Hos. 4:1-6; 6:1-4; Mic. 1:3-6; Zech. 9:4-6; 12:8, 9. Thus the word of the prophet passes right into that of the Lord without any formal transition. The two are simply fused, and thus prove to be one. Some passages clearly indicate that the word of the Lord and that of the prophet are equally authoritative, Jer. 25:3; 36:10, 11. Isaiah even speaks of his own written prophecies as "the book of Jehovah." 34:16. (3) *The designation of the Old Testament as he graphe or hai graphai.* In the New Testament we find that the Lord and the apostles, in their appeal to the Old Testament, frequently speak of it as *he graphe* (a term sometimes applied to a single passage of Scripture, Mark 12:10; Luke 4:21; John 19:36), or as *hai graphai* in view of the fact that it consists of several parts, Luke 24:27; Rom. 1:2. Cf. also *ta hiera grammata* in II Tim. 3:15. They evidently regarded this collection as authoritative. An appeal to it was equivalent to "God says," as appears from the fact that the formula *he graphe legein* (the Scripture says) is used interchangeably with others, which clearly indicate that what is quoted is the Word of God, and from cases in which the word quoted is really spoken by God in the Old Testament, Rom. 9:15-17; Gal. 3:8. (4) *Formulae of quotation.* The Lord and His apostles do not always use the same formula in quoting the Old Testament. Sometimes they simply say, "It is written," Matt. 4:4; John 6:45, or "Scripture says," Rom. 4:3; Gal. 4:30. In some cases they mention the human author, Matt. 15:7; 24:15, but frequently they name the primary author, that is, God or the Holy Spirit, Matt. 15:4; Heb. 1:5 ff.; 3:7. Paul in some cases personifies Scripture, so that it is represented as identical with God, Rom. 9:17; Gal. 3:8, 22; 4:30; cf. also Rom. 4:3; 10:11; 11:2; I Tim. 5:18. The writer of the Epistle to the Hebrews usually names the primary author, 1:5 ff.; 3:7; 4:3; 5:6; 7:21; 8:5, 8; 10:15, 16.

b. *Direct assertions.* There are several passages in which the divine authority of the Old Testament is clearly asserted, Matt. 5:17; Luke 16:17, 29, 31; John 10:35; Rom. 15:4; I Pet. 1:10-12; II Pet. 1:19, 21. This is true especially of the *locus classicus,* II Tim. 3:16: "All (every) Scripture is given by inspiration of God, and is profitable for teaching, for reproof, for correction, for instruction which is in righteousness." We read here in the original: *Pasa graphe theopneustos kai ophelimos pros didaskalian,* etc. This passage has been interpreted in various ways, and that not infrequently with the scarcely concealed intention of destroying its evidential value. On the basis of transcriptional evidence some proposed to leave out the word *kai,* but the weight of evidence clearly favors its retention. Because *pasa* stands without the article, some insist on translating *pasa graphe* by "every Scripture"; but such passages as Matt. 2:3; Acts 2:36; Eph. 2:21; 4:16; I Pet. 1:15, bear evidence of the fact that the word *pas* may mean "all" in the New Testament even when the article is wanting. Materially, it makes very little difference, whether we read "all Scripture," or "every Scripture," since the expression certainly refers back to *ta hiera grammata* in the 15th verse, and this serves to designate the Old Testament writings. There is also a strong tendency (cf. even the Am. Rev. Version) to regard *theopneustos,* not as the predicate, but as a part of the subject, and therefore to read: "All (or, "every") scripture inspired of God is also profitable for teaching," etc. But it would seem that, if it were so intended, the verb *estin* should have been used after *ophelimos,* and there is no good reason why *kai* should have been used before it. There is nothing that compels us to depart from the usual interpretation of the passage. In connection with this statement of Paul, the word of Peter in II Pet. 1:21 deserves special attention: "For no prophecy ever came by the will of man, but men spake from God being moved by the Holy Spirit." The writers of the New Testament were conscious of the guidance of the Holy Spirit in their writing, and therefore their written productions are authoritative, I Cor. 7:10; II Cor. 13:2, 3; Col. 4:16; I Thess. 2:13; II Thess. 3:14. Peter places the Epistles of Paul on a level with the writings of the Old Testament, II Pet. 3:15, 16. And Paul himself says: "If any man thinketh himself to be a prophet, let him take knowledge of the things which I write unto you, that they are the commandments of the Lord." I Cor. 14:37.

C. Nature and Extent of Its Inspiration

There has been no general agreement as to the nature and extent of the inspiration of Scripture, and with a view to a proper understanding of these, it may be well to consider the most important views that were held in course of time.

1. THE NATURE OF INSPIRATION. In dealing with the nature of inspiration, we shall consider first of all two erroneous views, which represent opposite extremes, and then state what we consider to be the correct view.

a. *Mechanical inspiration.* There is a rather common misunderstanding, against which we must be on our guard. It is often represented as if verbal inspiration were necessarily mechanical, but this is not the case. The two terms are certainly not synonymous, for they refer to different aspects of the work of inspiration, the one being an indication of the extent, and the other, of the nature of inspiration. And while it is true that mechanical inspiration is from the nature of the case verbal, it is not true that verbal inspiration is necessarily mechanical. It is quite possible to believe that the guidance of the Holy extended to the choice of the words employed, but was not exercised in a mechanical way. According to the mechanical view of inspiration God dictated what the *auctores secundarii* wrote, so that the latter were mere amanuenses, mere channels through which the words of the Holy Spirit flowed. It implies that their own mental life was in a state of repose, and did not in any way contribute to the contents or form of their writings, and that even the style of Scripture is that of the Holy Spirit. This theory has very unfairly and rather persistently been ascribed by its opponents to all those who believe in verbal inspiration, even after these have repeatedly disclaimed that view. It must be admitted that some of the early Church Fathers, the Reformers, and some Lutheran and Reformed theologians of the seventeenth century occasionally used expressions that savoured of such a view; but it should be added that their general teachings clearly show that they did not regard the writers of the Bible as mere passive instruments, but as real authors, whose intellectual powers were alert and operative and who gave expression also to their individuality in their writings. As far as the Reformers are concerned, this appears very clearly from the fact that many of those who do not believe in any real doctrine of inspiration, vie with each other in their attempts to prove that Luther and Calvin did not hold the strict view of inspiration which was current in the seventeenth century. The great historical Confessions, with the exception of the *Formula Consensus Helvetica* (1675) do not express themselves as to the precise nature of the inspiration of Scripture. The one Confession named comes closest to the presentation of a mechanical view of inspiration, but this Confession was recognized only by a few cantons in Switzerland, the land of its birth, and was even there set aside by a following generation. Moreover we should not lose sight of the fact that this Confession represents a reaction against the loose views on inspiration, which were sponsored by Cappelus of the school of Saumur. It may well be doubted, whether there ever has been a considerable number of Reformed theologians who consciously adopted a mechanical view of inspiration. This view is not found in our own *Confessio Belgica*, and is certainly not now the accepted doctrine of Reformed theology. Reformed theologians now generally have an organic conception of inspiration. They do not believe that the *auctores secundarii* of Scripture were mere passive instruments in the hand of God; that they were mere amanuenses who wrote what God dictated; that what they wrote did not in any sense of the word originate in their own consciousness; nor that their style in simply the style of the Holy Spirit. To the contrary, they adopt a view which recognizes them as real authors and does full justice to their personal share in the production of their writings.

b. *Dynamical inspiration.* If we desire on the one hand to avoid the mechanical view of inspiration, we are equally desirous, on the other hand, to steer clear of the so-called dynamical view. The term 'dynamic inspiration' is sometimes used to denote what we would call 'organic inspiration',[1] but is employed here to designate the theory of inspiration that owes its inception to the teachings of Schleiermacher. This theory renounces the idea of a direct operation of the Holy Spirit on the production of the books of the Bible, and substitutes for it a general inspiration of the writers, which really amounts to nothing more than a spiritual illumination, differing only in degree from the spiritual illumination of Christians in general. Strictly speaking, it eliminates the supernatural, transforms the idea of inspiration, and transfers it from the intellectual to the moral sphere. The writers of the New Testament (the Old Testament is not even taken into consideration) were holy men, who moved about in the presence of Jesus and lived in the sphere of revelation, which naturally had a sanctifying influence on their character, thought, and speech. Says Ladd: "The general conception of inspiration is that of a divine influence coming like a breath of wind, or some other fluid, into the soul of man, and producing there a transformation."[2] Bannerman correctly says that in Schleiermacher's theology inspiration is held to be "the natural, or at most the gracious, agency of God illuminating the rational or the spiritual consciousness of a man, so that out of the fulness of his own Christian understanding and feelings he may speak or write the product of his own religious life and beliefs."[3] This view is entirely subjective, makes the Bible a purely human product, and allows for the possibility of errors in the Word of God. Inspiration so conceived was a permanent characteristic of the writers, and in so far naturally also influenced their writings, but was by no means a supernatural operation of the Holy Spirit, which served to qualify the writers for the specific task of committing the divine revelation to writing. It terminated on the writers rather than on their writings. While it naturally influenced their writings, it did not affect them all in the same measure. On the one hand the Bible contains the highest truths, but on the other hand it is still imperfect and fallible. This theory, which is also called the theory of *spiritual insight* or *spiritual intuition*, certainly does not do justice to the Scriptural data on inspiration. It robs the Bible of its supernatural character and destroys its infallibility.

1. f.i. by Girardeau, *Discussions of Theological Questions*, p. 295.
2. *The Doctrine of Sacred Scriptures* II, p. 468.
3. *Inspiration of the Scriptures*, p. 142.

c. *Organic inspiration.* The term 'organic inspiration' is also somewhat ambiguous, because some use it to designate what is usually called 'dynamic inspiration.' The term 'organic' serves to stress the fact that God did not employ the writers of the books of the Bible in a mechanical way, just as a writer wields a pen; did not whisper into their ears the words which He wanted them to write; but acted upon them in an organic way, in harmony with the laws of their own inner being. He used them just as they were, with their character and temperament, their gifts and talents, their education and culture, their vocabulary, diction, and style. He illumined their minds, prompted them to write, repressed the influence of sin on their literary activity, and guided them in an organic way in the choice of their words and in the expression of their thoughts. This view is clearly most in harmony with the representations of Scripture. It testifies to the fact that the writers of the books of the Bible were not passive but active. In some cases they searched out beforehand the things of which they wrote, Luke 1:1-4. The authors of the books of Samuel, Kings, and Chronicles repeatedly refer to their sources. The messages of the prophets are generally determined by historical circumstances, and the New Testament Epistles also have an occasional character. The psalmists often sing of their own experiences, of sin and forgiveness, Ps. 32 and 51, of surrounding dangers and gracious deliverances, Ps. 48 and 116. Each one of the writers has his own style. Alongside of the sublime poetry and poetical language of poets and prophets, we have the common prose of the historians; alongside of the pure Hebrew of Isaiah, the Aramaic-tinted Hebrew of Daniel; and alongside of the dialectic style of Paul, the simple language of John. The writers put on their literary productions their own personal stamp and the stamp of their times. Thus the Bible itself testifies to the fact that it was not mechanically inspired. The Holy Spirit used the writers as He Himself had formed them for their task, without in any way suppressing their personality. He qualified them and guided them, and thus inspired the books of Scripture organically.

2. THE EXTENT OF INSPIRATION. Different views were held in the course of history, not only respecting the nature of inspiration, but also as to its extent. The three views that come into consideration here especially may be designated as partial inspiration, thought inspiration, and verbal inspiration.

a. *Partial inspiration.* Under the influence of eighteenth century Deism and Rationalism lax views of inspiration were zealously propagated and found ready acceptance in the theological world, and in some cases even met with adherents in the Churches. Le Clerc, who was originally a Reformed theologian, but later on became an Arminian professor at Amsterdam, denied the inspiration of many of the historical portions of Scripture, resolved that of the apostles into a sort of spiritual enlightenment and a strengthening of the faculties of the soul, and limited that of the prophets to the time when they received their revelations. From his time on it became quite common for theologians, who desired to maintain the doctrine of inspiration, at least in some sense of the word, to speak of degrees of inspiration. They distinguished between the doctrinal and the historical portions of Scripture, and regarded the former, containing essential truths, with which the writers were made acquainted by revelation, as plenarily inspired; and the latter, containing nonessential truths, of which the writers had knowledge apart from revelation, as only partially inspired, and as marred by inaccuracies and mistakes. There were also theologians, however, who were even more completely under the influence of Rationalism, and who accepted the idea of a partial inspiration devoid of supernaturalism. According to them the writers of the Bible simply enjoyed a special spiritual enlightenment and guidance, which offered no guarantee against all kinds of historical, chronological, archaeological, and scientific mistakes, but did make the writers reliable witnesses in moral and spiritual matters. Among those who adopt a partial inspiration of Scripture there is no unanimity whatsoever. Some would limit inspiration to doctrinal matters. others to the New Testament, others to the words of Jesus, and still others to the Sermon on the Mount. This shows as clearly as anything can that the theory is purely subjective, and lacks all objective basis. The moment one accepts it in any one of its many forms one has virtually lost one's Bible.

According to the Bible inspiration extends equally to all parts of the Word of God. The Law and the historical books, the Psalms and the Prophets, the Gospels and the Epistles,—they were all written under the guidance of the Holy Spirit, and are therefore all in the same measure *he graphe*. An appeal to any part of it, is an appeal to the Word of God, and therefore to God Himself. This is indicated in various ways. The Epistles of Paul are placed on a level with the writings of the Old Testament, which are clearly regarded as inspired and authoritative by Jesus and the apostles, II Pet. 3:15, 16. It should be noted that the New Testament contains quotations from twenty-five Old Testament books, and among these are several of a historical character, which in the estimation of some are least, if at all, inspired. The Lord Himself and the New Testament writers evidently regarded each one of these books as a part of *he graphe,* and ascribed to them divine authority. Moreover, there are several collective quotations, or catenae of quotations, that is, quotations gathered from several books, which are all advanced as equally authoritative to prove the same point, Rom. 3:10-18; Heb. 1:5-13; 2:12, 13. We cannot explain the interpenetration of the divine and the human factors in Scripture, any more than we can explain that of the two natures in Christ. Scripture presents itself to us as an organic whole, consisting of several parts, that are interrelated in various ways, and that find their unity in the central, all-controlling, and progressively unfolding, thought of God reaching out to man, in order to redeem him from sin and to bestow upon him the blessings of eternal salvation. And therefore we should not ask where the divine ends and the human begins, nor where the human ends and the divine begins. We might just as well ask where in man the soul ends and the body begins. No such line of demarcation can be pointed out. Scripture is in its entirety both the Word of God and the word of man.

b. *Thought inspiration.* Some who would defend the doctrine of inspiration against its complete denial, are of the opinion that the advocates of the doctrine should retrench somewhat, and speak of thought—rather than of word—inspiration. The thoughts, they say, were evidently divinely inspired, but the words in which they are clothed were freely chosen by the human authors, and that without any divine guidance. In that way they consider it possible to satisfy the requirements of the Biblical teaching respecting inspiration, and at the same time account for the imperfections and errors that are found in Scripture. But such an inspiration of thoughts without words is an anomaly, and is really inconceivable. Thoughts are formulated and expressed in words. Girardeau correctly remarks: "Accurate thought cannot be disjoined from language. Words are its vehicles both subjectively and objectively. When we think accurately and precisely, we think in words. To give the thought therefore, is to give the words."[1] And Dr. Orr, who would himself rather speak of plenary than of verbal inspiration, admits that the latter name expresses a true and important idea, where it "opposes the theory that revelation and inspiration have regard only to thoughts and ideas, while the language in which these ideas are clothed is left to the unaided faculty of the sacred penman." Moreover, he says: "Thought of necessity takes shape and is expressed in words. If there is inspiration at all, it must penetrate words as well as thought, must mould the expression, and make the language employed the living medium of the idea to be conveyed."[2] As we shall point out in the sequel, Scripture clearly teaches the inspiration of the words of Scripture.

c. *Verbal inspiration.* There are some who believe in the inspiration of every part of the Bible, but would rather not speak of verbal inspiration, because this is apt to suggest the mechanical idea that God dictated what the secondary authors wrote.[3] They would prefer to use the term "plenary inspiration." Others, however, reject the idea of verbal inspiration altogether, because they do not believe in any plenary inspiration. It may be well therefore to call particularly attention to the Scriptural data on this point. (1) *References to verbal communications.* The Pentateuch repeatedly refers to verbal communications of the Lord. The expressions, "The Lord said unto Moses" and "The Lord spoke unto Moses," serve so frequently to introduce a written message, that they almost have the force of a formula, Ex. 3 and 4; 6:1; 7:1; 8:1; 10:1; 12:1; Lev. 1:1; 4:1; 6:1, 24; 7:22, 28; 8:1; 11:1. The Lord certainly did not speak to Moses without words. The word of the Lord repeatedly came to Joshua in the same way, Jos. 1:1; 4:1; 6:2; 8:1. (2) *Prophets are conscious of bringing the very words of the Lord.* The prophets were conscious of the fact that the Lord spoke through them. Isaiah begins his prophecy with the words: "Hear, O heavens,

---

1. *Discussions of Theological Questions*, p. 324f.
2. *Rev. and Insp.*. p. 209.
3. Cf. Orr, *Revelation and Inspiration*, p. 209.

and give ear, O earth, for Jehovah hath spoken, 1:2; and he and other prophets constantly use the well known prophetic formulae, "Thus saith the Lord" and, "Hear the word of the Lord." Jeremiah even says: "Then Jehovah put forth His hand, and touched my mouth; and Jehovah said unto me, Behold, I have put my words in thy mouth," 1:9. In Ezekiel we read: "Son of man, go, get thee unto the house of Israel, and speak with my words unto them . . . . Son of man, all my words that I shall speak unto thee receive in thy heart, and hear with thine ears. And go, get thee to them of the captivity, unto the children of thy people, and speak unto them, and tell them, Thus saith the Lord Jehovah," 3:4, 10, 11. It is not necessary to multiply the examples. (3) *The apostles speak of the words of the Old Testament and of their own words as the words of God.* Paul explicitly says that he gives instruction, not in words of his own choosing, but in Spirit-taught words, I Cor. 2:13, and claims that Christ is speaking in him, II Cor. 13:3. And in the Epistle to the Hebrews several words of the Old Testament are quoted, not as words of some human author, but as words of God, or of the Holy Spirit, 1:5 ff.; 2:11-13; 3:7; 4:4, 5, 7; 8:8; 10:15-17. (4) *Arguments based on a single word.* There are three cases in which Jesus and Paul base a whole argument on the use of a single word of the Old Testament, John 10:35; Matt. 22:43-45; Gal. 3:16. In doing this they give clear evidence of the fact that they regard the separate words as inspired and infallible, and that the readers share their conviction. If this were not the case, they would not have been able to consider their arguments as conclusive.

D. Attempts to Discredit the Doctrine of Inspiration

Several attempts have been made to discredit or set aside the doctrine of inspiration. Of these the following may be considered as the most important.

1. THEY WHO DEFEND IT ARE REASONING IN A CIRCLE. We are often accused of reasoning in a circle, when we derive our proof for the inspiration of the Bible from Scripture itself. Because the Bible is true, we accept its testimony respecting its inspiration, and because it is inspired, we regard it as true. Apologetically, this argument can be met, and has frequently been answered. It is possible, for the sake of argument, to start out with the assumption that the books of the Bible are purely human productions, which, however, as the productions of eye-and ear-witnesses, which are known as men of high moral standing, can be regarded as entirely trustworthy. Then it can be shown that, according to these books, Christ and the apostles held the strictest view of the inspiration of the Old Testament. From that point it is quite possible to reach the conclusion that the Old Testament necessarily required a complement such as is found in the New Testament. And on the basis of this it can be said that therefore the whole Bible must be regarded as an inspired book. By reasoning in that fashion the circle is avoided. This line of argumentation is followed by Bannerman, Patton Warfield, Van Oosterzee, and others. But it is a question, whether the circle referred to is really as vicious as some would have us believe. Jesus evidently did not think so, when a similar objection was raised against His testimony concerning Himself as

the incarnate Word of God, John 8:13 f. In social life people frequently move in the same circle. If they are firmly convinced that a person is thoroughly reliable and trustworthy, they do not hesitate to receive his testimony concerning himself and his actions, when others accuse him of deception and dishonesty. Girardeau pertinently remarks: "Suppose we should use the argument: God declares that He is true; therefore God is true. Here God's truth would be proved by His truth. Would that be a vicious reasoning in a circle? The atheist might say, You assume that there is a God of truth. So we do, and so do all sensible men."[1] Through the testimony of the Holy Spirit in his heart the Christian stands in the unwavering faith that God is true in His revelation, and therefore it is a matter of course that he accepts the testimony of Scripture respecting itself.

2. JESUS DID NOT TEACH THE DOCTRINE OF INSPIRATION. Though modern liberal scholars generally admit that Jesus and the apostles accepted the Old Testament as the inspired Word of God, there are some among them who, in their denial of the doctrine of inspiration, appeal to Jesus as over against the apostles, and especially Paul. The apostles, they say, firmly believed that the writings of the Old Testament were written under inspiration, but Jesus did not share their opinion. And because they regard the testimony of Jesus as decisive, they feel justified in rejecting the doctrine of inspiration. But their fundamental assumption is contrary to the data of Scripture, and apart from these we have no knowledge of what Jesus thought on this subject. They point in quite another direction. The positive statements of Jesus respecting the abiding significance, authority, and inviolability of the Old Testament, Matt. 5:17, 18; 24:35; Luke 16:17; John 10:35, His quotations from it as an authoritative source, and His repeated use of it, leave no doubt as to the fact that He, as well as the apostles, recognized the divine authority of the Old Testament. Some who feel constrained to admit the force of the available evidence, but are not willing to draw the inevitable conclusion, seek refuge in the old accommodation theory of Semler. We fully agree with Dr. Burrell, when he says: "One thing is clear: when Jesus referred to the Scriptures as written by men under the influence of the Spirit, He separated those Scriptures generically from all other 'literature' whatsoever. To his mind, the inspiration of these writers was a singular sort of inspiration, which produced a singular book. In his teaching it is represented as the one book having authority."[2] Moreover, it should be remembered that such a contradistinction between Jesus and the apostles as the opponents assume, in which the attempt is made to play off the former against the latter, is absolutely false, and results in the loss of the Word of God. We know nothing about Jesus save through the testimony of the apostles. He who discredits the apostles bars the way for himself and will never be able to discover what Jesus taught. He even contradicts Jesus, who appointed the apostles as faithful witnesses and promised them the Holy Spirit, to guide them in all the truth.

---
1. *Discussions of Theological Questions*, p. 297.
2. *The Teaching of Jesus Concerning the Scriptures*, p. 134.

3. The Phenomena of Scripture Contradict the Doctrine of Inspiration. Under the influence of historical criticism still another method has been employed to set aside the doctrine of inspiration. They who employ this method are, at least in some cases, willing to admit that the Bible teaches its inspiration, but at the same time maintain that a correct conception of this inspiration can be obtained only by taking account of the peculiar phenomena of Scripture, such as doublets, mistakes, contradictions, misapplied quotations, and so on. Only such a doctrine of inspiration can be regarded as true, which will enable one to account for all these phenomena. The reasoning of those who take this position often sounds very plausible. They do not want a theory of inspiration that is imposed on Scripture from without, but one that is based on an inductive study of the facts. But, however plausible this representation may seem, it does not fit the case. According to it man faces the phenomena of Scripture just as he faces the phenomena of nature and the facts of history, which he must interpret and set forth in their true significance. It loses sight of the fact that the Bible contains a very clear doctrine respecting itself, which man must accept with childlike faith. Even the phenomena of Scripture may not be cited as a witness against this testimony of Scripture. He who does this *eo ipso* rejects the authority of the Bible and virtually adopts a rationalistic standpoint. Instead of humbly accepting the testimony of Scripture, he places himself above it as judge, and opposes to the testimony of Scripture his own scientific insight. History clearly teaches us that the historical-critical method does not lead to a generally accepted and permanent result. The representations vary according to the different standpoint of the critics, and do not lead to a satisfactory doctrine of Scripture. It has already become abundantly evident that this method leads to various views of Scripture, which are absolutely contrary to the teachings of Scripture itself,—a veritable babel of confusion. Ladd, whom no one will accuse of being prejudiced in favor of a strict view of inspiration, says that, while the old conception of Scripture as the Word of God was brushed aside as untenable, and several other theories were suggested as alternatives, not a single one succeeded in entrenching itself in the hearts and minds of Christian people in general.[1]

4. The Doctrine of Inspiration applies only to the Autographa, and Therefore Has No Real Practical Value. The fact that the doctrine of inspiration, as set forth in the preceding pages, applies only to the autographa (the original writings of the Biblical authors), which are no more in our possession, has led some to the rather hasty conclusion, that the problem of inspiration is of a purely academic character and has no practical bearing whatsoever. How can the inspiration of the originals be of any value for us, they ask, if we have in our possession nothing but defective manuscripts? They often give the impression that this renders the entire contents of Scripture uncertain, and that consequently no one can appeal to it as a divine and authoritative Word. But something may be said in answer to this. We would certainly

---

1. *What is the Bible*, p. 71 ff.

THE INSPIRATION OF SCRIPTURE

expect that the Holy Spirit, who so carefully guided the writers of Scripture in the interest of future generations, would also guard and watch over His revelation, in order that it might really serve its purpose. Hence Reformed theologians have always maintained that God's special providence watched over Scripture. Inspiration naturally called for conservation. And history certainly favors this idea in spite of all the variations that exist.

If we bear in mind that there are more than 4000 Greek MSS. of the New Testament, and in addition to that 6000 MSS. of the Vulgate, and 1000 of other Latin translations, then we understand that it was practically impossible that Scripture should be lost to the world for centuries, just as many of the writings of the Church Fathers were. Then we also understand what Kenyon, an eminent authority on the subject, says: "The number of manuscripts of the New Testament, of early translations from it, and of quotations from it in the oldest writers of the Church is so large, that it is practically certain that the true reading of every doubtful passage is preserved in some one or other of these ancient authorities. This can be said of no other ancient book in the world."[1] Textual errors did creep into the text in the course of frequent transcriptions, and the number of the existing variations even sounds very considerable. Nestle speaks of 150,000 in the New Testament, but adds that about nineteen-twentieths of these are devoid of real authority, and that of the remaining 7,500 nineteen-twentieths do not alter the sense of Scripture in any way. Moses Stuart points out that about ninety-five percent of all the existing variations have about as much significance as the question in English orthography, whether the word 'honour' should be spelled with or without the 'u'. According to Nestle there are about 375 variations that bear on the sense of Scripture, and even among these are several of little importance. While admitting the presence of variations, we should bear in mind what Moses Stuart says: Some change the sense of particular passages or expressions, or omit particular words or phrases; but no one doctrine of religion is changed, not one precept is taken away, not one important fact altered, by the whole of the various readings collectively taken."[2] From the existence of these variations it does not follow that the doctrine of verbal inspiration has no practical value; but only *that we do not know at present in what reading we have the Word of God on those particular points.* The important fact remains, however, that apart from the relatively few and unimportant variations, which are perfectly evident, we are in possession of the verbally inspired Word of God. And therefore it is of great practical importance that we maintain the doctrine of verbal inspiration.

E. Objections to the Doctrine of Inspiration

Several objections have been raised against the doctrine of inspiration, and particularly against the doctrine of verbal inspiration, and it cannot be

---

1. *Our Bible and the Manuscripts*, p. 11.
2. Quoted by Patton, *Inspiration of the Scriptures*, p. 114.

denied that some of them present real difficulties. It will not do to ignore them, nor to laugh them out of court. They deserve careful consideration and a more detailed discussion than we can devote to them here. We cannot even begin to discuss separate objections here with the necessary care. This must be left to works which deal exclusively with the doctrine of inspiration, such as Lee, *The Inspiration of Scripture;* Brannerman, *The Inspiration of the Scriptures;* and McIntosh, *Is Christ Infallible and is the Bible True?* We can only indicate the general nature of the objections, and give some general suggestions as to the way in which they can be met.

1. GENERAL NATURE OF THE OBJECTIONS. Some of the objections result from the application of the philosophy of evolution to the origin of the books of the Bible, a scheme which does not fit the facts, and is then made to militate against them. Their force naturally depends entirely on the truth or falsity of that philosophy. Others are derived from the supposed inner discrepancies that are found in Scripture as, for instance, between the numbers in Kings and Chronicles, between the account of Jesus' public ministry in the Synoptics and in the Gospel of John, and between the doctrine of justification in the Epistles of Paul and in the Epistle of James. Still others are drawn from the way in which the Old Testament is quoted in the New. The quotations are not always taken from the Hebrew, but frequently from the Septuagint, and are not always literal. Moreover, the quoted words are often interpreted in a way which does not seem to be justified by the context in which they are found in the Old Testament. There are objections, which result from a comparison of the Biblical narratives with secular history as, for instance, that of the taking of Samaria by Shalmanezer; that of Sennacherib's march against Jerusalem and the slaying of 185,000 Assyrians by an angel of the Lord; that of Esther's elevation to the position of queen; and that of the enrollment mentioned in the second chapter of Luke. Again, it is found that the miracles of Scripture cannot be harmonized with belief in the inflexible laws of nature. The narratives of these miracles are simply declared to be exaggerated, naive representations of historical events which made a deep imprssion, and after the lapse of years assumed the proportions of miracles in the consciousness of a credulous people. Some objections are the products of the moral judgment passed on Biblical injunctions and practices. Attention is called to the *jus talionis* in the law of Moses, to the polygamy that was prevalent among the Israelites, to the terrible scene of moral corruption in the last chapters of the book of Judges, to David's immorality, to the harem of Solomon, and so on. Finally, texual criticism also gives rise to objections. Scripture in its original text, we are told, is corrupt, and its translations are defective. The MSS. reveal all kinds of variations, which testify to the corruption of the original, and the translations are not always a correct representation of it.

2. GENERAL REMARKS ON THE OBJECTIONS RAISED. First of all the general remark must be made that, though we cannot ignore the objections that are raised but must take account of them, no one has the right to demand of us

that we make our belief in the inspiration of Scripture contingent on our ability to remove all objections by solving the problems which they present. The objections raised do not constitute a sufficient reason for setting aside the doctrine of inspiration, which is clearly taught in Scripture. The doctrines of the Trinity, of creation and providence, and of the incarnation, are all burdened with difficulties, but these do not justify anyone in rejecting the clear teachings of Scripture with respect to those truths. Many of the teachings of science are similarly burdened and present problems which cannot be solved at present, but are not therefore necessarily discounted. People confidently speak of atoms and electrons, of genes and chromosomes, though these still present many problems. We should always bear in mind the statement of Dr. Warfield, that it is "a settled logical principle that so long as the proper evidence by which a proposition is established remains unrefuted, all so-called objections brought against it pass out of the category of objections to its truth into the category of difficulties to be adjusted to it."[1]

In connection with the common objections against the doctrine of inspiration the following points should be borne in mind:

a. The present day opposition to Scripture and its inspiration is to a great extent, not merely scientific, but ethical. It clearly reveals the aversion of the natural heart to the supernatural. Opposition is evoked by the very fact that Scripture demands absolute subjection, the subjection of human reason to its authority. This ethical conflict is clearly seen in the opposition to the miracles, the incarnation, the virgin birth, the resurrection of Christ, and other supernatural events.

b. Many of the so-called objections have no factual basis, but are born of faulty assumptions. They often result from the wrong *scientific* attitude, which the opponent assumes to Scripture. If one takes for granted *a priorily* that the contents of Scripture is not the fruit of revelation but of natural evolution, then many facts and events appear to be out of place in the framework in which the Bible places them. Then the laws of Moses become an anomaly at the beginning of Israel's national existence, and the books of Chronicles must be regarded as unhistorical. Then Jesus especially becomes an historical enigma. Again, if it is taken for granted that all the events of history are controlled by an iron-clad system of natural laws, and the supernatural is eliminated, then there is, of course, no place for the miracles of Scripture. And if in the study of the Synoptics a double or triple source theory is taken for granted, *and these sources are made the standard of truth,* a great deal of material will naturally be set aside. But all such objections are the result of false assumptions, and therefore need not be taken seriously.

c. Several of the objections are exaggerated and can easily be reduced. Discrepancies and contradictions are sometimes hastily assumed, which on closer inspection prove to be no discrepancies or contradictions at all. There are so-called doublets in Joshua, Judges, and the books of Samuel, which in

---

1. *Revelation and Inspiration*, p. 174.

fact are merely complementary narratives, introduced in characteristically Hebrew fashion. The Gospel of John has been declared unhistorical, because its representation of the life of Jesus differs from that of the Synoptics; but even these differences can largely be explained in the light of the character and purpose of the different Gospels. A book like that of Gregory, *Why Four Gospels?* is very illuminating on this point.

d. There are also a number of objections that would apply on the assumption of a mechanical conception of inspiration, but lose their force entirely if the inspiration of Scripture is organically conceived. Verbal inspiration is sometimes denied, because the writers indicate that their literary work is based on previous investigations, because the individuality of the writers is clearly reflected in their writings, or because there are marked differences of style and language. But it is quite evident that these objections militate only against a mechanical view of inspiration.

e. Finally, objections are frequently derived from the low moral conditions which are reflected in the Bible, especially in its earliest books, and from the imperfections, deceptions, polygamy, and even immorality of some of the chief Bible characters, such as Noah, Abraham, Jacob, Eli, David, and Solomon. But the fact that the Bible gives a faithful picture of the times and the lives of these saints can hardly constitute an objection against its inspiration. The situation would be different, of course, if the Bible approved of such conditions or acts, or even if it condoned them; but as a matter of fact it does quite the contrary.

QUESTIONS FOR FURTHER STUDY: What is plenary, in distinction from verbal, inspiration? Does the fact that the Bible contains truths which transcend reason prove anything as to its inspiration? Is the doctrine of inspiration consistent with the evolutionary view of Scripture? If the Bible is not verbally inspired in all its parts, how can we determine which parts are, and which are not, inspired? What is the difference between prophetic, lyric, chokmatic, and apostolic inspiration? Does the doctrine of inspiration imply that the evangelists always recorded the *ipsissima verba* of Jesus? How does it square with the fact that the human authors of the Bible sometimes derive their material from written sources? Is it possible to deny the doctrine of inspiration and maintain the veracity of Jesus and the apostles? How did the inspiration of the writers of Scripture differ from the ordinary illumination of Christians? How, from the inspiration of the great poets?

REFERENCES: Bavinck, *Geref. Dogm.*, I, pp. 406-476; Kuyper, *Enc. der Heil, Godgel.*, II, pp. 369-511; id., *Dict. Dogm.*, *De Sacra Scriptura*, I, pp. 86-100; II, pp. 3:179; id., *De Hedendaagsche Schriftcritiek*; Honig, *Is de Bijbel op Bovennatuurlijke Wijze Geinspireerd?* Daubanton, *De Theopneustie der Heilige Schrift*; Bannerman, *Inspiration of the Scriptures*; Lee, *The Inspiration of the Scripture*; McIntosh, *Is Christ Infallible and is the Bible True?*, Patton, *Inspiration of the Scriptures*; McGregor, *The Revelation and the Record*, pp. 79-117; Given, *Revelation, Inspiration, and the Canon*, pp. 104-202; Orr, *Revelation and Inspiration*, pp. 155-218; Ladd, *The Doctrine of Sacred Scriptures*, II, pp. 452-494; Sanday, *Inspiration*; Warfield, *Revelation and Inspiration*, pp. 51-456; Girardeau, *Discussions of Theological Questions*, pp. 273-384; Cunningham, *Theological Lectures*, pp. 343-411; Mead, *Supernatural Revelation*, pp. 279-317.

F. The Perfections of Scripture

The Reformation naturally brought the doctrine of Scripture to the foreground. During the Middle Ages the fiction of an apostolic tradition, which was supposed to have come down in oral form from the days of the apostles gradually crystallized and secured a firm hold on the Church. This tradition was placed on a level with the Bible as an authoritative source of theological knowledge, and in practice was often treated as superior to the Bible. It was regarded as the necessary warrant for the authority of the Bible, and as the indispensable guide for the interpretation of Scripture. Moreover, the hierarchical Church of Rome, with its claim to infallibility, placed itself above them both. It posed as the only body which could determine infallibly what was, and what was not, apostolic tradition, and which could give an infallible interpretation of Scripture. Great emphasis was placed on the fact that the Bible owes its origin to the Church, and stands in constant need of the testimony of the Church. The Reformers clearly saw that this position of the Church of Rome was the fruitful source of many errors, and therefore felt that it was incumbent on them to call the people back to the Bible, which had been greatly neglected, and to stress its *autopistia*. To offset the errors of Rome they deemed it necessary to develop the doctrine of the perfections of Scripture. They themselves did not yet include a systematic presentation of this in their works, but their successors did. It occupies a very important place in the writings of Musculus, Zanchius, Polanus, Junius, and others. We conclude our study of the *principium cognoscendi externum* with a brief discussion of the perfections of Scripture.

1. THE DIVINE AUTHORITY OF SCRIPTURE. The divine authority of Scripture was generally accepted until the chill winds of Rationalism swept over Europe and caused the enthusiasm of faith to go down to the freezing point. This means that in the days of the Reformation the Church of Rome as well as the Churches that parted company with it, ascribed divine authority to Scripture. But in spite of the fact that Roman Catholics and Protestants had the principle of authority in common, they were not altogether agreed as to the nature of this authority. There was a very important difference of opinion with respect to the ground on which it rests. On the part of Rome there was an ever-increasing denial of the *autopistia* of Scripture, that is, of its inherent authority. It maintained that the Church temporarily and logically precedes Scripture, and therefore does not owe its existence to Scripture, but exists in and by itself, that is, through Christ or the indwelling Spirit of God. Scripture rather owes its existence to the Church, and is now further acknowledged, preserved, interpreted, and defended by it. Without the Church there is no Scripture, but without Scripture there is still a Church.

Over against this position of Rome, the Reformers emphasized the *autopistia* of Scripture, the doctrine that Scripture has authority in and of itself as the *inspired* Word of God. They did not hesitate to ascribe great importance to the testimony of the Church to Scripture *as a motivum credibilitatis*, but refused to regard this testimony of the Church as the final ground for the acceptance of Scripture. They firmly maintained the position that the Bible must be believed for its own sake. It is the inspired Word of God and therefore addresses man with divine authority. The Church can and should *acknowledge* the Bible for what it is, but can in no sense of the word *make* it what it is. The Protestant principle is, says Thornwell, "that the truths of the Bible authenticate themselves as divine by their own light."[1]

In Protestant circles, however, a dispute arose in the seventeenth century respecting the authority of Scripture. While Scripture as a whole was recognized as the only and sufficient rule of faith and practice, the question was raised, whether every part of it should be regarded as authoritative. In seeking an answer to this question it became evident that it was necessary to distinguish between the Word of God in a formal and in a material sense, and between an *auctoritas historica* and an *auctoritas normativa*. Scripture has first of all historical authority, that is, it is a true and absolutely reliable record, and as such is entitled to a believing acceptance of all that it contains. But in addition to that it also has normative significance, as a rule of life and conduct, and as such demands absolute subjection on the part of man. And in connection with this the difficult question arose, in how far the normative value that is ascribed to Scripture as a whole also belongs to its separate parts. Do the historical parts of the Bible, do the laws of Moses, and do the words of the speakers that are introduced in Scripture have normative significance for us? Happily, we need not grope about entirely in the dark here, for the Bible itself teaches us to make distinctions with respect to this point. It does not demand that we keep every one of the precepts which it contains. It disapproves of some and calls attention to the temporary character of others. Reformed theologians never attempted to lay down hard and fast rules by which we can be governed in this matter. Heppe gives some examples of the manner in which they dealt with the matter.[2] Voetius says that absolute normative significance must be ascribed to the words and works (a) of God, (b) of Christ as God and man, and (c) of the angels. Moreover, he regards those words of the prophets and of the apostles as normative, in which they as public teachers, orally or in writing, edify the Church. He ascribes normative authority to their deeds only when they are approved by Scripture. On the other hand, he does not regard *all* the words of Job as normative, nor the words of the friends of Job. Others explicitly exclude the words of the devils and of wicked persons. Voetius holds that the writings of the Old Testament are just as normative as those of the New Testament.[3] Grosheide calls attention to the fact that absolute normative significance must be ascribed to those statements or commands of God which are clearly intended for all ages, and to all positive statements of an ethical or dogmatical character; but that no such authority can be ascribed to the words of Satan, of wicked persons, or even

---

1. *Collected Writings*, I, p. 49.
2. *Dogmatik der evangelich-reformirten Kirche*, p. 22 ff.
3. *Catechisatie* I., p. 71 ff.

of the pious, except when they are clearly speaking in the name of God or make statements that are fully in harmony with the moral law; nor to purely historical narratives pertaining to the things of every day life.[1] In general it will not be difficult to determine, whether a certain part of Scripture has normative value for us. Yet there are cases in which the decision is not easy. It is not always possible to say, whether a certain Scriptural precept, which was clearly normative for the original readers, still has normative significance for us. On the whole it is well to bear in mind that the Bible is not exactly a code of laws, and is far more interested in the inculcation of principles than in the regulation of life by specific precepts. Even the laws of Moses and the history of Israel as the Old Testament people of God embody principles of permanent validity. Sometimes we may come to the conclusion that, while certain laws no more apply in the exact form in which they were cast, yet their underlying principle is just as binding today as it ever was. In dubious cases we shall have to be guided to a great extent by the analogy of Scripture and by the moral law.

In modern liberal theology very little remains of the normative significance of the Bible. Schleiermacher denied the normative character of the Old Testament altogether, and regarded only the New Testament as a norm for the Church. And he ascribed this significance to the New Testament, not on account of its supernatural inspiration, for he did not believe in this, but because he saw in it the record of the religious experiences of men, who, as the immediate associates of Jesus, enjoyed a special measure of spiritual illumination. Ritschl did not ascribe normative significance even to the New Testament, but saw in it only a valuable historical record of the beginnings of Christianity, and in no sense of the word a rule of faith. He felt free to reject all those elements which did not harmonize with the postulates of his own system and had no real value for the revelation in Christ as the real founder of the Kingdom of God, nor for the Christian life, as he conceived of it. In general it may be said that these two men determined the attitude which modern liberal theology assumes with reference to the Word of God. Strange to say, some present day Dispensationalists, who are strongly opposed to all Liberalism, also maintain that the Old Testament is not normative *for us*. They fully recognize the inspiration of the Old Testament, and consider it to be normative for the Jews, but not for New Testament believers. Cook expresses himself very clearly on this point, when he says that "in all the Old Testament there is not a sentence that applies to the Christian as a Rule of Faith and Practice—not a single command that is binding on him, as there is not a single promise there given him at first hand, except what is included in the broad flow of the plan of Redemption as there taught in symbol and prophecy."[2]

2. THE NECESSITY OF SCRIPTURE. Because the Church of Rome proceeds on the assumption that the Church takes precedence over Scripture, it

---
1. *Schriftgezag* p. 28.
2. *God's Book Speaking for Itself*, p. 32.

cannot very well acknowledge the absolute necessity of the latter. The Church, which derives its life from the Holy Spirit, is self-sufficient and therefore *autopistos*. While it does need tradition, it does not really need Scripture, no matter how useful this may be as a norm. The Lord referred those to whom He brought His doctrine, not to a book, but to the living voice of His apostles and of the Church. "He who heareth you," He said to the apostles, "heareth me." Moreover, nearly twenty years elapsed after the ascension of Christ before a single book of the New Testament came into existence, and during all that time an appeal to the New Testament was naturally out of the question. According to Rome it is far more correct to say that the Bible needs the Church than that the Church has need of the Bible. The denial of the necessity of Scripture, however, was not limited to the Church of Rome. Even in the early Church some of the mystical sects, such as the Montanists and the Cathari regarded the Bible as quite superfluous. And in the days of the Reformation the Anabaptists and the Libertines of Geneva were of the same opinion. The Anabaptists especially exalted the inner word at the expense of the external. They did not regard the Bible as the true Word of God, but only as a testimony, a description, a dead and thoroughly impotent letter. In their estimation the real and true Word of God was spoken by the Holy Spirit in the hearts of God's people. Schleiermacher also taught that Scripture was produced by the Church, and is simply the supreme, and therefore also authoritative, expression of its religious life. This may be said to be the prevalent view in modern Liberalism, which draws for its theology far more on the Christian consciousness, informed by the current teachings of science and philosophy, than on the Bible as the Word of God.

When the Reformers defended the necessity of Scripture over against Rome and the Anabaptists, they did not deny that the Church existed before Moses' day, nor that the New Testament Church was in existence long before there was a canon of the New Testament. Neither did they defend the position that Scripture was *absolutely* necessary, in the sense that God could not have made man acquainted with the way of salvation in some other way. They considered Scripture to be necessary in virtue of the good pleasure of God to make the Word the seed of the Church. Even before the time of Moses the unwritten word served that purpose. And the New Testament did not come into existence apart from the spoken word of Jesus and the apostles. As long as these witnesses of the facts of redemption lived, there was little need of a written word, but when they fell away, this changed at once. The historical character of God's revelation, the history of redemption, and the redemptive facts which did not admit of repetition, and were yet of the greatest significance for all coming generations, made it necessary to commit God's special revelation to writing. From that point of view Scripture remains necessary to the very end of time. In this sense of the word Reformed theology has always defended the necessity of Scripture. Even Barth, who does not share the Reformed conception of the Bible as the infallible Word of God, feels constrained to defend its necessity as a witness to the divine revelation.

3. The Perspicuity of Scripture. In the estimation of Rome the Bible is obscure, and is badly in need of interpretation even in matters of faith and practice. It contains deep mysteries, such as the doctrine of the Trinity, of the incarnation, and others, and is often so obscure that it is liable to be misunderstood. For that reason an infallible interpretation is needed, and this is supplied by the Church. Peter says distinctly that some parts of the Bible are hard to understand, and the experience of centuries proves conclusively that, without the infallible interpretation of the Church, it is impossible to reach the desired unity in the interpretation of Scripture. Over against this position of the Roman Catholic Church the Reformers stressed the perspicuity of Scripture. They did not intend to deny that there are mysteries in the Bible which transcend human reason, but freely admitted this. Neither did they claim such clarity for Scripture that the interpreter can well dispense with scientific exegesis. As a matter of fact, they engaged in exegetical labors far more than the votaries of Rome. Moreover, they did not even assert that the way of salvation is so clearly revealed in Scripture that every man, whether he be enlightened by the Holy Spirit or not, and whether or not he be deeply interested in the way of salvation, can easily understand it. Their contention was simply that the knowledge necessary unto salvation, though not equally clear on every page of Scripture, is yet conveyed to man throughout the Bible in such a simple and comprehensible form that one who is earnestly seeking salvation can, under the guidance of the Holy Spirit, by reading and studying the Bible, easily obtain for himself the necessary knowledge, and does not need the aid and guidance of the Church and of a separate priesthood. Naturally, they did not mean to minimize the importance of the interpretations of the Church in the preaching of the Word. They pointed out that Scripture itself testifies to its perspicuity, where it is declared to be a lamp unto our feet, and a light unto our path. The prophets and the apostles, and even Jesus Himself, address their messages to all the people, and never treat them as minors who are not able to understand the truth. The people are even declared to be able to judge and to understand, I Cor. 2:15; 10:15; I John 2:20. Because of its perspicuity the Bible can even be said to be self-interpretive. The Reformers had this in mind, when they spoke of an *interpretatio secundum analogiam fidei* or *Scripturae*, and laid down the great principle, *Scriptura Scripturae interpres*. They did not regard the special task of the Church in the interpretation of the Bible as superfluous, but explicitly recognized the duty of the Church in this respect. Hence they spoke of the *potestas doctrinae* of the Church.

4. The Sufficiency of Scripture. Neither Rome nor the Anabaptists regarded the Bible as sufficient. The latter had a low opinion of Scripture, and asserted the absolute necessity of the inner light and of all kinds of special revelations. They attached very little importance to the ministry of the Word. One of their pet slogans was, "The letter killeth, but the Spirit maketh alive." From the time of the Middle Ages Rome maintained the absolute necessity of

oral tradition as a complement to the written word. This tradition was not always clearly defined. The term originally covered oral teachings and customs of apostolic origin. But in the measure in which the Church moved farther and farther away from the apostolic age, it became increasingly difficult to determine, whether certain teachings really came down from the apostles. Hence it became necessary to define the characteristics of what might truly be regarded as apostolic tradition. An attempt at this was made in the rule of Vincentius Lerinensis, who declared that to be apostolic which was believed everywhere, always, and by all (*ubique, semper, et ab omnibus, creditum est*). Real apostolic tradition could therefore be recognized by the fact that it was believed everywhere, at all times, and by the whole Church. This definition was adopted by all later Roman Catholic theologians, though in actual practice it was modified. It was very difficult to determine, whether a certain truth was *always* believed, and therefore the question gradually took on the more contemporaneous form, whether such a truth is at any particular time generally believed. The antiquity of the truth was sacrificed to its universality, and the really important question was ignored. It was tantamount to saying that it could not be determined, whether a certain teaching actually came down from the apostles. But even so a formidable difficulty remained. In seeking an answer to the question who was to pass on this question of universality, it was held that the Church in general could not do this, but only the *ecclesia docens*, the bishops in their councils. This is still the position of the Old Catholic Church. But even this position proved untenable. The question arose, When are the bishops infallible in determining the nature of a tradition, always, or only when they are met in council? And if they can give infallible decisions only when they have come together, must their vote be unanimous or is a majority sufficient to lend weight to their decision? And if a majority is sufficient, how great must this be; is a majority of one sufficient? The result of all these deliberations was that the Pope was finally declared infallible in matters of faith and practice, when speaking *ex cathedra*. If the Pope now declares something to be apostolic tradition, that settles the matter, and what is so declared thereby becomes binding on the Church.

Over against the position that Scripture needs some complement, the Reformers asserted the *perfectio* or *sufficientia* of Scripture. This doctrine does not mean that everything that was spoken and written by the prophets, by Christ, and by the apostles, is incorporated in Scripture. The Bible clearly proves that this is not the case, I Kings 4:33; I Cor. 5:9; Col. 4:16; II Thess. 2:5. Neither does it mean that all the articles of faith are found in finished form in Scripture. The Bible contains no dogmas; these can be derived from it only by a process of reflection. The Reformers merely intended to deny that there is alongside of Scripture an unwritten Word of God with equal authority and therefore equally binding on the conscience. And in taking that position they took their stand on Scriptural ground. In Scripture each succeeding book connects up with the preceding (except in contemporary narratives), and is based on it. The Psalms and the Prophets presuppose the Law and appeal to it, and to it only. The New Testament comes to us as the fulfilment of the Old and refers back to nothing else. Oral traditions current in the time of Jesus are rejected as human inventions, Matt. 5:21-48; 15:4, 9; I Cor. 4:6. Christ is presented to us as the acme of the divine revelation, the highest and the last, Matt. 11:27; John 1:18; 17:4, 6; Heb. 1:1. For the knowledge of the way of salvation we are referred to Scripture only, to the word of Christ, and of the apostles, John 17:20; I John 1:3. The Reformers did recognize a Christian tradition, but only a Christian tradition based on, and derived from, Scripture, and not one that equalled or even surpassed it in authority.

QUESTIONS FOR FURTHER STUDY: How do Roman Catholics defend the authority of tradition alongside of that of Scripture? Why do they attach so much importance to apostolic tradition? Is it right to limit the normative authority of Scripture to those parts which teach the doctrine of salvation? Has Scripture any authority in matters of science and art? Does the Bible in any way testify to its necessity? How does modern liberal theology judge of this? Do not the many contradictory interpretations of Scripture disprove its perspicuity? How do the oral law of the Jews and the oral tradition of the Roman Catholics compare? Is the appeal of the Mystics to II Cor. 3:6 to disprove the sufficiency of Scripture, tenable?

REFERENCES: Bavinck, *Geref. Dogm.* I, pp. 476-527; Kuyper, *Dict. Dogm., De Sacra Scriptura* II, pp. 190-241; Ladd, *The Doctrine of Sacred Scripture* II, pp. 514-610; Cunningham, *Theol. Lectures*, pp. 459-516; D. S. Schaff, *Our Fathers' Faith and Ours*, pp. 147-170; Wilmers, *Handbook of the Chr. Rel.*, pp. 120-151; Heppe, *Dogm. der ev. ref. Kirche*, pp. 9-31; id., *Dogm. des deutschen Protestantismus im zechzehnten Jahrhundert* I, pp. 211-257; Mead, *Supernatural Revelation*, pp. 318-355; Schmid, *Doct. Theol. of the Ev. Luth. Church*, pp. 61-101; Gravemeijer, *Leesboek over de Geref. Geloofsleer* I, pp. 244-267; Burgess, *The Protestant Faith*, pp. 59-94.

V. THE PRINCIPIUM COGNOSCENDI INTERNUM

The knowledge of God presupposes, not only that God has revealed Himself, but also that man is capable, either constitutionally or by virtue of a gracious work of renewal, of receiving and appropriating this revelation. If man did not have that ability, the divine revelation, while existing objectively, would forever remain foreign to him and exercise no influence on his life. All knowledge, and consequently also all science, requires a certain correspondence between subject and object. This means that alongside of the *principium cognoscendi externum* there must also be a *principium cognoscendi internum*, a principium in man which enables him to discern and to appropriate God's special revelation. Naturally, the absolute Idealist would not subscribe to this position, for according to him knowledge not only calls for a *correspondence* between subject and object, but for the *identity* of the two. Even the Theology of Crisis feels constrained to put the matter in a different form. It recognizes no objectively existing revelation; nor does it believe in a point of contact in the life of man for special revelation. Revelation simply is not revelation until it is brought home to the heart of man in faith. But this faith is not a permanent receptivity in man for an objectively existing revelation, but is given in and with the revelation itself whenever God reveals Himself. This means that on this point the distinction between the subjective and the objective is really cancelled. Reformed theology, however, recognizes the existence of a *principium cognoscendi internum*, and the question naturally arises, What is the nature of this principium? In the course of history several answers have been given to that question. The organ by which man judges and appropriates the revelation of God was sought successively: (A) in the human understanding, (B) in speculative reason, (C) in devout feeling, and (D) in the moral consciousness. We shall consider these successively.

A. The Human Understanding

Some sought the *principium cognoscendi internum* in the human understanding in general, as distinguished from what is more specifically called the speculative reason. It was their persistent attempt to establish the truth on *historico-apologetical* grounds.

1. HISTORICAL STATEMENT OF THIS POSITION.

a. *Up to the time of the Reformation.* In view of the fact that the revelation of God in Christ does not minister to the pride of man but rather humbles him, it naturally met with a great deal of opposition and was repeatedly in need of defense. This was necessary even in the apostolic age, so that the

Bible itself contains apologetical elements. In the second century the Apologetes defended the truth of Christianity over against Jews and Gentiles, and gave an account of the grounds on which it rests. They did not take their starting point in doubt or in any so-called neutrality, but in an unwavering faith and called attention to the superior excellency of Christianity, to the redemptive message of special revelation, to the antiquity and unity, the simplicity and sublimity, the fulness and many-sidedness of Scripture, to prophecies and miracles, and to the testimony of the Church and the blessings of the gospel. These arguments were repeated in the writings of the anti-Gnostic fathers and in later theology, though they were sometimes treated in other connections and did not always assume the same character.

Scholasticism also took its starting point in faith, but by its attempt to change religious truths into concepts of reason effected a separation of natural and supernatural truths that was detrimental to both. According to them the former could be proved by reason, but the latter could only be accepted on authority. In the former scientific certainty was possible, but in the latter it was not possible to rise above the level of faith. The order which they usually followed, though with several variations, was the following: first they sought to demonstrate by rational argumentation the truths of natural revelation; then they proved in a similar way the possibility, necessity, and reality of special revelation; and finally they urged reason, on the mere ground of the existence of a special revelation, to accept its contents blindly in faith. The motives that were adduced for belief in a special revelation were generally called *motiva credibilitatis*. The argument that Scripture as a divine revelation rests on the testimony of the Church was developed by the Roman Catholics especially after the Reformation. All such arguments, however, though they may demonstrate the reasonableness of accepting Scripture as the Word of God, can only produce a *fides humana* and never a *fides divina*. Even among the Roman Catholics some are willing to admit this, though on the whole they have a high opinion of Apologetics. The general Roman Catholic representation as to the way in which man arrives at the knowledge of God's revelation is the following: (1) Supernatural revelation rises on the basis of natural revelation, and can only be appropriated successively by degrees. (2) By various proofs man in his natural state is first led to the natural theology, which constitutes the preamble of faith. At this point even science is possible, since the proofs are demonstrative. Ordinarily we cannot yet speak of faith at this stage. (3) He who has reached this point is now, through the motives of credibility, of which the Church is the most important, put in a position to see and admit the trustworthiness of God's revelation and the reasonableness of faith. (4) After man has thus been led to the *fides humana* (human faith) he is raised by an infused grace to the supernatural order and prepares himself by good works for the vision of God.

b. *After the Reformation.* The Protestants took a different position, but did not always consistently maintain it. The Reformers did not take their starting point in human reason, but in the Christian faith, and stressed the fact that this faith rests only on divine authority and is wrought by the Holy Spirit. Protestant theologians did not always remain true to this principle, but frequently returned to the doctrine of a natural theology, and to the historical proofs for the truth of revelation. Under the influence of Cartesius, who took his starting point in doubt, Rationalism gradually found its way into the Churches, and the historico-apologetical method came into vogue. It clearly came to the foreground in Supranaturalism. In the application of this method the purpose was to prove that God has revealed Himself in a supernatural way rather than to exhibit the reasonableness of revelation. And in order to prove this, attention was called to the miracles of Scripture, to the fulfilment of prophecies, often of a very special character, to the striking correspondence of the various parts of Scripture, to the moral influence of the gospel, and so on. The purpose was to lead men to faith by such intellectual considerations. It cannot be denied that some who followed this method did it with the best intentions. Some of their works are even now mentioned with honor in Christian Apologetics, though the method now followed and the arguments adduced are quite different. Yet this method was bound to lead to Rationalism. Even Butler could pen a sentence like the following: "For though natural religion is the foundation and principal part of Christianity, it is not in any sense the whole of it."[1] Reason is accorded the right to examine and explain the credentials of revelation, and is thus placed above Scripture. For that reason this method stands condemned from a theological point of view. Moreover, its untenableness clearly appeared from the history of Supranaturalism itself, and from the sharp criticism of Rousseau and Lessing, of Kant and Schleiermacher. For a long time even Reformed authors continued to speak of natural theology as *fundamental* theology, but in many Reformed circles it is entirely discredited at present.

2. EVALUATION OF THIS POSITION. As intimated in the preceding, the historico-apologetical method does not meet with approval from a theological point of view, because it underrates both religious truth and faith. Religious truth is not like some theorem of science, and faith is not purely intellectual insight into some result of scientific investigation. Baillie calls attention to the fact that this whole method of reasoning is called in question today.[2] It also does scant justice to the Christian religion. The Word of God presupposes the darkness and error of the natural man, and would therefore contradict itself, if it submitted itself to the judgment of that man. It would thereby acknowledge one as judge whom it had first disqualified. Finally, this method does not lead to the desired result. In the beginning of the previous century miracles and prophecies could serve as proofs, but in the present day they themselves require proof.

This does not mean, however, that Apologetics is devoid of all real value. It may undoubtedly serve a useful purpose in some respects, but cannot, with-

---

1. *Analogy*, Part II, Chap. 1.
2. *Our Knowledge of God*, p. 129.

out forfeiting its theological character, precede faith nor prove the truth of revelation *a priorily*. It presupposes in its votaries a believing acceptance of the truth. A threefold value may be ascribed to it: (a) It compels theology to give an account of its contents and of the grounds on which it rests, and thus promotes theological self-consciousness. (b) It makes the Christian conscious of the fact that he need not feel embarrassed in the presence of the enemy, but finds support in nature and history, in science and art, and in the heart and conscience of every man. (c) Though it cannot of itself bring any man to the acknowledgment of the truth by compelling proofs, it may, like the ministry of the Word, give him a profound impression of the truth, which he cannot easily shake off.

In actual practice, however, Apologetics has often moved in the wrong direction. (a) It has divorced itself from faith, assuming a place outside of, above, and preceding theology, and has thereby laid claim to an authority to which it is not entitled. (b) It has separated faith and knowledge in such a way as to cause religious truth to rest wholly or in part on purely intellectual grounds, something that is entirely contrary to the nature of that truth. (c) The result was that it cherished exaggerated expectations with reference to its scientific labors, as if it could change the heart through the intellect, and by means of sound reasoning could cultivate piety.

B. Speculative Reason

The position of those who regarded speculative reason as the organ by which to discern, and judge, and appropriate religious truth, did not differ essentially from those who ascribed these functions to the human understanding in general. The one as well as the other made human reason the arbiter of the truth as well as its appropriating organ. Both belong to that broader category generally known as Rationalism. And one of the fundamental assumptions of Rationalism, says Paterson is, "that the mind has been restricted to the use of its natural powers in the discovery and appropriation of religious and moral truth. The notion is rejected that at any stage of the process the mind has been aided by an immediate action upon it of the Divine Spirit, as the result of which it is enabled to take possession of truth that would otherwise lie beyond its ken and grasp."[1] At the same time they who exalted speculative reason to the place of honor presented a system that was far more profound and comprehensive than that of vulgar Rationalism, that is, the Rationalism of the Wolffian type. They made speculative reason not only the norm and the necessary faculty for the reception of the truth, but even regarded it as the source of the truth, and by so doing broke the more effectively with the idea of a special divine revelation.

1. HISTORICAL STATEMENT OF THIS POSITION. The vulgar Rationalism of the eighteenth century, represented by Deism and the Wolffian school of philosophy, finally yielded to the critical onslaughts of Rousseau and Lessing,

---

1. *The Rule of Faith*, p. 113.

of Kant and Schleiermacher. The superficial structure which it reared was swept from its foundation. With Kant and Schleiermacher the autonomy of the subject began. At first the reaction went so far as to discount the objective world. According to Kant man cannot know *noumena* or the essence of things, but knows merely phenomena, and even these only in the forms which the thinking subject imposes on them. The subject thus produces the form of the phenomenal world. Fichte went a step farther and denied the existence of an objective world, in distinction from the subject. In his opinion the world of external things exists only in the one universal mind and is the product of this mind. At first Schleiermacher also assumed this standpoint. In course of time it was felt, however, that there must be something that has objective reality and therefore normative value. That consideration led to the so-called restauration, in which the attempt was made to get back to the objective, while retaining the same subjective starting point. Hegel was the great representative of this tendency. He raised the subjective, ethical Idealism of Fichte to an objective, logical Idealism, and substituted for the idea of being that of becoming. In his system of thought the whole world became a process, a development of the logical idea, in which all being is simply represented as thought. In that evolution religion also has its place. It, too, is pure thought or knowledge, namely, the knowledge which the Absolute has of itself in forms of the imagination. It is clothed in forms and symbols, or pictorial representations, of which only speculative reason can fathom the deep significance. According to Hegel it is the task of philosophy to rid the dogmas of religion of their historical forms, which are after all mere husks, and to discover and elucidate the idea, which is the precious hidden kernel. Thus the great truths of Christianity, such as the doctrine of the Trinity, of the incarnation, of the atonement, and others, not only became objects of philosophical speculation, but in their essential nature and ideal form really became the fruits of this speculation. Apart from Scripture and every other authority, these truths were represented as *necessary thoughts of reason*, and were therefore shown to be highly reasonable. The real proof for the truths of religion was found in the fact that they presented themselves to the mind as *necessary thoughts*. This was in harmony with the fundamental principle of Hegel: "All that is rational is real." Whatever one thought *with logical necessity* and proved to be a coherent part of the whole system of truth, was regarded as true. Logical necessity of thought or coherence was thus made the standard of truth in matters of religion. This method was applied in theology by Daub, Marheineke, Strauss, Vatke, Weisse, Biedermann, and others, though not always to the same degree, nor with the same result. It also found some favor among the followers of Schleiermacher, the father of modern theology, who shared the subjective starting point of Hegel, though he took position in the affections rather than in reason.

2. EVALUATION OF THIS POSITION. They who regard speculative reason as the criterion of religious truth are wedded to the speculative method in appropriating and judging this truth. This method undoubtedly has an ad-

vantage over the historico-apologetical method. Supranaturalism pretended to be able to demonstrate the dogmas of religion so clearly as to silence all objections. It made a determined effort to give a definite and clear representation of the truth, so that the reasonableness of it could at once be seen. But its sharp distinctions led to an intellectualism in which truth was divorced from life. The speculative method broke with this demand for *clearness*, and recognized the deep sense of the dogmata, and the mysterious elements in religion. Moreover, it emphasized the fact that religion occupies a unique place in human life, and therefore demands a corresponding organ in human nature. Hegel found this in speculative reason, and Schleiermacher, in the feelings. Both were mistaken, but nevertheless called attention to an important matter, when they stressed the necessity of a proper organ for religion, a matter that is of the greatest importance for the study of theology, and is therefore entitled to grateful recognition.

But the speculative method did not stop at the thought that thinking and being necessarily correspond to each other; it proceeded to the identification of the two. This is the fundamental error of speculative philosophy. The great question is, Do we think a thing because it exists, or does it exist because we necessarily think it. Speculative philosophy claims the latter, but without any warrant. At this point Hegel took an impossible leap. The existence of a thing does not follow from the fact that we think it, for existence is not an emanation of thought, but rests on an act of power. It is true that God thought things eternally, but He brought the things which existed *ideally* into *real* existence only by a creative act. We can only reflect on what God thought long before and has creatively brought to our consciousness in the existing world of reality. If we reject all that comes to us from without, we retain only a vague principle without any content, from which nothing can be derived. Notwithstanding its high pretensions and its, ostensibly, good intentions, the speculative method did not succeed in changing the despised doctrines of the Christian religion into a philosophical system of universal truth, quite acceptable to the world. The word of the cross remained foolishness to them that perish. It broke away from the objective basis of God's revelation, and therefore could not succeed in constructing a real system of theology.

C. Devout Feeling or Religious Intuition

A third position with respect to the *principium cognoscendi internum* of theology, is that of those who find the organ by which religious truth is acquired and discerned in devout feeling or religious intuition. Schleiermacher is generally recognized as the father of this view. This conception of the internal or subjective principle of knowledge in theology has this in common with that of Hegel, that it does not involve any preliminary assumption as to the derivation of the subject-matter from revelation. But in distinction from those who championed the speculative method and virtually changed theology into philosophy, the advocates of this method are inclined to banish all philosophy from theology. They are like the speculative philosophers and theologians, however, in their failure to distinguish between the norm or criterion and the source of religious truth. Since they recognize their own subjective feelings as the source of this truth, the question for them is not so much a question of the appropriation, as of the appraisal, of religious truth or, to express it in a different way, a question of recognizing it *as religious truth.* Their special characteristic is that they seek religious certitude in a religious-empirical way. Devout feeling is the criterion of religious truth, and the test applied to it is the test of experience.

1. Historical Statement of the Position. When both of the preceding methods led to no result, many theologians took refuge in religious experience and sought support in it for the certainty and truth of Christianity. It is particularly in the application of this method that the influence of Schleiermacher is felt. He and his followers had the laudable desire to restore theology to honor again, and they attempted to accomplish this by taking position in the believing consciousness. In answer to the question, What prompts us to accept the truths of Christianity? the advocates of this method do not appeal to historical or rational proofs, nor to the authority of Scripture or of the Church, but to the experience of salvation in the heart of the sinner. Schleiermacher wants the theologian to start with the data given in the confession of a particular Church, and by these data he means, not so much the doctrines that are formulated in the Creeds, as the living and effectual beliefs, which are voiced in the preaching and teaching of the Church. Then these doctrines or beliefs must be traced to their original source, which is not found in Scripture, but in the devout feeling which results from the relation of the soul to Jesus Christ. And, finally, they must be reproduced in a systematized form in the light of the fact that they are the reflex of distinctly pious feelings. This means that the doctrines are derived from pious or religious feelings, and also find in these the ground of their certitude. It is only in the light of such feelings that their truly religious character stands out.

Frank, one of the outstanding theologians of the Erlangen school of theology, is also one of the most representative advocates of this theory. His system already marks a real advance upon that of Schleiermacher, since he does not start from a general state of feeling, but from the specific experience of regeneration. In his work on *The System of the Christian Certainty* he seeks the answer to this question: What leads man to depend on the objective factors of salvation, such as God, Christ, Scripture, and others, and to accept Scripture as the Word of God? And his answer is that this is not due to historical or rational proofs, nor to the authority of Scripture, of the Church, or of tradition, but only to the experience of regeneration. The Christian certainty of which he speaks is not the assurance of salvation, but the assurance respecting the reality of the truth. Christian certitude, in the sense of certainty respecting the truth, finds its basis, according to Frank, in the Christian life, that is, in the believer's moral and spiritual experience. The Christian knows that a mighty change has taken place in his life, and from this experience of regeneration he infers the whole content of Christian truth. This truth arranges itself in three groups around the experience of regeneration. (a) There are truths which are immediately involved in that experience, such as the reality of sin, of judgment, and of future perfection (immanent and central truths). (b) Then there are truths which must be assumed, in order to explain the new condition, such as the reality of a personal God, the existence of God as triune, and the redemption wrought by the God-man (transcendent truths). (c) Finally, these lead right on to the means by which the preceding agents work, such as the Church, the Word of God, the sacraments, miracles, revelation, and inspiration (transeunt truths). This answer of Frank undoubtedly contains an important truth, since regeneration is indeed necessary, in order to see the Kingdom of God. But the manner in which he elaborates his thought is very dubious, and this is probably the necessary result of his subjective standpoint. He does not consistently work out a single thought, but constantly confuses the manner in which religious truths are derived, and the manner in which certainty respecting these is obtained. Since his work is entitled *The System of the Christian Certainty*, it raises the expectation that the author simply desires to show how the believer reaches Christian certitude. But in that case he should have limited himself to the task of elucidating the origin and nature of Christian certainty, and should not in addition have discussed the contents of the religious consciousness. Then he would not have given us a system of the objects to which this certainty pertains; and yet this is exactly what he does, when he derives all religious truths from the experience of regeneration.

2. EVALUATION OF THIS POSITION. There are many objections to this starting point and method. (a) Regeneration and all other experiences of the Christian are always connected with the objective factors of the Church, the Scriptures, and so on, while Frank divorces the two. (b) In his second work, *The System of the Christian Truth*, he himself gives precedence to these objective factors, and thus recognizes their priority. For that very reason he should have maintained this order throughout his system. (c) The method in which he derives the objective dogmata from the certainty of the Christian, is one that does not fit in theology. It is borrowed from speculative philosophy, which derives religious truth from the necessity of logical coherence. (d) This method goes contrary to all religious experience. No Christian ever obtained certainty respecting objective truths in the manner described by Frank. Scarcely anyone has adopted his method. And even among those who have adopted it in a modified form there is a difference of opinion as to the significance of experience for the *principia* of theology. The application of this method carries with it a threefold danger. (a) It easily leads into the danger of forming a wrong conception of religious experience, and of expecting from it what it cannot yield. While it is possible to experience certain emotions, such as those of penitence, fear, hope, and so on, it is not possible to experience historical facts. (b) It really makes it impossible for uneducated Christians to obtain knowledge and certainty respecting the historical facts of Christianity,

since these can only be deduced from experience by an elaborate process of reasoning. (c) It is apt to rob historical Christianity ever increasingly of its real significance. Experience is loaded down with a burden which it cannot bear. The truth of Christianity cannot rest on it as a final ground. And the consciousness of this may easily lead to a reduction of the burden by divorcing the contents of faith from all historical facts and limiting it to religious and ethical experiences.

D. The Moral Consciousness

Finally, there is still another view of the norm of religious truth, and of the manner in which we come to recognize and acknowledge it as such, a view that is somewhat akin to the preceding, but which, in distinction from the preceding, with its emotional appeal, stresses the ethical element in religion. It is a view that finds its roots in the moralism of Kant, and that became popular in theology through the influence of the Neo-Kantianism of Ritschl and his followers. It makes the moral consciousness the real judge of religious truth. The real emphasis in this view is not on emotional experience, but on ethical self-maintenance. The great and determinative question is, whether a certain truth satisfies the moral requirements of the heart or the conscience, and thus answers to a real practical need. Hence the method applied by its advocates is called *ethical-psychological* or *ethical-practical*.

1. HISTORICAL STATEMENT OF THE POSITION. If the immediately preceding method connects up with Schleiermacher, this method finds its main support in Kant. For its adherents Christianity in general is not so much a doctrine that must be demonstrated and accepted as true, nor a historical fact that calls for proof, but a religious and ethical power that addresses itself to the heart and the conscience of man. According to them Christianity cannot be made acceptable to all men without distinction, but only to those who have a proper moral disposition, a feeling of dissatisfaction, a sense of the good, a desire for redemption, and so on. When Christianity comes in contact with such men, it commends itself to their hearts and consciences as divine truth without any reasoning or further proof. It satisfies their religious needs, answers to their higher aspirations, reconciles them with themselves, brings them peace, comfort, and salvation, and thus proves itself to be the consolation and the wisdom of God.

This kind of argumentation did not begin with Kant. Tertullian already appealed to the testimony which the soul involuntarily gives to Christ. The Apologetes pointed out that the heathen religions of their day were not able to satisfy the religious needs of man, nor to foster a truly ethical life. Duns Scotus called attention to the moral influence of God's revelation and to its sufficiency in enabling man to reach his destiny. Both Roman Catholic and Protestant theologians sought to prove the truth of the Christian religion by pointing to its operation and influence on the intellectual, moral, social, and political life of individuals and nations. Pascal and Vinet especially brought this method to honor, but did not yet place it in opposition to historical argumentation. The former even admitted the great value of historical proofs, though he did not assign to them their usual place; and the latter did not despise them, though he regarded them as inferior to the moral and religious proof. In later years this method was adopted by Astie, Pressencé, Secretan, de la Saussaye, and others, who generally neglected and sometimes even disdained historical proofs.

However, the influence of Kant was of great significance for this method. According to him the theoretical reason necessarily yields three ideas, namely, those of God, freedom, and immortality. These three are therefore general. It does not assure us, however, that there are corresponding realities, nor enlighten us as to the nature of these realities. The corresponding realities are demanded, however, by the practical reason with its categorical imperative. This clearly testifies to the existence of a moral order, and demands that this order shall finally triumph over the natural order. This being so, it naturally follows that man must be free, that there must be a future life in which the moral will be really triumphant, and that there must be a highest Judge to punish vice and reward virtue. Only that view of the world is true that answers to our inner life and satisfies our moral needs.

When the insufficiency of the speculative method appeared, there was a tendency to go back to Kant. In theology Kantianism was reintroduced especially by Ritschl and Lipsius, though these men differed from Kant in several particulars. It is especially in the school of Ritschl that the ethico-psychological method is brought into prominence. This school regards Christianity as a historical phenomenon, but especially as a religious and ethical power of the greatest significance for the heart and conscience of man. Ritschl finds in religion especially two elements: on the one hand that of dependence on God, and on the other, that of spiritual freedom or supremacy over nature, which, in the estimation of Ritschl, is its main element. The Christian religion gives answer to the question, how man as a free moral being, who is yet hemmed in by nature and in many ways dependent on it, can maintain his freedom and rise superior to nature. And the answer is that man can gain the mastery over nature through communion with God in Christ and by making God's end his own, that is, by seeking the Kingdom of God in a life for God, motivated by love. In this practical power of Christianity Ritschl finds the real proof for the truth of the revelation of God in Christ and of the Christian religion. It is not a theoretical, but a practical proof. Like Schleiermacher, he too would banish all metaphysics from theology. In science theoretical proofs apply, but in religion only judgments of value. As a matter of fact, however, neither one of the two succeeded in excluding philosophy. Moreover, Kaftan, one of the most prominent and one of the ablest followers of Ritschl, stressed the fact that judgments of value cannot be divorced from theoretical judgments of being.

2. EVALUATION OF THIS POSITION. This and the immediately preceding method undoubtedly deserve to be preferred above the historical and specula-

tive methods. The method now under consideration does not regard religion merely as a doctrine to be proved, nor as a condition of the subject to be analyzed intellectually, as the first two methods do respectively. It looks upon the Christian religion as a historical, objective power that answers to the moral needs of man, and finds in this its proof and justification. Nevertheless, there are serious objections to this method. (a) Though a religion that does not satisfy the religious and ethical life, that offers no comfort in sorrow and death, and does not give strength unto the battles of life, is not worthy of the name of religion; yet the fact that the Christian religion does do this, is no absolute proof of its truth, since there are other religions which also give a certain degree of satisfaction in this respect. (b) It is dangerous to make the truth of Christianity dependent on judgments of value. There would be no great objection, if it were only intended to stress the fact that a dogma must always have religious and ethical value, or that intellectual reasoning can never give us perfect certainty respecting religious truths, while this can be obtained by experiencing the religious values expressed by the dogmas. In that case the subjective evaluation would presuppose the objective reality of the religious truths and would only serve as a means to obtain certainty respecting that reality. Then the value of a thing would not be represented as the ground of its existence, but would simply enable us to acknowledge it subjectively. In the system of Ritschl it is quite different, however, since the judgments of value are divorced from all metaphysics. (c) Moreover, in this way we can never reach objectivity. The needs that find satisfaction in the Christian faith are virtually created by that same faith through the work of the ministry. Hence the question arises, whether those needs are real in the life of man, or have merely been awakened artificially and are therefore purely imaginary. In other words, the question of the truth of the Christian religion remains.

QUESTIONS FOR FURTHER STUDY: What is the difference between a *fides humana* and a *fides divina*? Can we be satisfied with historical certainty in theology? How can the transition from the historico-apologetical, to the speculative, method be explained? Is subjectivism, which makes the human reason or human experience the source of Christian truth, compatible with absolute certainty? Can absolute Idealism ever lead to a satisfying Christian certitude? Is the test of experience and the pragmatic test ever applied to the truth in Scripture? What makes these tests so popular in the present day? What more objective test does Troeltsch recommend? How should we judge of the psychological approach to religion, as exhibited in Horton's *A Psychological Approach to Theology*? Does the position taken by Baillie in his *Our Knowledge of God* differ materially from that of Schleiermacher?

REFERENCES: Bavinck, *Geref. Dogm.* I, pp. 528-602; Miley, *Syst. Theol.*, I, pp. 34-47; Macintosh, *Theol. as an Emp. Science*, pp. 7-26; Dorner, *System of Chr. Doct.*, I, pp. 58-168; Girardeau, *Discussions of Theol. Questions*, pp. 73-125; Paterson, *The Rule of Faith*, pp. 92-173; Kaftan, *The Truth of the Chr. Rel.*, I. pp. 230-316; Frank, *The System of the Chr. Certainty*; Baillie, *The Interpretation of Religion*, pp. 174-339; Heffern, *Apology and Polemic in the N. T.*; Wenley, *Contemporary Theology and Theism*, pp. 11-124; Schaeder, *Theozentrische Theologie*, Vol. I and II, pp. 1-55; Horton, *A Psychological Approach to Theology*; Baillie, *Our Knowledge of God*; Dickey, *Revelation and Response*; Mackintosh, *Types of Modern Theology*.

E. Faith, the Proper Principium Internum

Under the influence of Schleiermacher most theologians have come to the conclusion that religion is a unique phenomenon in human life, and can only be understood in a manner corresponding to its nature. By assuming this position theology takes its starting point in the subject, but should not, simply for that reason, be accused of subjectivism. No science has another starting point, since the objective world exists for us only as it is reflected in our consciousness. There must always be a *principium internum* that answers to the *principium externum*. Moreover, Christian theology from the very beginning took its starting point in the believing subject, was born of faith, and was guided and controlled by the rule: *per fidem ad intellectum*. And this is also entirely in harmony with Scripture, which speaks not only of a revelation of God outside of us, but also of an inner illumination of the Holy Spirit. If the accusation of subjectivism could be lodged against this starting point with any degree of justice, it could also be urged against all science, against theology as a whole, and even against Scripture itself. Such an accusation is warranted only, however, when the subjective condition absolutely necessary for the knowledge of a thing is made the source of that knowledge. An organ by which we take cognizance of the objective world round about us, is not the source from which that world proceeds.

1. THE NAME OF THE PRINCIPIUM COGNOSCENDI INTERNUM. The *principium internum* is usually called *faith* in Scripture. Other terms are also used, such as *regeneration*, John 3:3; I Cor. 2:12, 14, *purity of heart*, Matt. 5:8, *love to the will of God*, John 7:17, and *the Spirit of God*, I Cor. 2:13. For several reasons, however, the term *faith* deserves preference. (a) It is the term that stands out prominently in Scripture. (b) It directs attention at once to the conscious life, and thus involves a recognition of the fact that all the knowledge of man is mediated by his consciousness. And (c) it indicates better than any other name the close connection between religious knowledge and all other knowledge of man. In general it may be said that we obtain knowledge in no other way in religion than we do in the other sciences. We should remember that faith is not a new organ of science. Men sometimes speak of believing and knowing as opposites, but in such cases they use the word 'believe' in the weak sense of having an opinion for which the proper evidence is lacking. The word 'faith' has a far more profound meaning, however. It is frequently used to denote *the positive knowledge that does not rest on external evidence nor on logical demonstration, but on an immediate and direct insight*. In that sense it can ever be said to be fundamental to all the sciences. Intuitive knowledge and immediate insight occupy an important place in human life. There is not a single field of endeavor, nor a single phase of life in which we can get along without it.

2. DISTINCTIVE NATURE OF THE KNOWLEDGE OF FAITH. The correspondence between general and religious knowledge should not cause us to lose sight of the existing difference. There is a very important difference between

faith in the sense of immediate certainty and faith in the religious sense. In the Christian religion faith has a unique significance, as the following points will show. (a) In the New Testament it denotes a religious relation of man to God, and includes not only a *certain* knowledge, that is, an assured knowledge, but also a heartful trust in God, a complete surrender to Him, and a personal appropriation of the promises of the gospel. (b) While the faith we exercise in connection with the external world, for instance with respect to the reliability of our senses, the pertinency of the laws of thought, and so on, rests on our own inner observation, Christian faith is directed to that which is invisible and cannot be observed, Heb. 11:1. (c) Faith in the religious sense is distinguished from that in the sense of immediate certainty in this that it rests on the insight of others rather than on our own. We are made acquainted with the grace of God in Jesus Christ through the testimony of prophets and apostles. (d) Finally, Christian faith differs from faith as immediate certainty also in the fact that it does not arise spontaneously in human nature. While it is perfectly human, and may even be called the restoration of human nature, it grates on the pride of the natural man and arouses hostility in his heart. God is not only its object, but also its author. Barth and Brunner go so far as to call God, rather than man, the subject of faith. While they also speak of it as man's response to the divine revelation, they really regard it as that in which God completes His revelation. The revelation itself gives birth to the response. As long as it does not do this, there is no revelation.

According to Scripture this faith carries its own certainty with it. It does this, not because it is so firm and certain in itself, but because it rests on the testimony and the promises of God. It makes the invisible blessings of salvation just as certain for man, yea even more certain, than his own insight or any scientific proof can ever make anything. Scripture represents certainty as one of the characteristics of faith. Alongside of the certainty of science we have, therefore, the certainty of faith, practically demonstrated in the believing Church, in its martyrs and steadfast confessors, and theoretically professed and developed in Christian theology. It is a certainty that is unwavering and indestructible. But this faith does not necessarily involve the truth of that which is believed. There is a great difference between subjective certainty and objective truth. In this respect everything depends on the grounds on which faith rests.

F. The Ground of Faith

By faith we accept the testimony of God as it is contained in Scripture. But now the question arises, How do we know that that testimony is true, and therefore perfectly reliable? What is the ground on which our faith in the Word of God rests? Or, perhaps better still, By what means is the conviction respecting the truth of the special revelation of God wrought in our hearts? In answer to these questions Reformed theologians point to the testimony of the Holy Spirit. It is this subject that calls for a brief discussion in this concluding chapter.

1. **The Doctrine of the Testimonium Spiritus Sancti in the Church.** It was admitted from the earliest Christian centuries on that none of the intellectual or historical proofs adduced for the truth of the Christian religion provide an adequate assurance. While they may lead to a *fides humana*, divine grace is necessary to engender faith in the heart. Augustine was the first one of the Church Fathers who clearly saw and taught the absolute necessity of inward grace for the acceptance of Scripture as the Word of God. It is true that he also attached great value to the testimony of the Church as a *motivum credibilitatis*, but he did not regard this as the last and deepest ground of faith. Theoretically, even the Church of Rome held that only the Holy Spirit can give one absolute certainty respecting the truth of revelation, but in practice there was a tendency to replace the testimony of the Holy Spirit by the testimony of the Church.

The Reformers consciously and deliberately placed testimony of the Holy Spirit in the foreground. They derived their certainty respecting the truth of the divine revelation from the work of the Spirit of God in the hearts of believers. They took position against the Church of Rome with its undue emphasis on the testimony of the Church, and also against the Anabaptists and other Mystics, who revealed a tendency to divorce the testimony of the Holy Spirit from the external testimony contained in Scripture. Calvin was the first one to give a detailed exposition of the doctrine of the testimony of the Holy Spirit.[1] Since his day this doctrine is quite generally accepted by both Lutheran and Reformed theologians. Of late, however, it has suffered eclipse. This is due in part to the fact that many confuse the testimony of the Holy Spirit with the argument from experience, which is so popular in many circles today, and in part, to the mystical conception which some have of the testimony of the Holy Spirit, in connection with the widespread aversion to the supernatural. It is not unnecessary therefore to indicate precisely what is meant with the testimony of the Holy Spirit.

We should bear in mind, that the particular work of the Holy Spirit described by that name does not stand by itself, but is connected with the whole work of the Holy Spirit in the application of the redemption wrought in Christ. The Spirit renews the sinner, not only in his being, but also in his consciousness. He removes the spiritual darkness of the understanding and illumines the heart, so that the glory of God in Christ is clearly seen. It is only in virtue of the special operation of the Holy Spirit that man confesses Jesus Christ as Lord, I Cor. 12:3. The work of the Holy Spirit enables him to accept the revelation of God in Christ, to appropriate the blessings of salvation, and to attain to the assurance of faith. And the testimony of the Holy Spirit is merely a special aspect of His more general work in the sphere of redemption. For that reason the two should never be dissociated.

---

1. *Institutes* I. p. 7.

2. MISTAKEN NOTIONS OF THE TESTIMONIUM SPIRITUS SANCTI. There are especially two views of the testimony of the Holy Spirit against which we must be on our guard.

a. *That it brings a new revelation.* The Mystics conceived of it as an inner revelation to the effect that the Bible is the Word of God. This was evidently the conception which Strauss had of it, for he maintained that, when Protestants accepted the doctrine of the *testimonium Spiritus Sancti*, they virtually adopted the principle of Mysticism. He interpreted it as the communication of a new truth, namely, *that the Bible is really the Word of God.* If this interpretation were correct, his assertion would be justified, for then the Christian would indeed be receiving a new revelation through the testimony of the Holy Spirit, just as the prophets did in the days of old. This revelation would then, of course, call for a new attestation, and so on *ad infinitum.* Such a conception of the testimony of the Holy Spirit makes our belief in Scripture as the Word of God dependent on this new revelation, and naturally involves a denial of its *autopistia.* The older Protestant theologians never had such a conception of the testimony of the Holy Spirit. They all stressed the *autopistia* of Scripture and were strongly opposed to the mysticism of the Anabaptists. Even the somewhat related representation, that we must conceive of the testimony of the Holy Spirit as an influence producing in believers a blind or unfounded conviction that the Bible is the Word of God, proved unacceptable to them. Faith is a conviction founded on a testimony, which in the absence of proper evidence does not make its appearance.

b. *That it is identical with the argument from experience.* The testimony of the Holy Spirit should not be confused, as is often done, with the testimony of experience. The Holy Spirit does indeed work in believers the experience of salvation in Christ, which cannot be explained apart from Scripture, but is wrought through the instrumentality of the Word, and therefore implicitly testifies to the fact that the Bible is of divine origin. This is an inference, in which we conclude, from an experience which we regard as divine, that the Bible, through which the experience is wrought in us, is the inspired Word of God. This argument has been elaborated, though not in the same form, by such theologians as Frank, Koestlin, Ihmels, Stearns, and many others. In itself it is perfectly legitimate and is not devoid of evidential value, but it is something quite different from the testimony of the Holy Spirit. They who identify the two do not distinguish properly between the efficient cause of faith and the motives for faith. The testimony of experience may certainly be a motive for faith, but just as certainly cannot be the origin of it, since it already presupposes faith. The testimony of the Holy Spirit, on the other hand, is the *causa efficiens* of faith. Without it all the motives for faith would have no convincing power. Moreover, the testimony of experience respecting Scripture is no objective testimony of God, but simply the testimony of our own heart respecting the Scriptures. Finally, it has the character of a mere inference, or may even be said to involve more than one inference, since it concludes from a certain experience to Scripture as its origin, and from the fact that this experience is wrought through to the instrumentality of the revealed Word to the fact that this revelation is indeed the Word of God. It does not, therefore, have the character of an immediate testimony of the Holy Spirit. And because the testimony of experience is entirely subjective, the faith that is founded on it rests, in the last analysis, on the inner experience of the soul rather than on the objective testimony of God in His Word, which is after all the ground of all Christian certitude.

3. CORRECT VIEW OF THE TESTIMONIUM SPIRITUS SANCTI. Calvin absolutely rejects the idea that the authority of Scripture rests on the testimony of the Church, as well as some other erroneous views. He finally says: "Let it therefore be held as fixed, that those who are inwardly taught by the Holy Spirit acquiesce implicitly in Scripture; that Scripture, carrying its own evidence along with it, deigns not to submit to proofs and arguments, but owes the full conviction with which we ought to receive it to the testimony of the Spirit. Enlightened by Him, we no longer believe, either on our own judgment or that of others, that the Scriptures are from God; but, in a way superior to human judgment, feel perfectly assured—as much so as if we beheld the divine image visibly impressed on it—that it came to us, by the instrumentality of men, from the very mouth of God."[1] The Testimony of the Holy Spirit is simply the work of the Holy Spirit in the heart of the sinner, by which he removes the blindness of sin, so that the erstwhile blind man, who had no eyes for the sublime character of the Word of God, now clearly sees and appreciates the marks of its divine nature, and receives immediate certainty respecting the divine origin of Scripture. Just as one who has an eye for the beauties of architecture, in gazing up into the dome of the St. Peter's Church at Rome, at once recognizes it as the production of a great artist, so the believer in the study of Scripture discovers in it at once the earmarks of the divine. The redeemed soul beholds God as the author of Scripture and rests on its testimony with childlike faith, with a *fides divina*. It is exactly the characteristic mark of such faith that it rests on a testimony of God, while a *fides humana* merely rests on a human testimony or on rational arguments. Of course, rational arguments may be adduced for the divine origin of Scripture, but these are powerless to convince the unrenewed man. The Christian believes the Bible to be the very Word of God in the last analysis on the testimony which God Himself gives respecting this matter in His Word, and recognizes that Word as divine by means of the testimony of God in his heart. The testimony of the Holy Spirit is therefore, strictly speaking, not so much the final ground of faith, but rather the means of faith. The final ground of faith is Scripture only, or better still, the authority of God which is impressed upon the believer in the testimony of Scripture. The ground of faith is identical with its contents, and cannot be separated from it. But the testimony of the Holy Spirit is the moving cause of faith. We believe Scripture, not because of, but through the testimony of the Holy Spirit.

---

1. *Institutes* I. vii, 5.

QUESTIONS FOR FURTHER STUDY: In how many different senses is the word 'faith' used? How do faith and knowledge compare in the estimation of Locke, and in that of Kant? What do the Ritschlians mean when they speak of "faith-knowledge"? Is faith a matter of the intellect, of the will, of the emotions, or of all three combined? How does Calvin work out the doctrine of the testimony of the Holy Spirit? What is the difference between the *testimonium Spiritus Sancti generale* and *speciale?* Does the testimony of the Holy Spirit apply to the different parts of the Bible separately?

REFERENCES: Bavinck, *Geref. Dogm.* I, pp. 603-670; Kuyper, *Enc. der Heil. Godgel.,* II, pp. 501-511; Hodge, *Syst. Theol.,* II, pp. 69-86; Wisse, *Geloof en Wetenschap,* pp. 41-212; Foster, *Studies in Theol., Proleg.,* pp. 74-246; Hall, *Dogm. Theol.,* Introd., pp. 84-141; Frank, *The System of Chr. Certainty;* Stearns, *The Evidence of Chr. Experience;* Ihmels, *Centralfragen der Dogm.,* pp. 1-21, 134-165; Kaftan, *The Truth of the Chr. Rel.,* II; Hepp, *Testimonium Spiritus Sancti, Generale;* C. W. Hodge, *Witness of the Holy Spirit,* Princeton Review, Vol. II, p. 41 ff.

SELECT LITERATURE

I. General Works on Introduction

Barth, *Dogmatik I. Prolegomena*, Muenchen, 1927; *The Doctrine of the Word of God*, New York, 1936.
Bavinck, *Gereformeerde Dogmatiek I.*, Kampen, 1906.
Foster, *Studies in Theology, Prolegomena*, Cincinnati, 1891.
Girardeau, *Discussions of Theological Questions*, Richmond, Va., 1905.
Hall, *Dogmatic Theology I., Introduction to Dogmatic Theology*, New York, 1907.
Ihmels, *Centralfragen der Dogmatik in der Gegenwart*, Leipzig, 1921.
Kaftan, *The Truth of the Christian Religion*, 2 vols., Edinburgh, 1894.
Lobstein, *An Introduction to Protestant Dogmatics*, Chicago, 1910.
Mackay, *A Preface to Christian Theology*, New York, 1941.
Smith, *Introduction to Christian Theology*, New York, 1882.
Ten Broeke, *A Constructive Basis for Theology*, London, 1914.
Van Dijk, *Begrip en Methode der Dogmatiek*, Utrecht, 1877.
Weidner, *Introduction to Dogmatic Theology*, Chicago, 1895.

II. Dogmas, Creeds, and Authority in Religion

Allen, *Freedom in the Church*, London, 1907.
Dreyer, *Undogmatisches Christentum*, Berlin, 1901.
Forsyth, *Theology in Church and State*, London, 1915.
Harris, *Creeds or no Creeds*, New York, 1927.
Hepp, *De Waarde van het Dogma*, Kampen, 1920.
Hospers, *The Reformed Principles of Authority*, Grand Rapids, 1924.
Lamont, *The Church and the Creeds*, Boston, 1923.
Leckie, *Authority in Religion*, Edinburgh, 1909.
Meyrick, *Is Dogma a Necessity?* London, 1883.
Miller, *The Utility and Importance of Creeds and Confessions*, Philadelphia.
Paterson, *The Rule of Faith*, London, 1914.
Patton, *Fundamental Christianity*, New York, 1926.
Sabatier, *Religions of Authority*, New York, 1904; *Outlines of a Philosophy or Religion*
Stewart, *Creeds and Churches*, London, 1916.

III. Theology and Theological Encyclopaedias

Bavinck, *Kenenis en Leven*, Kampen, 1922.
Cave, *Introduction to Theology and Its Literature*, Edinburgh, 1896.
Hagenbach, *Encyclopaedie und Methodologie der theologischen Wissenschaften*, Leipzig, 1889.
Hastie, *Theology as Science*, Glasgow, 1899.
Hodge, C. W., *The Significance of the Reformed Theology Today*, Princeton.
Honig, *Dogmatiek en Ethiek*, Kampen, 1930.
Kuyper, *Encyclopaedie der Heilige Godgeleerdheid*, vol. II, Amsterdam, 1894. Translated by Dr. H. De Vries.
Marshall, *Theology and Truth*, London, 1906.
Raebiger, *Theological Encyclopaedia*, 2 vols., Edinburgh, 1884.
Ten Broeke, *A Constructive Basis for Theology*, London, 1914.

Warfield, *The Idea of Systematic Theology;* and *Task and Method of Systematic Theology,* in *Studies in Theology,* New York, 1932.

IV. Religion, Philosophy of Religion, and Apologetics

Baillie, *The Interpretation of Religion,* New York, 1928.
Beattie, *Apologetics,* Richmond, Va., 1903.
Bruce, *Apologetics,* New York, 1922.
Caldecott, *The Philosophy of Religion,* London, 1901.
Edwards, *The Philosophy of Religion,* New York, 1924.
Galloway, *The Philosophy of Religion,* New York, 1921.
Hepp, *Gereformeerde Apologetiek,* Kampen, 1922.
Lidgett, *The Christian Religion,* London, 1907.
Kellogg, *A Handbook of Comparative Religion,* Philadelphia, 1899.
Menzies, *History of Religion,* New York, 1895.
Ormond, *The Philosophy of Religion,* Princeton, 1922.
Patton, *Fundamental Christianity,* New York, 1926.
Puenjer, *History of the Christian Philosophy of Religion,* Edinburgh, 1887.
Sabatier, *Outlines of a Philosophy of Religion,* New York.
Smith, *Apologetics,* New York, 1882.
Warfield, *Apologetics* (in *Studies in Theology*), New York, 1932.
Wright, *A Student's Philosophy of Religion,* New York, 1925.

V. Revelation and Inspiration

Baillie and Martin, *Revelation,* New York, 1937.
Bannerman, *Inspiration of the Scriptures,* Edinburgh, 1865.
Bavinck, *Wijsbegeerte der Openbaring,* Kampen, 1908.
Daubanton, *De Theopneustie der Heilige Schrit.*
Dickie, *Revelation and Response,* New York, 1938.
Engelder, *Reason or Revelation,* St. Louis, 1941.
Ewald, *Revelation, Its Nature and Record,* Edinburgh, 1884.
Fisher, *Nature and Method of Revelation,* London, 1890.
Gilson, *Reason and Revelation in the Middle Ages,* New York, 1938.
Girardeau, *Discussions of Theological Questions,* Richmond, Va., 1905.
Given, *Revelation, Inspiration, and the Canon,* Edinburgh, 1881.
Honig, *Is de Bijbel op Bovennatuurlijke Wijze Geinspireerd?* Baarn, 1909.
Kuyper, *De Hedendaagsche Schriftcritiek,* Amsterdam, 1881.
Ladd, *The Doctrine of Sacred Scripture,* 2 vols., New York, 1883.
Lee, *The Inspiration of Scripture,* New York, 1857.
Lewis, *A Philosophy of the Christian Religion,* New York, 1940.
MacGregor, *The Revelation and the Record,* Edinburgh, 1893.
M'Intosh, *Is Christ Infallible and is the Bible True?* Edinburgh, 1901.
Orr, *Revelation and Inspiration,* New York, 1910.
Warfield, *Revelation and Inspiration,* New York, 1927.

VI. History of Theological Study

Boardman, *A History of New England Theology,* 1899.
Briggs, *History of the Study of Theology,* 2 vols., New York, 1916.
Burggraaf, *The Rise and Development of Liberal Theology in America,* New York, 1928.
Foster, *A History of New England Theology,* New York, 1907.
Frank, *Geschichte und Critik der neueren Theologie,* Leipzig, 1898.
Gruetzmacher, *Textbuch zur systematischen Theologie,* Leipzig, 1923.
Haroutunian, *Piety Versus Moralism,* New York, 1932.
Heppe, *Dogmatik des deutschen Protestantismus in sechzehnten Jahrhundert,* 3 vols., Gotha, 1857.
Lichtenberger, *History of German Theology in the Nineteenth Century,* Edinburgh, 1899.
McGiffert, *Protestant Thought Before Kant,* New York, 1911; *A History of Christian*

Thought, New York, 1932, 2 vols.
Moore, *History of Christian Thought Since Kant*, New York, 1922.
Pfleiderer, *The Development of Theology in Germany Since Kant*, London, 1890.
Randall, *The Making of the Modern Mind*, New York, 1926.
Scholten, *De Leer der Hervornde Kerk*, Vol. I, Leiden, 1870.
Schweizer, *Die Glaubenslehre der evangelisch-reformirten Kirche*, Zuerich, 1844, 2 vols.
Storr, *The Development of English Theology in the Nineteenth Century*, New York, 1913.
Walker, *The Theology and Theologians of Scotland*, Edinburgh, 1888.
Workman, *Christian Thought to the Reformation*.

INDICES

Index of Authors

A

Allen, on freedom from creeds, 63.
Aquinas, Thomas, on object of theology, 37; his definition of religion, 102; on reason and revelation 126 f.

B

Bacon, on speculative method, 68.
Baillie, on revelation, 117 f.
Bannerman, on Schleiermacher's view of inspiration, 146, 152.
Barnes, denial of scientific character of theology, 45.
Barth: conception of dogma, 20-25; authority of dogma, 25-34; relation of dogma to dogmatics, 36; object of theology, 23, 44; task of dogmatics, 44, 56 f; source of theology, 61 f; on Reformed doctrine, 62; authority of the creeds, 63 f; on empirical method, 70; on God as subject in the study of theology, 96; on religion, 104 ff.; on revelation, 70, 97 f., 122 f.; on general revelation, 61; 130; on special revelation, 138 f.; on revelation as act, 137; On purpose of revelation, 138; on inspiration, 146; on necessity of Scripture, 166; on God as subject of faith, 182.
Bavinck: his definition of dogmatics, 44; on relation of apologetics to dogmatics, 50; on principium cognoscendi externum, 96; on principium cognoscendi internum, 97; on psychological explanation of religion, 113; on method of determining revelation, 126.
Beattie, conception of apologetics, 49.
Beck, on Bible as source of theology, 61.
Brown, W. A., opposition to church creeds, 63.
Bruce, on apologetics, 50.
Brunner: on authority of creeds, 63 f.; on revelation, 122; on general revelation, 130; on special revelation, 138 f; on revelation as object, 139; on inspiration, 146; on God as subject of faith, 182.
Burrell, Jesus' teaching on inspiration, 157.

C

Caird, on natural religion, 116.
Caldecott, on speculative method, 68.
Calixtus, on analytical method, 73.
Calvin, and trinitarian method, 72; on derivation of 'religion,' 99; definition of religion, 102; on general revelation, 128 f.; on testimony of the Holy Spirit, 185.
Camfield, on revelation, 122.
Chantepie de la Saussaye, on derivation of dogma, 22 f.
Cicero, on derivation of 'religion,' 98.
Cocceius, on covenantal method, 73.
Cook, on Old Testament as norm for Christians, 165.
Curtiss, on subscription to creeds, 63.

D

Dreyer, on undogmatic Christianity, 27.
Durkheim, on origin of religion, 111.

E

Edghill, on Schleiermacher's conception of dogmas, 22; on Erlangen school, 53.
Edwards, D. M.; on Schleiermacher's view of religion, 108; on historical method of studying the origin of religion, 109 f.; on psychological method of studying the origin of religion, 111 f.; on origin of religion, 113, 115; on revelation, 121; on reasoning in a circle, 125.

F

Fichte, his subjective idealism, 174.
Fleming, on speculative method, 68.
Forsyth, his conception of dogma, 20, 35; on relation of dogmas to dogmatics, 35.
Foster, G. B., on dogmas, 24; on Schleiermacher's view of the encyclopaedic place of dogmatics, 49; on revelation, 121.
Frank, on Christian certainty, 176 f.
Frazer, on origin of religion, 111.
Fulton, on natural revelation, 116.

INDEX OF AUTHORS

G

Garvie, on Ritschlian view of dogma, 65.
Gellius, on derivation of 'religion,' 98.
Gibbons, on rule of faith, 62.
Girardeau, definition of theology, 41; on thought-inspiration, 155; on reasoning in a circle, 157.
Grosheide, on normative authority of Scripture, 164 f.

H

Harnack, on formation of dogmas, 24; on special element in dogmas, 32; on relation of dogma to dogmatics, 35.
Harris, on nature of science, 46 f.
Hegel, and opposition to dogma, 26 f.; and rehabilitation of dogma, 26 f.; on relation between philosophy and religion, 69; on religion, 26 f., 104; on seat of religion, 106; and speculative method, 68 f., 174.
Hodge, A. A., definition of theology, 41.
Hodge, Chas., definition of theology, 42; on revelation and inspiration, 144.
Huxley, on science, 47.

K

Kaftan, on break-up of dogma, 10; on relation of dogma to dogmatics, 35; on task of dogmatics, 54; on dogmatics as science of the Christian faith, 65; on speculative method, 68.
Kant, and opposition to dogmas, 26; on knowledge of God, 40; on religion, 104; on seat of religion, 107; on origin of religion, 112; on revelation, 118 f.; his phenomenalism, 174.
Kenyon, on New Testament manuscripts, 159.
Kuyper, definition of theology, 42 f.; on object of theology, 42 f.; on relation of ethics to dogmatics, 51; on the Bible as the principium cognoscendi of theology, 60, 96.

L

Lactantius, derivation of 'religion,' 98; Definition of theology, 101.
Ladd, on modern conception of inspiration, 152, 158.
Laidlaw, on 'heart' in Scripture, 109.
Le Clerc, on inspiration, 145 f., 153.
Leidenroth, derivation of 'religion,' 98 f.
Leydekker, and trinitarian method, 72.

Lobstein, on derivation of dogmas, 22; on formulation of dogmas by church, 24, 26; on authority of dogmas, 26, 34; on relation between dogmas and dogmatics, 38; definition of dogmatics, 40; on task of dogmatics, 55; on faith as source of dogmatics, 65.
Lowrie, on Barth's view of revelation, 124.

M

Machen, on Christianity, 28.
Macintosh, on scientific character of theology, 45, 47; on variations of empirical method, 69; on God as object of theology, 70.
Mackintosh, on Schleiermacher's view of dogmas, 22.
McGiffert, on social element in dogmas, 32; on revelation, 120.
Micklem, his conception of dogma, 20.

N

Neander, on distinction between apokaluptein and phaneroun, 126, 133.
Nestle, on variations, 159.

O

Orr, on connection between religion and revelation, 116; on church fathers' view of inspiration, 144; on thought-inspiration, 155.
Otto, on character disposition in religion, 103.

P

Paterson, on Rationalism, 173.
Pfleiderer, on origin of religion, 111.

R

Rainy, on origin of dogmas, 36.
Reville, on liberal Christianity, 33.
Ritschl, on origin of religion, 112; on normative significance of the Bible, 165; and ethical-psychological method, 179; on elements in religion, 179.
Rolston, on Barth's Subjectivism, 70.

S

Sabatier, on social element of dogmas, 32; on authority of dogmas, 34.
Sanday, on church fathers' view of inspiration, 144.
Schaeder, on object of theology, 43; on task of dogmatics, 56.

INDEX OF AUTHORS

Schleiermacher, on authority of dogmas, 26, 34; on relation between dogmas and dogmatics, 35, 38; definition of dogmatics, 40; on encyclopaedic place of dogmatics, 48 f.; on apologetics, 49; conception of task of dogmatics, 53; on Christian consciousness as source of theology, 60, 64; and empirical method, 69 f.; on religion, 104; on seat of religion, 107 f.; on origin of religion, 112; on revelation, 118 f., 120; on normative significance of the Bible, 165; on Scripture as product of the church, 166; on principium internum of theology, 175 f.

Scholten, on difference between apokaluptein and phaneroun, 133.

Schultz, on Christological method, 74.

Schweizer, theological works of, 57.

Seeberg, on formation of dogmas, 23; on origin of dogmas, 36; on Calvin's view of inspiration, 145.

Shedd, definition of theology, 41; on theology as a science, 48.

Smith, H. B., on apologetics, 50; on Christological method, 74.

Smith, G. B., on revelation, 121.

Spencer, on origin of religion, 110 f.

Spirago, definition of religion, 102.

Strauss, on testimony of the Holy Spirit, 184.

Strong, A. H., definition of theology, 41.

Stuart, Moses, on variations, 159.

T

Thornwell, definition of theology, 41; on Catholic view of source of theology, 63; on significance of creeds, 64; on autopistia of Scripture, 164.

Troeltsch, on Protestant dogma, 27; on task of dogmatics, 55.

Tyler, on origin of religion, 110 f.

V

Van Dijk, on relation between dogmas and dogmatics, 38 f.; on derivation of subject-matter of dogmas, 23; on task of dogmatic, 53 f.

Van Oosterzee, and distribution of the material of dogmatics, 74.

Vinet, on practical proofs for Christianity, 178 f.

Voetius, on normative authority of Scripture, 164.

W

Warfield, definition of theology, 42, 43; on relation of apologetics to the rest of theology, 49 f.; on source of theology, 59 f.; on significance of Christian consciousness for theology, 66 f.; on objections to inspiration, 161.

Wilmers, on rule of faith, 25; on source of theology, 62.

Index of Subjects

A

Activism, inimical to dogmas, 28.
Anabaptists, on necessity of Scripture, 166; on sufficiency or Scripture, 167.
Angel of the Lord, means of revelation, 134.
Apologetics, relation of to dogmatics, 49; views of Schleiermacher, Ebrard, Warfield, Kuyper, Bavinck, and Hepp on, 49 f.; value of, 50, 173.
Arminians, theology of, 82.
Authority of Scripture: Rome on, 163; Protestant view of, 163 f.; historical and normative, 164 f.

B

Belgic Confession, on general revelation, 129.

C

Christian consciousness: as source of theology, 64 f.; objections to it as source, 6 f.; significance of for dogmatics, 67; Warfield on, 66 f.
Church, in defining dogmas, 24 ff.; and authority of dogmas, 25, 33 f., 163 f.; and need of sogmas, 29 ff.; and origin of dogmas, 23 f., 36 f.
Communications, as means of revelation, 134 f.
Confessions, as source of theology, 62 ff.
Creeds, opposition to, 26 f.; as source of theology, 62 ff.; significance of for theology, 41.

D

Deism, and denial of special revelation, 119.
Dispensationalism, on normative value of the Old Testament for Christians, 165.
Distribution of dogmatics, 72 ff.
Dogmas. derivation of the name, 18; biblical use of the name, 18 f.; use of the term in theology, 19 f.; matter of derived from Scripture, 21 ff.; fruit of reflection, 23 f.; defined by the church, 24 ff.; necessity of, 26 ff.; opposition to, 26 ff.; elements included in, 31 ff.; relation of to dogmatics, 35 ff.

Dogmatic theology: and dogmas of the church, 16 ff.; different views of object of, 37 ff.; definition of, 39 ff.; encyclopaedic place of, 48 f.; relation of to apologetics, 49 f.; relation of to ethics, 50 f.; task of, 53 ff.; distribution of, 72 ff.; of the Old Catholic church, 76 f.; of the Middle Ages, 77 ff.; of the Reformation, 79 f.; of Protestant Scholasticism, 80 f.; of Pietism, *Rationalism*, and Supranaturalism, 83 f.; of the modern period, 84 ff.
Dogmatics, work on of: Origen, 76; Augustine, 76 f.; John of Damascus, 77; Vincentius, 77; Anselm, 78; Lombardus, 78; Halesius, 78; Aquinas, 78 f.; Melanchton, 79; Zwingli, 79 f.; Calvin, 80; Gerhard, 80; Calixtus, 80 f.; professors of Leyden, 81; Mastricht, 81; Turretin, 81; Burmannus, 82; Witsius, 82; Episcopius, 82; Grotius, 82; Limborch, 82; Bellarmin, 82; Petavius, 82; Jansen, 82; Priestly, 83; Brettschneider, 84; De Wette, 84; Schleiermacher, 84 f.; Schweizer, 85; Scholten, 85; Marheineke, 86; Strauss, 86; Biedermann, 86; Thomasius, 86; Kahnis, 86; Frank, 86 f.; Philippi, 87; Dorner, 87; Mueller, 87; Martensen, 87 f.; Ritschl, 88; Herrmann, 88; Kaftan, 88; Haering, 88.

E

Encyclopaedic place of dogmatics, 48; Schleiermacher's view of, 48 f.
Erlangen school, on task of dogmatics, 53.
Ethical-psychological method: historical statement of, 178 f.; evaluation of, 178 f.
Ethicals: their definition of dogma, 23; their view of task of dogmatics, 53 f.
Ethics, relation of to dogmatics, 50 f.
Evolutionists, on origin of religion, 112.

F

Faith; as principium internum of theology, 181; knowledge of, 181 f.; ground of, 182 f.
Feelings, as seat of religion, 107 f.; as principium internum, 175 ff.
Formula Consensus Helvetica, on inspiration, 145.

INDEX OF SUBJECTS

G

General revelation: relation of to special revelation, 128 f.; significance of: for the Gentile world, 130 f.; for the Christian religion, 131 f.; insufficiency of, 132.

God: as object of theology, 39 ff.; as principium essendi: in science, 73 f.; in theology, 95 f.

H

Heart, as the seat of religion, 108 f.

Historico-apologetical method: history of up to the Reformation, 170 f.; after the Reformation, 171 f.; evaluation of, 172 f.

Holy Spirit, in inspiration, 151 f.; testimony of, 182 ff.

Human understanding, as principium internum, 170 ff.; up to the time of the Reformation, 170 f.; after the Reformation, 171; evaluation of, 172 f.

I

Idealism, deniel of special revelation, 119 ff.

Image of God in man, according to the Belgic Confession and the Canons of Dort, 100 f.

Inspiration of Scripture: in history, 144 ff.; Scripture proof for, 146 f.; inspiration in oral teaching, 147 f.; inspiration of written Word, 148 ff.; mechanical, 151 f.; dynamical, 152; organic, 153; partial, 153 ff.; of thoughts, 155; verbal, 155 f.; attempts to discredit, 156 ff.; Jesus' teachings on, 157; objections to, 159 ff.; of autographa only 158 f.; value of doctrine of verbal inspiration, 159.

Intellect, as seat of religion, 106 f.

L

Lutherans, dogmatics of, 80; neo-Lutherans, 86 f.

M

Meditating school, its theology, 87.

Method of dogmatics, 67 ff.; method of securing and dealing with the subject-matter of dogmatics: speculative, 67 ff.; empirical, 69 ff.; genetico-synthetic, 71 f.; Method of studying the origin of religion: historical, 109 ff.; psychological, 111 f.; theological, 113 ff.; method of judging and appropriating the truth: historico-apologetical, 170 ff.; speculative, 173 ff.; religious-empirical, 175 ff.; ethico-psychological, 178 ff.

Method of distributing the subject-matter of dogmatics, 72 ff.; trinitarian, 72 f.; analytical, 73; covenantal, 73; Christological, 74; based on kingdom idea, 74; synthetical and logical, 74 f.

Miracles: names of, 136; as means of revelation, 135 f.

Modern liberal theology: on authority of dogmas, 34; on Scripture as source of theology, 33; on relation between dogmas and dogmatics, 38; its definition of theology, 40 f.; its denial of scientific nature of theology, 44 f.; on source of theology, 64 ff.; on empirical method, 69 ff.; its conception of religion, 103 f.; on the origin of religion, 109 ff; its denial of special revelation, 119 ff.; its denial of inspiration, 156 ff.; on the authority of Scripture, 165; on the significance of the Christian consciousness, 64 ff.

Moral consciousness, as principium internum, 178 ff.

N

Natural revelation, 126 f.; relation of to supernatural revelation, 126 f.

Natural theology, before and after the Reformation, 126 f.

Necessity of Scripture: Rome on, 165 f.; Anabaptists on, 166; Reformers on, 166.

O

Object of theology: God as, 39 f., 41 ff.; religious faith as, 40 f.; religion as, 40; revelation as, 41 ff.; facts and truths of Scripture as, 42.

P

Pantheism, involves denial of God as principium essendi, 94, 96; involves denial of revelation, 119 f.

Pantheistic Idealism, involves denial of world as principium cognoscendi, 94; involves denial of revelation, 119 f.

Partial inspiration, 153 f.

Pelagianism, and revelation, 132.

Perfections of Scripture: its authority, 163 ff.; its necessity, 165 f.; its perspicuity, 167; its sufficiency, 162 ff.

Perspicuity of Scripture: Rome on, 167; Reformers on, 167.

Pietism, unfavorable to dogmas, 28.

Positivism, its denial of scientific character of theology, 45.

INDEX OF SUBJECTS

Principia: definition of, 93; essendi and cognoscendi, 93; non-theological sciences, 93 ff.; of religion or theology, 95 ff.; cognoscendi externum of theology, 96 f.; cognoscendi internum of theology; human understanding, 170 ff.; speculative reason, 173 ff.; devout feeling, 175 ff.; moral consciousness, 178 ff.; faith, 97, 181 ff.
Prophets: function of, 147; consciousness of, 147; formulae of, 147 f.; failure to understand their own message, 148.

Q

Quotations, formulae of, 148; in the New Testament, 149.

R

Rationalism, dogmatics of, 83 f.; on authority of dogmas, 34, 163.
Reason, as principium internum of science, 94 f.; of theology, 173 ff.
Reformed: on formation of dogmas, 24 f.; on task of dogmatics, 58 f.; on source of theology, 60 f.; dogmatical study among, 88: on inspiration, 145; on conservation, 159; on principium internum, 182 f.
Reformers: conception of dogmas, 19; of religion, 102; on natural and supernatural revelation, 127; on authority of Scripture, 163 f.; on necessity of Scripture, 166; on perspicuity of Scripture, 167; on sufficiency of Scripture, 168 f.; apologetics of, 171 f.; on testimony of the Holy Spirit, 183.
Religion: derivation of word, 98; definitions of, 101 ff.; Scripture terms for, 99; objective and subjective, 99 f.; historical conceptions of, 100 ff.; of the early church, 101; of the scholastic period, 101 f.; of the Reformers, 102; of modern liberal theology, 103; of Barth, 104; seat of, 106 ff.; origin of, 109; and revelation, 116 f.
Religious-empirical method, 175 ff.; historical statement of, 176; evaluation of, 177 f.
Revelation, general, cf. General revelation.
Revelation, special: as principium cognoscendi externum, 96 f.; and religion, 116 f.; idea of, 117 ff.; historical conceptions of, 117 ff.; proper conception of, 124 ff.; natural and supernatural, 126 f.; general and special, 125; means of, 134 ff.; and Scripture, 139 f.; historical views of this relation, 139 ff.; Reformed conception of this relation, 141.

Ritschlianism: on derivation of dogmas, 19, 22; on authority of dogmas, 26, 34; on relation between dogmas and dogmatics, 38; its conception of dogmatics, 40; on task of dogmatics, 54 f.; on Christian consciousness as source of theology, 65; the ethico-phychological method, 178 ff.

Roman Catholics: their conception of dogmas, 19, 21; on authority of dogmas, 25, 33; on source of theology, 62 ff.; on tradition as source, 62 f.; dogmatical study of, 82; on authority of Scripture, 163; on necessity of Scripture, 165 f.; on perspicuity of Scripture, 167; on sufficiency of Scripture, 167 f.; on apologetics, 171.

S

Scholasticism: general nature of, 77 f.; on principium internum of theology, 171; Protestant scholasticism, 80.
Science: theology as, denied, 44 f.; maintained, 46 ff.
Scripture: as principium unicum of theology, 60; as source of dogmas, 21 ff.; and revelation, 139 ff.; inspiration of, 144 ff.; perfections of, 162 ff.; authority of, 163; necessity of, 165 f.; perspicuity of, 167; sufficiency of, 167 ff.
Source of dogmatics: Scripture as, 59 ff.; church and confession as, 62 ff.; Christian consciousness as, 64 ff.
Special revelation, cf. Revelation, special.
Speculative method: historical statement of, 173 f.; evaluation of, 174 f.
Speculative school in dogmatics, 85 f.
Sufficiency of Scripture: Rome on, 167 f.; Anabaptists on, 167; Reformers on, 168 f.
Supernatural revelation, 126; relation to natural revelation, 126 f.
Supranaturalism, dogmatics of, 84.

T

Task of dogmatics: views of modern liberal theology, 53 ff.; Reformed view of, 58.
Testimony of experience and the testimony of the Holy Spirit, 184 f.
Testimony of the Holy Spirit, 183 ff.; Reformers on, 183; mistaken conceptions of, 184 f.; and testimony of experience, 184; correct view of, 185.

INDEX OF SUBJECTS

Theology: function of in forming dogmas, 35 ff.; as science, 44 ff.; and teaching of the church, 62 ff.; of the early church, 76 f.; of the Middle Ages, 77 ff.; of the Reformation, 79 f.; federal, 81; of Pietism, 83; of Rationalism, 83 f.; of supranaturalism, 84; of Schleiermacher and his school, 84 f.; of the neo-Lutherans, 86 f.; of the Mediating school, 87; of Ritschl and his school, 88; of the Reformed, 88 f.

Theology of Crisis: on religion, 104 f.; opposed to modern conception of revelation, 122; on revelation, 122 ff.; on special revelation, 130; on inspiration of Scripture, 141; on faith as completing revelation, 170.

Theophanies, as means of revelation, 134 f.
Tradition, as source and norm of theology, 62 ff.; Rome on apostolic, 167 f.

V

Verbal inspiration, 153 f.; objections to, 159 ff.; value of doctrine of, 159.
Vatican council, on authority of dogmas, 33; on source of theology, 62 f.

W

Will, as seat of religion, 107.
World, as principium externum of science, 94.